THE ROMAN AMPHITHEATRE
IN BRITAIN

THE ROMAN AMPHITHEATRE
IN BRITAIN

TONY WILMOTT

*For Dan Garner, Stewart Ainsworth, Keith Mathews,
Dai Morgan Evans and all who worked on the
Chester Amphitheatre Project, 2004–2006*

First published in 2008
Reprinted 2010

The History Press
The Mill, Brimscombe Port,
Stroud, Gloucestershire, GL5 2QG
www.thehistorypress.co.uk

© Tony Wilmott, 2008

The Right of Tony Wilmott to be identified as the Author
of this work has been asserted in accordance with the
Copyright, Designs and Patents Act, 1988.

All rights reserved. No part of this book may be reprinted
or reproduced or utilised in any form, or by any means, electronic,
mechanical, photocopying, recording or otherwise, without the prior
permission of the publisher and copyright holder.

British Library Cataloguing in Publication Data.
A catalogue record for this book is available from the British Library.

ISBN 978 0 7524 4123 8

Typesetting and origination by
The History Press.
Printed in England

CONTENTS

	Acknowledgements	6
1.	Introduction	7
2.	Origins and development of the amphitheatre	10
3.	Discovery and exploration	21
4.	Type, distribution and context	44
5.	Planning, construction and architecture	62
6.	The sites: the south and east	92
7.	The sites: the north and west	135
8.	The arena spectacle	161
9.	After the Romans	183
10.	Conclusions: amphitheatres and spectacles in Britain	190
	Appendix: Visiting the amphitheatres	198
	Notes	203
	Select Bibliography	217
	Index	220

ACKNOWLEDGEMENTS

I would like to thank my wife Carol for her patience during the preparation of this book. Various colleagues have discussed aspects of the work and their comments have been helpful. I would like to thank David Bomgarner, Nick Bateman, Dan Garner, David Mattingley and Pete Wilson in particular. Most of the original line drawings are the work of Chris Evans and I thank both him and Sue Evans very sincerely. Permission for the reproduction of copyright illustrations has kindly been granted by a number of individuals and organisations, identified in figure captions. I am particularly grateful to the Society for the Promotion of Roman Studies, Professor Mike Fulford, the Museum of London especially Nick Bateman and Andy Chopping, Karl Schmotz and Sebastian Sommer, the Chester Amphitheatre Project (Chester City Council, English Heritage), Colchester Museum, Jeremy Cooper and the Whitehill Farm Roman Villa Project, Andrew Birley and the Vindolanda Trust, Neil Holbrook and Cotswold Archaeology, Richard Brewer and the National Museum of Wales, English Heritage, David S. Neal, Luigi Thompson and Bryn Walters, the Saffron Walden Museum, Roy Friendship-Taylor, Ralph Jackson and the Trustees of the British Museum.

1

INTRODUCTION

> We may affirm, there was scarce any colony or free city, of considerable note, in their extensive empire, that wanted these places of public pastime; and scarce any province now, where their footsteps at least are not visible, and many almost intire, particularly what we are now treating upon, amphitheatres: yet I believe it will appear a novelty to most people, when we shall talk of such curious antiquities in Britain.[1]

To many people the arena is perhaps the pre-eminent symbol of the Roman Empire, although it is also a source of puzzlement. There is a general idea that Roman society is familiar – that the Romans were 'like us', they had baths and central heating. Those who hold this view are often confused, but also fascinated and repelled in equal measure, by the idea that these people, 'civilised, like us' and 'way ahead of their time' also had a tremendous propensity for violence and public blood-lust satiated by mass slaughter in the arenas of the Roman world, especially, of course, in the Colosseum. There is actually no conflict here. Both pictures are distorted, driven partly perhaps by the early age at which Roman civilisation is taught in schools, and certainly by the popularity of such movies as *Gladiator*. This is one of my favourite films, for many reasons, but not because it is an accurate portrayal of the Roman world or the Roman amphitheatre. The Roman world, like any ancient culture, should be looked at holistically in its own terms and this is what the popular view has tended not to do. The arena is one part (some would argue not a terribly important part[2]) of Roman civilisation as a whole, and needs to be placed in context with the rest of that civilisation in order to be properly understood. This warning is necessary as a preface to this book, which deals solely with the Roman amphitheatre as it was experienced in one province on the fringe of the Empire – Britain.

The amphitheatre certainly is a quintessentially Roman phenomenon. The types of spectacles which were eventually housed in the amphitheatre long pre-dated the appearance of the first stone built amphitheatres in the last decades of the Roman Republic. Function dictated form and amphitheatres were invented to accommodate the spectacles, which became increasingly important, especially in the early years of the *Principate* (the imperial system). The Romans were conscious that the amphitheatre was a building type they invented, which did not derive from Greek prototypes and which had greater potential to demonstrate *Romanitas* (Roman-ness) than any other architectural symbol. The amphitheatre spread as Rome spread. The spectacles extended through the Greek and Hellenistic provinces, but in these regions they took place largely in existing buildings such as theatres and stadia, which were often adapted to host spectacles in a safe way. Across the western Empire, from Spain though Gaul and the German provinces, along the Rhine and Danube frontiers, from the Balkans to Britain, amphitheatres were built. As the building style spread, however, it was adapted to local conditions and the extent to which the concept of the amphitheatre and its activities was adopted into the lifestyles of the myriad communities and cultures that participated in the Roman Empire varied enormously from place to place.

The first scholarly recognition that there were amphitheatres in Britain came in 1723 and the first excavations on an amphitheatre site in 1849. Since then excavation, discovery and research has revealed much, but the amphitheatre remains something of a sideshow in Romano-British archaeology and in most general works on Roman Britain the subject merits only a few lines. This reflects both the relative lack of research on amphitheatres in Britain and also a lack of enthusiasm to engage with the subject because of its bloodthirsty connotations. This is, perhaps, exemplified by the value-laden comments of the late George Boon on the amphitheatre at Caerleon, of which he said with distaste that:

> we may ... be certain that the bloody and degrading spectacles for which the name of Imperial Rome stands forever condemned, were witnessed here and in every such building.[3]

Excavations have not tended to be extensive and, where they were, have not tended to be published rapidly. Until the publication of work at Dorchester and Chester in 1975, the only major archaeological report on a British amphitheatre was that on Caerleon, excavated in the 1920s by Mortimer and Tessa V. Wheeler.[4] The extensive excavations of Michael Fulford at Silchester in the 1970s, the discovery of the London amphitheatre in 1988 and further work at Chester from 2004-6 have moved our understanding of the British amphitheatres on apace, to the point at which, for the first time, a book-length treatment of the subject seems both possible and desirable. The production in 1988 of a major study of amphitheatres across the Empire by the French scholar, Jean-Claude Golvin,[5] established a new era for amphitheatre studies, but as David Bomgardner pointed out in his review of Golvin's work,[6] the treatment in this volume of the amphitheatres in Britain is less than thorough and, despite the pioneering work of Fulford[7] (to whose name we should now add that of Nick Bateman[8]), 'no satisfactory survey of the British amphitheatres exists'. Though a brief gazetteer of amphitheatre sites by Roy Wilding appeared in 2005,[9] I hope that I am justified in claiming this book as a first attempt at such a survey.

Chapter 2 will briefly summarise the rise of the spectacles and the development and spread of amphitheatres throughout the western Empire. This makes no pretence to being either exhaustive or original, but sets the scene. In Chapter 3, I trace the history of the exploration of the amphitheatres, and the ways in which they have been studied and appreciated since Stukeley's first words on the subject in 1723, which are liberally quoted below my chapter headings. Chapters 4 and 5 draw from the evidence of the British amphitheatres to draw down themes, similarities and contrasts. Firstly, I suggest a typology based upon the sorts of communities served by the amphitheatres and look at the possible motivations and contexts for their construction. I then compare their planning and architecture. Chapters 6 and 7 summarise what is known of each amphitheatre in turn. Here I also give the grounds for the rejection of some structures which have been thought to be amphitheatres in the past and which are still from time to time quoted in the literature as such. Chapter 8 changes emphasis and examines the material evidence for the arena and for what went on there, drawing on a wide range of depictions of the arena in the material culture of Roman Britain. In Chapter 9 I will examine the fate of amphitheatres after Rome, and in Chapter 10 I attempt to reach conclusions on the way in which the amphitheatre was received, understood and appreciated in the British provinces.

One of the pleasures of writing this book has been the opportunity to visit all of the sites mentioned in the text. Not all of the sites are impressive, but many are surprising. I have added as an appendix a brief gazetteer and guide for the visitor to the more worthwhile sites.

2

ORIGINS AND DEVELOPMENT OF THE AMPHITHEATRE

> This, I suppose gave occasion to the building of regular amphitheatres, of which Caesar made the first in the *Campus Martius*, but of wood, when he was dictator. The first of stone was erected in Augustus, his time, by Statilius Taurus, in the place of the former, which was the only one till Vespasian, whose work was the monstrous *Collisaeum*, but finished by his son, Titus.[1]

By the time of the Roman conquest of Britain the amphitheatre and the games were long-established institutions in the Roman world. In order to place the British evidence into its wider context, we need to look at the origins of the amphitheatre and to trace its spread. There are three threads to this story; the first is the origin and history of the spectacles that eventually became associated with the amphitheatre, the second is the development of the architectural form. These have frequently been described in works on the amphitheatre, and in this chapter we will basically summarise existing knowledge and established ideas. The final thread relevant to this book is the spread of amphitheatres and the acceptance of the spectacles in the western Roman Empire.

The amphitheatre was, as the Romans themselves readily recognised, one of the very few building types that they, solely, invented. Most of the other sorts of public buildings that they used derived ultimately from Greek prototypes; Roman temple architecture was mostly developed from Greek styles, the *basilica* and *forum* of the Romans originated in the *stoa* and *agora* of Greek civic planning, and the theatre, of course, was a Greek invention. It is perhaps worth at the outset distinguishing between the theatre and the amphitheatre as one still finds the terms confused in the popular imagination. A theatre has a semi-circular auditorium, with a stage along the diameter of the circle, behind which rises a wall, usually ornamented with columns and niches. An amphitheatre is generally oval or elliptical, with seating all the way around. In a theatre the audience's eyes are drawn to the stage, in an amphitheatre to the open space in the centre of the ring of seating – the *arena*. The amphitheatre resembles two theatres, set face-to-face, with the stage and its equipment removed. The word 'amphitheatre' literally means 'theatre on both sides'.

The form of the amphitheatre developed during the later decades of the Roman Republic, at a time of political rivalry, during which individuals and factions would effectively bribe the electorate by staging spectacles. With the end of the Republic and the beginning of the Imperial system under the first emperor, Augustus (27 BC-AD 14; sole ruler from 30 BC), the amphitheatre and the events within it became one of the supreme symbols and expressions of *Romanitas*, the state and the emperor's role within it. This, of course, saw its greatest expression in the construction of the Colosseum under the Flavian dynasty (AD 69-96). The buildings were built to house events of a type that had taken place previously without specific structures designed for the purpose, *venationes* and *munera*.

The *venationes* were wild animal hunts, designed at least in part to demonstrate the dominance of man (particularly of civilised Roman man) over the natural world. Animal sacrifice as part of religious events was commonplace in the ancient world and some early Roman festivals incorporated spectacles involving animals. During the *Cerealia* animals such as hares and deer were hunted in front of spectators, and foxes and bulls took part respectively in the feasts of the *Floralia* and the *ludi Taurei*.[2] Animals were imported to Rome as novelties at various times, particularly after the first two Punic wars against Carthage (264-246 and 218-202 BC) when such creatures as elephants were displayed for the first time at Rome, though they were not initially slaughtered. The first recorded example of a *venatio* in Rome, in which ferocious wild animals fought together and were killed, was during votive games in 186 BC, given by M Fulvius Nobilior in fulfilment of a vow he had made in return for victory in campaigns in Greece, and featured a hunt of leopards and lions.[3] It is possible that the idea of this kind of entertainment was an import from North Africa to Rome following the Punic wars, though there is no absolute evidence for this. Certainly such spectacles were facilitated by the availability of North African animals, particularly the *africanae* or big cats, following the final destruction of Carthage in 146 BC. Significantly, this year also marked the first reference to the execution of non-Roman criminals in Rome by throwing them to wild beasts (*damnatio ad bestias*), when Scipio Aemilianus, the conqueror of Carthage, dealt with deserters from the auxiliary forces in his army in this way.

Games known as the *ludi circenses* were given annually by the newly elected *curule aediles*. These games began regularly to feature *venationes* in 169 BC.[4] This marks the point at which such spectacles began to be adopted in the regular festivals of the Roman political and religious calendar; the point in effect when they became institutionalised and therefore expected. Rival political figures competed to show the most novel, dangerous, or just plain numerous animals they could, thus 100 lions were shown in 104 BC following the north African war against Jugurtha and, in 58 BC, M Aemilius Scaurus showed 150 leopards, five crocodiles and a hippopotamus. The rival games of Pompey and Caesar continuously upped the ante, with Pompey slaughtering 20 elephants, 600 lions, 410 leopards, apes, lynx and a rhinoceros, and Caesar reciprocating in even more lavish style. Through the reign of Augustus and the early emperors lavish spectacles became even more extreme in an attempt to continually produce novelty, to the point where, at the inaugural games in the Colosseum, Titus had 9000 animals slaughtered in the arena.[5] Not only did these spectacles demonstrate the domination of man over nature, but by the introduction of new and unfamiliar species from strange places, the geographical extent of Rome's dominion was also symbolised. This was true particularly of Pompey, who was able to show many animals from the regions he had conquered in the east. These events were generally staged in the only structure in Rome which could house them, the *Circus Maximus*.

Gladiatorial displays were known as *munera*. The word has the meaning of 'duty' or 'obligation' and finds its origin in the idea of the duty of the living to provide obsequies for deceased relatives. The origins of gladiatorial combat were even lost to the Romans who did, however, generally believe that it was an imported practice. Its origins have been sought by historians in an adoption by the Etruscans of a Campanian practice, which was then transmitted to Rome during the time of the kings. The detail of this argument need not concern us here. The first known reference to a gladiatorial *munus* dates to 264 BC, when the funeral took place, in the *Forum Boarium* in Rome, of Decimus Brutus Pera.[6] Brutus' sons put on a spectacle at which three pairs of gladiators fought simultaneously. *Munera* were intended to draw attention to the virtues and the importance of the dead man and his family, and along with other aspects of funeral display, they also served to stress the importance and heritage of the family and its living members. *Munera* were only given for the most distinguished (and wealthy) citizens. Like the *venationes*, these events grew larger as families and individuals competed between themselves, not only competing with events staged by the living, but also against famous events from family pasts – thus in 212 BC the funeral of Marcus Aemilius Lepidus saw 22 pairs of gladiators and, in 183 BC, 60 pairs fought in memory of Publius Licinius.[7] *Munera*, however much they might have been contrived to elicit the maximum amount of public favour to the giver, were actually given by private individuals, and not by any intervention of the state. Despite this, lavish *munera* were presented as electoral bribes, often

ORIGINS AND DEVELOPMENT OF THE AMPHITHEATRE

1 External stair of the amphitheatre of Pompeii

at times well removed from the death of the individuals they purported to commemorate. So effective was this that in 63 BC, M Tullius Cicero introduced a law to forbid those in public life from holding *munera* during the two years prior to their standing for office. The idea was clearly to divorce the spectacles from the campaigning. Two years previously, in 65 BC, Julius Caesar, as *aedile*, had attempted to stage a *munus* of 320 pairs of gladiators.[8] Although the individuals staging *munera* were often public office holders, this does not equate to the state providing the events. The first *munus* which could be interpreted as state provision was held as part of the *Feriae Latinae*, the Latin festival, in 42 BC at the height of the civil war between Antony and Octavian on the one hand and the assassins of Julius Caesar on the other.[9]

During the late Republic, *munera* were held in public spaces within the city, often in the *Forum*. Dio Cassius describes *spectacula* staged by Caesar in the *Forum* of Rome, and also mentions the 'hunting theatre' built by Caesar for his triumph in 46 BC. This, according to Dio, 'was called an amphitheatre … for it had seating on all sides without a stage structure'.[10] It may well have been intended to be at least semi-permanent. By this time, the first stone-built, true amphitheatres were already in existence, primarily in the *coloniae* of Campania. These cities, many established by the dictator Sulla following the Social War (90-88 BC), were Roman planted towns in areas of Italy which were forcibly resettled and reorganised, and the amphitheatres may have begun to assume the symbolism which they were to acquire during the *Principate* even this early. The archetype is the amphitheatre of Pompeii (*1*), stone built and dated by its dedicatory inscription to *c*.70 BC. Other early amphitheatres include the first phases of structures that were to become much grander later, such as Pozzuoli (*2*) and Capua, and others that remained modest, such as Paestum (*29, 45*).[11] In Rome itself the provision of permanent public auditoria, such as theatres, had

2 Part of the façade of the amphitheatre at Pozzuoli, Italy

been banned for a long time, as they could have become venues for political and popular gatherings. The first stone theatre was not built in the city until that of Pompey in 55 BC. A structure mentioned by Pliny, which has excited comment at least since Stukeley discussed it in 1723,[12] is the double theatre of C Scribonius Curio. This novelty, built in 52 BC, comprised two wooden theatres placed back to back, which, after theatrical events, could be revolved to face each other, creating the seating around the arena of an amphitheatre.

The first stone-built amphitheatre in Rome was erected by C Statilius Taurus during the reign of Augustus, in 29 BC. At the same time Augustus placed limits on the size and frequency of *munera* given by others, while his own events were the most lavish ever seen, with 10,000 men participating in eight gladiatorial events according to his own account.[13] By 22 BC the spectacles were basically under Imperial control. The *praetors* were allowed public funding to produce two *munera* annually using a total of 120 gladiators, all other such events were produced by the emperor and members of the imperial family. By the time of Domitian (AD 81-96) no gladiatorial games could be produced except by the emperor or on his behalf.[14] From this point on, in Rome, it was the ruler who determined the scope, frequency, date and duration of the games, which generally would be celebrated on exceptional festivals and occasions. Although the distinction between public and private benefaction was blurred by this system, it remained the case that the ruler gave *munera* as a personal gift using his own resources. They did not strictly speaking come from the public purse. Another Augustan phenomenon was the bringing together of the strands of the *venationes* and the *munera* into a single event, the *munus legitimum*, and the beginning of a format which saw *venationes* in the morning of a festival, the execution of criminals at lunchtime and, the highlight of the show, gladiatorial fights in the afternoon.

The Statilian amphitheatre was probably not the only venue in Rome used for the spectacles held by the Julio-Claudian dynasty, which would also have continued to be held in the *Forum* and the *Circus Maximus*. The building certainly perished in the great fire of Rome in AD 64 during the reign of Nero. The chaos of the Year of Four Emperors (AD 69), which followed Nero's assassination in AD 68, ended in the accession of Vespasian and the beginning of the Flavian dynasty, which lasted until the death of Domitian and the accession of Nerva in AD 96. Vespasian lacked the legitimacy conferred by descent from Augustus, and needed to establish his rule and the stability of the succession. The supreme symbol of this need was the construction of the greatest stone-built amphitheatre of all – the Flavian amphitheatre, known to us as the Colosseum (*3*). Following the fire, Nero had planned a great palace, the *Domus Aurea*, or Golden House, built across much of the fire-damaged city. Nero's artificial lake, part of his ornamental park, was used by Vespasian as the site of the Colosseum, symbolically righting the injustice of Nero and turning his appropriated land back to public use. In Rome, the building of the Colosseum was a break with tradition, but became an instant symbol of 'being Roman' across the whole Empire, as it remains in many ways to this day. The Colosseum was a multi-layered symbol. It was the setting in which the ruler paraded and demonstrated his power to the people, but was also the place where the Roman people could sense and feel their own power and the glory of their Empire. It was a model of Roman society, with seating arranged hierarchically, the wealthy and powerful in the lower front seats and the masses, segregated by class, in the higher tiers. It was a place where emperor and people could see and be seen, where they could interact, and where often the political views of the masses could be represented to the emperor in chanting (whether he took any notice or not). The order imposed on the arena, the control of the organiser or *editor* of the games and the ritualisation of what was a chaotic and bloody process was similarly symbolic of the order imposed on the Empire and upon Roman society by the Imperial system.

The communities, first of Italy and then of the Empire at large, built amphitheatres and provided games in order to demonstrate that they were indeed part of the Roman nexus, and the buildings were erected and shows put

3 The Colosseum, showing the outer two arcades in section

on by provincial elites anxious to demonstrate their alignment with the Roman world. In the eastern provinces the spectacles spread, but amphitheatres did not,

ORIGINS AND DEVELOPMENT OF THE AMPHITHEATRE

4 The amphitheatre at Arles, France, with a modern audience awaiting the beginning of a bull fight

as the Greek world already had buildings such as stadia and theatres, which could be, and were, adapted for the purpose.[15] There are hints that in some western provinces the concept of gladiatorial combat was not wholly alien to aspects of native practice. For instance in Spain, gladiators appeared at the funeral of the chieftain Viriathus in 140 BC, and in Gaul, a native Celtic form of execution forced criminals to fight each other.[16] Roman settlers in southern Gaul had certainly imported *munera*, with the first recorded spectacle taking place in Arles (*4*) in 63 BC.[17]

Two of the most important influences in the spread of *Romanitas* in the western provinces were the Imperial cult and the army, and these elements also fostered the spread of the amphitheatre. The Imperial cult in the western provinces is characterised by the site of *Condate* near *Lugdunum* (Lyons). Here Drusus, in AD 12, established a cult centre around a temple and altar to Rome and Augustus on a site which was also the meeting place of the Council of the Three Gauls. The first stone amphitheatre on this site was built by a priest (*sacerdos*) of the cult, C Julius Rufus, during the reign of Tiberius. Inscriptions on the seating giving tribal affiliations suggest that seating was reserved for delegates to the Council[18] and that the arena was integral to the festival of the Imperial cult held annually on 1 August. Although the building may have been used for both ritual ceremonial and public debate, Roman gladiatorial combat was also introduced by Augustus in the context of the sanctuary.[19] The fourth-century account of Eusebius, recounting the martyrdom of a number of Christians at *Lugdunum* in AD 177, almost certainly in the amphitheatre at *Condate*, demonstrates that the amphitheatre was also used for executions.[20] The martyrs suffered flogging, burning and exposure to wild beasts. The chief priesthood was an annual magistracy, held in rotation by members of the various communities of the Gallic provinces, and there is evidence that the financial burden of providing fully trained gladiators became so onerous that the central authority intervened, providing condemned criminals to fight each other to the death.[21] *Munera* were associated with the cult from the outset, and the amphitheatres served to allow the spectators to affirm their loyalty and, as in Rome, to view the panoply of Roman power. The accession of Vespasian in AD 69 and the initiation of the Flavian dynasty opened up a new phase in the Imperial cult, and the amphitheatre seems to have taken a place in this, as shown by the large amphitheatre provided at the Imperial cult centre of Narbo, the charter for which includes mention of *spectacula*.

The use of the amphitheatre as an Imperial symbol is shown to effect on Trajan's column, which depicts episodes from the Dacian wars and may show amphitheatres erected on the frontier by the army. The first amphitheatre is shown in the portrayal of a siege and occurs next to a triumphal arch. The second is in the background of a scene showing Trajan and his retinue holding a parley with a group of Dacian dignitaries (*48*). This architectural backdrop combines with the togas worn by the Romans to show where the power resides.[22] Trajan's column is, of course, an exercise in Imperial military propaganda. The legions were fundamental to the expansion of the Roman Empire and the spread of Roman ideas, and were completely linked with the Imperial system. The army was imbued with Roman and Imperial identity above all other institutions. Recent studies have stressed the idea of the Roman army as a community among other communities in the Empire, with a unique general outlook and function. The military community was the basis of Imperial power and control, its role derived from the ruler, and its status deriving from its relationship with the emperor. Many legionary fortresses and some auxiliary forts had their own amphitheatres, with 28 scattered along the line of the *limes*, the Roman frontier in north-western Europe, broadly along the Rhine and Danube. Efforts have been made to identify these as *ludi*, or training grounds for the Roman army, an interpretation which long found favour in Britain (p. 58). It is, however, more likely that these amphitheatres were built for the celebration of festivals, especially those festivals associated with the Imperial cult. Amphitheatres at legionary fortresses served large groups of Roman citizens, as citizenship was a prerequisite for joining the legions. In some newly conquered provinces, like Britain, legionary fortresses housed the largest single groupings of Roman citizens, and their loyalty to and identification with the concept of the emperor need hardly be stressed. In these amphitheatres the soldiers would see military virtue enacted, the ability to fight well and to die well. Pliny wrote of gladiatorial combat that here was:

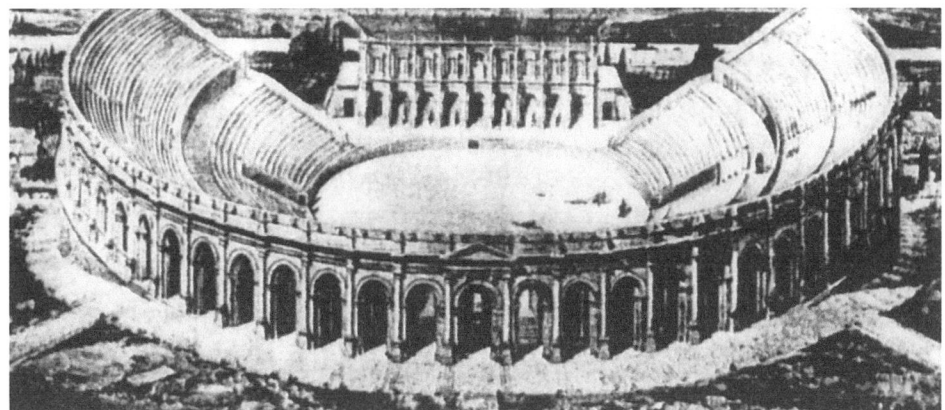

5 Reconstruction of the Gallic semi-amphitheatre at *Lutetia. Drawn by J. Formigé 1918*

nothing enervating or weak, nor anything that would soften or break the manly spirit, but something that awakens contempt for death and indifference to wounds, since even in the bodies of slaves and criminals a love of glory and desire for victory can be seen[23]

In the amphitheatre Roman legionaries would see the specifically military aspects of the Roman concept of *virtus*.[24] Importantly, in the gladiator, the soldier was seeing one aspect of *virtus* in its purest form, as the only claim a gladiator had to this quality came through fighting. In this way the military amphitheatre performed a didactic function, reinforcing the requirement in the Roman legionary for uncomplaining courage, skill at arms and the ability to die in combat without complaint. No gladiator ever fought as a Roman legionary. The equipment of the different forms of gladiators was ultimately derived from barbarian prototypes. The arena showed barbarians fighting with barbarian weapons. Perhaps this also reinforced for the legionary that he would be required to fight someone who had very different fighting styles to those in which he was himself trained.

Recent work has indicated that, outside the administrative and military context, different provinces adopted the amphitheatre and all it involved to different degrees and on their own terms.[25] Amphitheatres seem in general to have been an aspect of urbanisation, with every truly Romanised town aspiring to the construction of such a facility. Amphitheatres were part of a suite of buildings that were desirable adjuncts to urban life, but they were also sometimes connected to temples demonstrating a cult connection, thus the two amphitheatres at Augst (*Augusta Raurica*) were closely connected to the development of temples.[26] In Gaul a simple correlation between centres of population and the provision of amphitheatres is not the whole story. True amphitheatres tend to be situated in the cities of the southern, wealthier and more Romanised parts of the region. In the north the so-called theatre-amphitheatres were numerous. The site of Les Arénés in Paris, for instance, consisted of an elliptical arena flanked by a monumental stage (5). It may be that part of the motivation to create this kind of building was simply economic – the hybrid form would obviate the need for both a theatre and an amphitheatre, but it also seems likely that they were designed for specific purposes, perhaps catering to a specific provincial taste in entertainment.[27] Such buildings were not limited to the urban scene, but also appeared at significant rural shrines.

When an amphitheatre was located in an urban context it was almost always on the fringe of the town. Like many aspects of the games and the amphitheatre, this was symbolic. The amphitheatre was 'on the edge' in so many ways, marking the boundary between life and death, between savage and civilised, in the sense of both wild nature and wild humanity seen in the arena, between danger and security, order and disorder. It was 'visibly the place where civilisation and barbarism met, and civilisation for the Romans meant the city'.[28] Perhaps we can also see the prevalence of amphitheatres on the Imperial frontiers as this same idea writ large.

A final consideration is the frequency with which shows might have been presented in provincial amphitheatres. This is a difficult issue. Spectacles were part of the duties of municipal magistrates, and would be put on to celebrate religious events and the Imperial cult, as well as the dedication of public buildings or the fulfilment of vows. One of the very few indications of the frequency of spectacles in the Western Empire is the *Lex Ursonenis*, which regulates the scale of spectacles to be given in the city of Urso, in modern Portugal, during the time of Julius Caesar. The *aediles* of the city were to organise annual, three-day festivals of games. These were to last for the greater part of whole days and the *aedile* was expected to fund the shows with 2000 *sesterces* from his own pocket.[29] This is a statute of limitations intended to prevent ambitious local politicians bankrupting themselves, however even this seems ambitious for the northern Gallic or British scene, as does Augustus' legal maximum of 120 gladiators for a *munus* given by anyone but the emperor.[30] Frequency would depend on the resources of the individual, as *munera* were individual gifts, not state events. One is drawn to the inevitable conclusion that such events varied in frequency from area to area depending on the taste of the community and the wealth and liberality of individuals. However, the likelihood is that they were few and far between in many provincial locations, including in Britain.

3

DISCOVERY AND EXPLORATION

> The *area* in the middle was commonly called *arena*, from the sand it was strown over with, for the better footing of the combatants, and to drink up the blood: this again by intervals was fresh strown, or raked over to prevent slipperiness. Hence this word became a common appellation of an amphitheatre, and most of those beyond sea are still called *arena*.[1]

The discovery, interpretation and excavation of the British amphitheatres has taken place gradually over some 250 years. During the seventeenth and eighteenth centuries the first amphitheatres were identified. During the nineteenth century debate over the identification of amphitheatres took place alongside a very few proper investigations. The scientific study and discovery of the British amphitheatres has therefore been a largely twentieth-century phenomenon.

EARLY REFERENCES AND ANTIQUARIAN STUDIES

It is possible that the first 'modern' record of an amphitheatre was contained in the account of Caerleon written by the twelfth-century monk *Giraldus Cambrensis*, or Gerald of Wales. He wrote:

> This city was of undoubted antiquity, and handsomely built of masonry, with courses of bricks, by the Romans. Many vestiges of its former splendour may yet be seen … remarkable hot baths, relics of temples, and theatres, all inclosed within fine walls, parts of which remain standing. You will find on all sides, both within and without the circuit of the walls, subterraneous buildings, aqueducts, underground passages; and what I think worthy of notice, stoves contrived with wonderful art, to transmit the heat insensibly through narrow tubes passing up the side walls.[2]

There is no doubt that he saw impressive standing Roman ruins of which the amphitheatre would have been a part. His trustworthiness as an observer and interpreter of such things is shown by the description of a hypocaust, which is quite astonishing for 1191.

Later observers, such as the Tudor antiquarian John Leland, recorded sites but did not interpret them well. Of the British amphitheatres Leland noticed only that at Richborough, of which he wrote:

> There is a good flyte-shot of fro Ratesburgh ... a great dike caste yn a round cumpas as it had been fens of menne of warre. The cumpace of the ground within is not much above an acre, and that is very holo by casting up the yerth.[3]

The central hollow of the arena is at least well described. The diarist, John Aubrey, noted that 'Mr John Langley, the schoolmaster of [St] Paul's School found such a theatre-like place at Dorchester, Dorsetshire'. This was almost certainly the amphitheatre site of Maumbury Rings.[4] William Stukeley[5] later noted that this site had been spotted and identified as an amphitheatre by Sir Christopher Wren, a contemporary of Aubrey and Langley, when he travelled to Portland to find suitable stone for the building of St Paul's Cathedral.

Stukeley's observations at Dorchester earn him the title of the father of British amphitheatre studies. His dissertation '*Of the Roman amphitheatre at Dorchester*' was first published as a pamphlet and read to his Masonic lodge in 1723,[6] but is most accessible within in his magisterial work of 1776, the *Itinerarium Curiosum*.[7] He was the first to recognise what the earthworks at Silchester, Richborough and Dorchester (*6*) really were, and his analysis of Dorchester includes informed discussion of matters which remain at the forefront of amphitheatre studies today, including surveying schemes, estimates of audience capacity and a discussion of the origins of the architectural form. Many parts of his text are quoted in this book, particularly at the chapter headings. He also produced the first series of illustrations of British amphitheatres, including reconstruction drawings of the Dorchester site. Stukeley regretted that Christopher Wren had not produced illustrations, as these would have shown the amphitheatre 'in greater perfection, before the gallows were removed here by an unlucky humour of the sheriff'. As late as 1767 Maumbury Rings had been used for executions, which attracted huge crowds and caused the 'parapet to be much beaten down, by the trampling of horses and men at executions'. As many as 10,000 are reckoned to have attended the public strangling and burning of the 19 year-old murderess, Mary Channing, in 1706,[8] the execution of 'a woman for petit-treason, by burning' to which Stukeley referred in the context of his mathematical attempts to estimate actual seating capacity.[9] The practice of execution in the arena in the late

DISCOVERY AND EXPLORATION

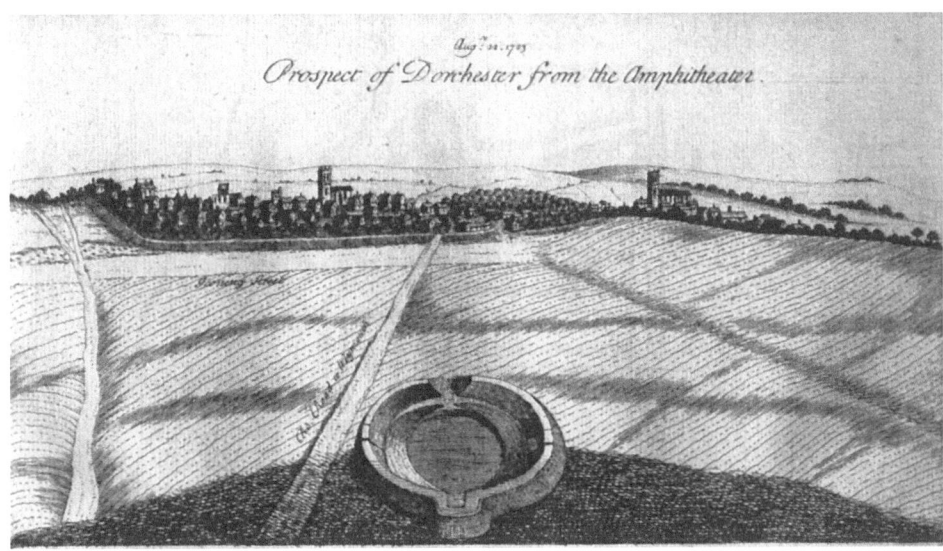

6 Prospect of Dorchester viewed from the amphitheatre, by William Stukeley (1723)

seventeenth and early eighteenth centuries presents a dark return to the Roman function of the site, unparalleled elsewhere.

Stukeley was not embarrassed to promote earthwork amphitheatres as being as interesting and grand, in their way, as their great, stone-built, Imperial counterparts:

> [This] piece of architecture ... Will give to the spectator a fine notion in the structures of this sort abroad, deservedly the admiration of travellers; and will present a person of understanding, the pleasure of observing the great and noble genius of the Romans in every production of their hands. Nor does the meanness of its materials debase, but rather inhance, its value and art; for though less costly and lasting than stone and marble, of which the others are built, yet for the same reason, less liable to rapine, and the covetous humour of such as plunder them for other uses: therefore I believe, in the main, it is as perfect as most abroad, if not so alluring to the eye, whence we must suppose it has so long escaped common observation.[10]

Though Stukeley recognised that Maumbury Rings was an amphitheatre, he erred in his belief that the monument as it stood was unaltered since Roman times. It had, in fact, been extensively altered when it was transformed into an artillery fortification only a century before, during the English Civil Wars. In his plan of the 'geometrical groundplot' of the amphitheatre (7) he attempted to identify features named in classical sources, such as the seat of the praetor and the wild-beast dens.

These interpretations were largely hopeful and mistaken. The ramps labelled *iter circulares*, for example, of which Stukeley makes a great deal his in text, were cut into the *cavea* during the 1640s to allow artillery to be taken to the ramparts. Much interpretation, including the statements on the orientation of the building to gain the most favourable effects from the sun and to shelter from wind and rain, and the long discussion of acoustics, would not now seriously be considered. None of this, however, detracts from the careful observation and description of the monument that marks Stukeley out as one of the greatest field observers among early antiquarians.

Two other amphitheatres were identified by Stukeley, Silchester (*8*) and Richborough (*9*), and up to the end of the century these were the only ones accepted, with the later addition of Cirencester, first noticed by Richard Gough, who described the amphitheatre in the area known as ' "the Querns" – an elliptical area called the Bull Ring.'[11] Stukeley mentioned a tombstone found in 'the Querns', but clearly did not visit the location.

THE NINETEENTH CENTURY

Stukeley's account of Dorchester is scholarly, restrained and scientific. It is very much in the spirit of the eighteenth-century Enlightenment. By the early nineteenth century the rise of Romanticism changed the mood such that no account of amphitheatres was complete without some lurid speculation on the horrors which the monument must have witnessed. I will quote only one representative sample of this school, which is contained in an anonymous pamphlet on the history of Silchester. A valuable observation, which notes the appearance of seating terraces, is followed by typical romantic imaginings:

> [The amphitheatre has] high and steep banks now covered with a grove of trees, and two entrances. Seats arranged in five rows, one above another. In one part close on the south side appears to have been the *cavea* or den, where the wild beasts were kept before they were let out into the arena.
>
> There the gladiators or naked prize fighters used to exhibit their skill ... wild beasts used to be brought forth to fight with each other and thus afford a brutal pleasure to the polished Romans.
>
> What scenes have taken place in this now silent and deserted spot! The lion's roar and the tiger's howl have echoed through these woodlands. The shrieks of the torn victim have here rent the air, while the shouts of the multitude, as cruel as the beasts which afforded them such a sanguinary pleasure, were still more awful.[12]

DISCOVERY AND EXPLORATION

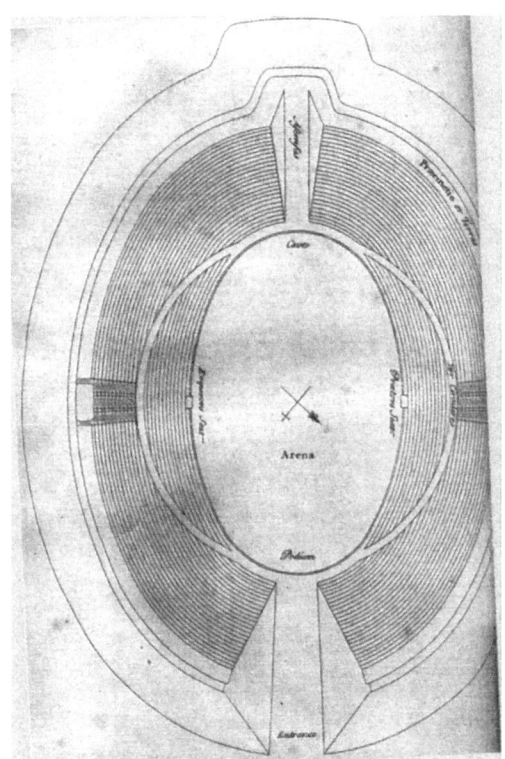

7 Conjectural reconstruction drawing of the original layout at Dorchester, by William Stukeley (1723)

8 View of the amphitheatre at Silchester, by William Stukeley (1775)

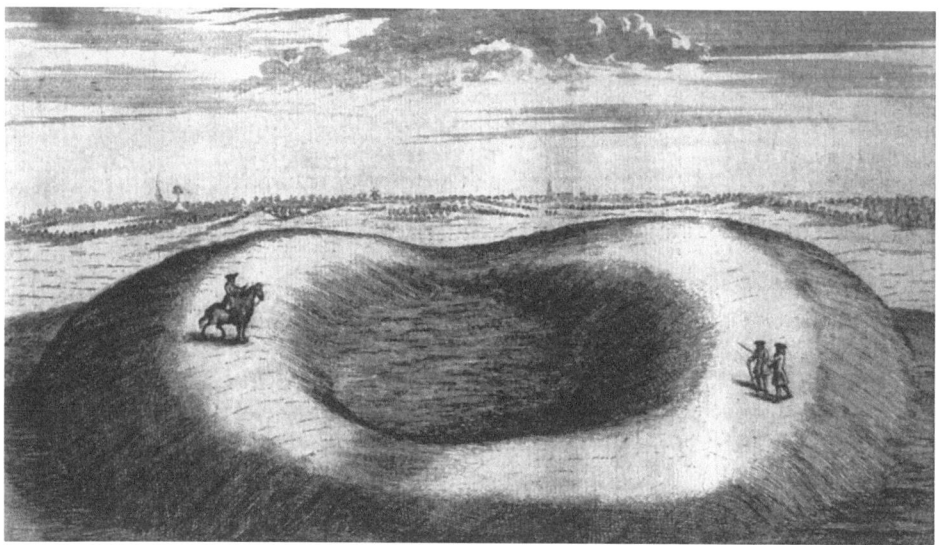

9 View of the amphitheatre at Richborough, by William Stukeley (1775)

The mid-century marked the beginning of practical research. The Verulamium theatre was discovered and first excavated in 1847 when a farmer notified the antiquary R. Grove-Lowe of the presence of curvilinear walls in his field. Though well conducted for its time, the excavation did not establish a chronological sequence for the building.[13] This was the first Roman site of entertainment to be excavated, but the earliest excavation on any British amphitheatre was undertaken only two years later, at Richborough. During the autumn of 1849 the local antiquarian Mr Rolfe 'resolved to test the cause of the appearances [of an amphitheatre] previously noted.'[14] Despite there being no obvious trace of buried masonry, excavation was begun. 'A small fragment of Roman mortar was at length detected on the surface, and the labourers being directed to dig beneath the spot, came to a wall at the depth of about one foot'. They had found the arena wall. The plan of the arena (*10*) leaves much to be desired and the report as published is confusing, but this was a major step in the study of British amphitheatres. Charles Roach Smith's expressed hope that the:

> researches which, under the personal guidance of Mr Rolfe, have so successfully terminated will, it is trusted, create a desire in individuals who may command the means, to institute an examination of analogous works in other parts of the country, with a view to decide their mode of construction.[15]

DISCOVERY AND EXPLORATION

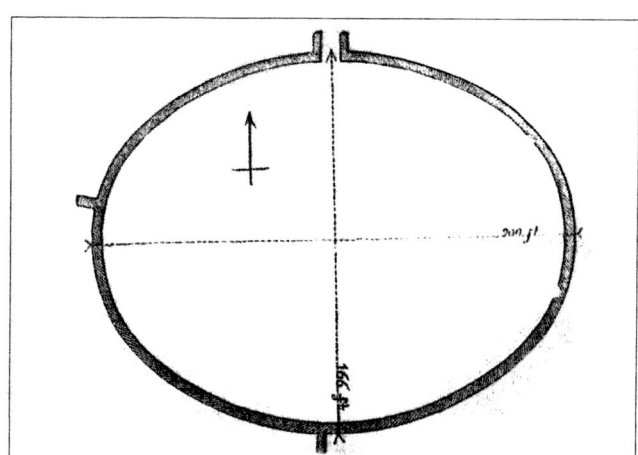

10 Plan of the arena at Richborough following the excavations of 1848. Roach Smith 1849

This was not to be fully realised until Bosanquet's work at Housesteads in 1898 and that of Gray at Maumbury Rings Dorchester in 1908. Roach Smith made note of the 'large theatre, for dramatic representations' at Verulamium and otherwise cited the amphitheatres known to him at Silchester, Dorchester and Caerleon.

Throughout the nineteenth century various sites were reported as possible amphitheatres, only for the claims never to resurface. There are many examples, of which I will quote only two. Firstly, in 1874, an earthwork at Castell, Llanidan on Anglesey was proposed by W. Owen Stanley[16] who identified stone seats at one end of an oval earthwork, concluding that 'it was a Roman, not a British work, as the British are, almost without exception, of earth'. In the modern Royal Commission Inventory of the island this site falls into the 'unclassified' category.[17] Stanley quoted a range of monuments, including many prehistoric sites as potential amphitheatres. He did, however, also mention the site of Arthur's Round Table at Caerleon and the earthwork near the auxiliary fort at Tomen-y-Mur, both of which are now accepted as amphitheatres, the latter being seriously put forward in 1888.[18]

The second example is to the south of Chichester, close to the Roman palace at Fishbourne, in the harbour village of Bosham. In 1886, H. Mitchell[19] reported on:

> ... a large excavation in the form of a basin, where tradition says the Romans burnt their dead. Mr Harris, whose family have resided in Bosham upwards of 200 years ... has been told by members of his family that they remember remnants of the tiers of seats where the spectators sat to watch the funeral pile ... This excavation Mr Lowther thinks much more likely to have been an amphitheatre. The remains of several of these exist in Britain in the vicinity of Roman camps.

Whatever this may have been, it has completely disappeared, but its proximity to the amphitheatre at Chichester, which was discovered in 1935, makes it unlikely that this was a Roman amphitheatre.

An example of a different sort was the 1858 suggestion that an oval depression lying to the north of Hadrian's Wall near Housesteads was an amphitheatre. The key to this was the discovery of an additional gate through the Wall (the so-called Knag Burn Gate). At the time it had only recently been found that gates were provided only at the forts and milecastles of the Wall, and this extra gate needed an explanation. This was simple – the gate existed to give access to the amphitheatre. The complication that the amphitheatre lay north of the Wall was solved by reference to the extra-mural position of the amphitheatres of Cirencester and Silchester, which for Albert Way[20] confirmed:

> in a certain measure ... the conjecture that the excavation adjacent to Housesteads had likewise been destined for those disports for which we find provision made in the most remote parts of the empire, on sites of any extensive or permanent occupation by the Romans.

The interpretation was completely accepted by the great Wall scholar John Collingwood Bruce[21] (*11*) who spoke of it in context with the Cirencester amphitheatre and, with no little relish, at the 1860 meeting of the Archaeological Institute at Gloucester:

> One interesting feature of *Corinium* is its extramural amphitheatre. We find the *amphitheatrum castrense* outside the walls at Dorchester, Silchester, Caerleon, Richborough and several other places. We also have one in the north of England adjacent to the mural station of Borcovicus. It is however, small in comparison with that of Cirencester, but large enough for the garrison, which consisted only of one cohort. In the sculptures of Trajan's column we perceive two amphitheatres erected during the Dacian campaigns. It was necessary to give the soldiers amusement. When the tribune of the Tungrian cohort at Borcovicus, on the great Northern Barrier, found that his men were suffering from the sameness of their daily toil, all he had to do was to catch a couple of Caledonians, and off with them to the amphitheatre.[22]

In the same year, 1858, the possible amphitheatre at Charterhouse-on-Mendip was identified by the Rev H.M. Scarth:

> at Charterhouse are very interesting remains of a Roman station and a perfect amphitheatre. ... The farmer pointed out the site of another amphitheatre about half a mile distant to the south.[23]

DISCOVERY AND EXPLORATION

11 Nineteenth-century view of the supposed amphitheatre at Housesteads. *Bruce 1853*

The suggestion that two amphitheatres existed on the same small site seems very doubtful, though recent ideas on the German auxiliary amphitheatres perhaps make the idea less outlandish (p. 61). It is also, of course, entirely possible that the two earthworks were built at different times and for different purposes.

During the British Archaeological Association's excursion to Cirencester in 1869, lively debate took place over the identification of the Cirencester amphitheatre and whether other British earthworks could be said to have been amphitheatres. The views were typical of the time. The amphitheatre had first been identified as such by Samuel Rudder in 1800 (p. 110),[24] and various small excavations had taken place. In 1868, T.C. Brown had made sections through the monument, but had found no 'stones or steps such as had been found in amphitheatres in foreign countries.'[25] He was, however, in no doubt of the function of the amphitheatre, stating that in the British climate stone seats would be uncomfortably cold and that seating of wood would have been provided, which had since perished. Others present were unconvinced – a Mr Roberts thought it to be quarry spoil heaps and Mr Turner, an 'encampment, nothing more'. The Rev. Prebendary H.M. Scarth was an amphitheatre enthusiast and was of the opinion that 'it was not fair to judge of the amphitheatres of England at Roman stations by those on the Continent'; a statement of a kind frequent at the time, implying that Roman Britain was special and 'different' from the rest of the Empire. Scarth claimed sites at Dorchester, Silchester, Old Sarum, Charterhouse-on-Mendip and Ilchester. He 'multiplied instances, and denied they were natural formations. People might as well say the barrows of the Wiltshire Downs were natural formations'. The Rev. Joyce had no doubt that Silchester had an amphitheatre, and Mr Black said that it was common among Roman legions to have gladiators, hence the necessity for amphitheatres. Indeed the presence of an amphitheatre strengthened his belief that Cirencester was the site 'of a military post formed by the Romans and not an ancient city taken by them'. Finally Mr Black hoped that further excavations would be made, and that 'opinion should be determined by example'.

The hopeful nature of earthwork studies and the identification of amphitheatres based on the flimsiest of evidence were shown in the Association's meeting the following year (1870) in St Albans. Though the theatre was not exposed for the Congress to view, its excavator, R. Grove-Lowe, was embarrassed when he conducted the participants to 'the site of the supposed Roman amphitheatre';

> [he] explained that he had been deceived by an extraordinary growth of mushrooms, which he had mistaken for the amphitheatre. He was very sorry to have misled them – he was not to have the honour of being the discoverer of both the theatre and the amphitheatre at Verulam.[26]

Two further nineteenth-century identifications should be mentioned at this stage, as they have, to varying degrees, both passed the test of time. The first of these is a small oval earthwork near the Roman auxiliary fort at Tomen-y-Mur in North Wales (*12*). First described in 1784 by Thomas Pennant,[27] it was not until 1888 that it was suggested that this was an amphitheatre and 'probably used for the gladiatorial exhibitions to which the Romans were so much addicted'.[28] Secondly, at Woodcutts there is a small Romano-British village settlement on Cranborne Chase in Dorset. It was excavated by General Pitt Rivers in 1885, and was thoroughly reported in the first of the General's celebrated and pioneering excavation reports.[29] The General described an earthwork close to the village as 'the amphitheatre known as "Church Barrow"' and produced evidence to show that it may have been a Roman work.

All nineteenth-century lists of places where amphitheatres were to be found contain a basic list – Dorchester, Silchester, Cirencester and Richborough being the most often cited – but these are almost always augmented by a number of varied and speculative locations identified through negligible evidence or flights of fancy. If mushrooms could become amphitheatres then more rigorous

DISCOVERY AND EXPLORATION

12 Nineteenth-century view of the amphitheatre at Tomen-y-Mur. Allen 1888

methods were needed. These were prefigured in 1898, when R.C. Bosanquet excavated the site of the so-called amphitheatre at Housesteads, and proved it to have been a Roman sandstone quarry, nothing more.[30]

THE TWENTIETH CENTURY

In 1908, Hadrian Allcroft published his *Earthwork of England*,[31] a classic volume on the earthwork monuments of the country, in which he looked at past interpretations with a sceptical and hypercritical eye. For the Roman period he singled out amphitheatres for special mention, dismissing or suspecting most, as he saw that many identifications were hopefully or romantically inspired:

> The fact is that amphitheatres, with their implication of butchery, are as much an obsession with the multitude as are the Druids with their supposed unholy rites. Antiquaries of repute have gone out of their way to voice the totally unwarranted assertion that "every Roman town in Britain had its amphitheatre". As well expect every petty town in India to boast an English-built theatre.[32]

He was particularly scathing about the more obscure identifications which had been made – those similar to the cases of Bosham and Llanidan which we have already noted:

31

… the determination to find amphitheatres all over the map has led to their being claimed for places as far apart as Mark Inch in Fifeshire and Redruth and Gwennap in Cornwall, although both these counties were regions which the Romans never occupied. As a matter of fact the so-called Cornish amphitheatres are for the most part Medieval works, and that of Gwennap was made about 1803 to accommodate miners who attended Wesleyan preachings! In plain truth any convenient hole in the ground has been fixed on by irresponsible visionaries as an amphitheatre.[33]

Allcroft evaluated the more likely cases, but was very careful to accept only those for which there was good evidence and to regard others with suspicion:

There is … reason to doubt whether Britain boasted so many amphitheatres. After all, and when one comes to examine the list even of those only alleged to exist, it scarcely bears out the broad generalisation that every Roman station had its own. There was one at Silchester … There was another at Richborough in Kent … There are said, on various authority, to be the remains of others at Colchester, Caerlleon [sic], Cirencester, Aldborough (Yorks) and Borcovicus [Housesteads] on the Wall; but of these only the case of Cirencester seems to be above suspicion, and that of Caerlleon probable. The so-called amphitheatre of Colchester has been suspected to be a medieval maze; that of Borcovicus may have been a quarry. That at Caerlleon called the Round Table stands in a field known as the Bear-House field, but while it may not be anything but a medieval baiting ring, on the other hand it may be a genuine Roman amphitheatre put to the use of bear baiting in subsequent times.[34]

Allcroft accepted the amphitheatre at Maumbury Rings near Dorchester,[35] although, in a shaft clearly aimed at the shade of William Stukeley, he expressed scorn for:

the imagination of some generations [which] has exercised itself in trying to fit in the details of the work with what is known of the arrangements of Roman amphitheatres – to identify the Praetor's box, the seats of the lesser notables and the dens of the wild beasts …[36]

The amphitheatre of Charterhouse-on-Mendip was regarded with suspicion as:

… an earthwork of peculiar character which passed as unquestioned as an amphitheatre since it was so styled by the late Prebendary Scarth in 1858 (he seems indeed to have seen two amphitheatres here, which only makes the matter doubly marvellous).[37]

His dismissal of the amphitheatre at Housesteads (Borcovicus) (he seems not to have known that this had been disproved 10 years previously) was accompanied by a footnote:

> ... It is of course quite possible that a quarry hole of convenient character may have actually been used by the Romans or Romano-Britons for purposes of sport, but even so to call such holes by the name of amphitheatres is misleading.[38]

In the case of Charterhouse-on-Mendip, one of Allcroft's criteria for rejection was simply the size of the earthwork, that the word 'amphitheatre' is too dignified for a work as small, and that the word 'raises false ideas of space and grandeur'. He may not have been aware of the claims of Tomen-y-Mur, but would probably have dismissed that site for the same reason. Effectively with this statement Allcroft opened up the question of definitions – just what is an amphitheatre? – which will be examined in detail in the next chapters.

Allcroft's scepticism was symptomatic of a new and more scientific approach to the examination of earthworks in general at the beginning of the twentieth century. Ninety-nine years after his work, the very small number of sites that he accepted (*13*) is somewhat startling, but also highlights the pace of discovery and interpretation during the course of the twentieth century. Allcroft's certain sites were Silchester, Richborough, Dorchester and Cirencester. Caerleon he accepted with reservations. The lack of excavation on any of the sites before Allcroft wrote is extraordinary in retrospect. Richborough was the only site proven by excavation, while Silchester and Cirencester had been trenched on a small scale with inconclusive results and no published reporting. Dorchester had seen small-scale trenching in its north entrance in 1879,[39] but the next century saw a mass of excavation work and of new discoveries.

The first site to be tackled on a large scale was Maumbury Rings, Dorchester (*14*). Funds were raised by public subscription and an excavation committee was formed representing the British Archaeological Association and the Dorchester Field Club. The excavation director chosen by the Committee was H. St George Gray, a highly respected field archaeologist, who had been General Pitt Rivers' principal assistant. Gray, who was recruited by the General in 1888, while still in his teens, remained with him until 1899,[40] and had subsequently excavated many sites, notably at Avebury. With a small team and on leave from his post as curator of the Taunton Museum, Gray undertook five seasons of work from 1908 to 1913. The publication of the excavations, however, had to wait a considerable time. Though interim accounts appeared every season, these did not include full plans and sections. Full publication awaited the analysis of Gray's archive by Richard Bradley, which was published in the *Archaeologia* in 1975.[41] Gray's job at

Site	Allcroft 1908	Collingwood & Richmond 1969	Fulford 1989	Futtrell 1997	Bateman 1997	Wilding 2005	This Volume
Aldborough	Poss.	Amph.	Amph.	Amph.	Uncertain	Amph.	Rejected
Baginton (the Lunt)	X	X	Gyrus	Amph.	Uncertain	Gyrus	Gyrus
Bosham	X	X	X	X	X	Amph.	Rejected p.28
Caerleon	Prob.	Ludus	Amph.	Amph.	Amph.	Amph.	Legionary Amph.
Caerwent	X	Amph.	Uncertain	Amph.	Amph.	Amph.	Urban Amph.
Caistor St Edmund	X	Uncertain	X	Amph.	Thea/Amph.	Amph.	Urban Amph.
Canterbury	X	X	X	Thea/Amph.	Thea/Amph.	Amph.	Thea/Amph.
Carmarthen	X	X	Amph.	Amph.	Thea/Amph.	Amph.	Urban Amph.
Catterick	X	X	X	X	Uncertain	Amph.	Rejected
Charterhouse-on-Mendip	Rejected	Uncertain	Amph.	Amph.	Uncertain	Amph.	Rural Amph.
Chester	X	Ludus	Amph.	Amph.	Amph.	Amph.	Legionary Amph.
Chesters	X	X	X	X	X	Amph.	Gyrus?
Chichester	X	X	Amph.	Amph.	Amph.	Amph.	Urban Amph.
Cirencester	X	Amph.	Amph.	Amph.	Amph.	Amph.	Urban Amph.
Dorchester (Maumbury)	X	Amph.	Amph.	Amph.	Amph.	Gyrus	Shrine/Amph?
Forden Gaer	X	X	X	X	X	Amph.	Gyrus?
Frilford	X	X	X	Amph.	Thea/Amph.	Amph.	Amph./Gyrus?
Inveresk	X	X	X	X	X	X	Auxiliary Amph.
London	X	X	Amph.	Amph.	Amph.	Amph.	Urban Amph.
Newstead	X	X	X	X	X	X	Auxiliary Amph.
Richborough	Amph.	Amph.	Amph.	Amph.	Amph.	Amph.	Urban/Military Amph.
Silchester	Amph.	Amph.	Amph.	Amph.	Amph.	Amph.	Urban Amph.
Tomen-y-Mur	X	X	Amph.	Amph.	Amph.	Amph.	Auxiliary Amph.
Verulamium	X	Ludus	Amph.	Amph.	Amph.	Amph.	Thea/Amph.
Walton	X	Thea	X	X	X	X	Rejected
Winterslow	X	Uncertain	Uncertain	X	Uncertain	Amph.	Rejected

13 Table to show the interpretations of British amphitheatres and amphitheatre-like structures by various authors

Taunton allowed him to excavate on many sites in Somerset, one of which was the proposed amphitheatre site at Charterhouse on Mendip. This was surveyed and partially excavated in 1909, while he was working at Dorchester, and it is possible that he was attempting to see the two sites together in order to compare results. The Charterhouse work, however, was inconclusive. The excavation took

DISCOVERY AND EXPLORATION

14 Excavation in progress at Maumbury Rings, Dorchester in 1909. The two figures are emptying one of the Neolithic pits. Behind them can clearly be seen the ring groove cut in the chalk for the timbers of the arena wall. *Bradley 1975*

place over two wet fortnights in June and July 1909, and even Gray found the results unsatisfactory.[42]

At the same time as the Dorchester excavations, exploration of the site of 'King Arthur's Round Table' at Caerleon began. The first formal work was conducted in 1909 under the aegis of the Liverpool Committee for Excavation and Research in Wales and the Marches. The excavation of the site, however, awaited the appointment of a dynamic director for the newly formed National Museum of Wales – Mortimer Wheeler. Wheeler saw excavation at the legionary fortress of Caerleon (*Isca*) as a strategic step in his exploration of Roman Wales, and decided to work on the amphitheatre, as it was well known, devoid of later buildings and 'likely to attract the considerable funds required for a long term programme of work'. Using the appeal of the name of King Arthur, Wheeler secured funding for the work in 1926 from the Daily Mail newspaper and the Loyal Knights of the Round Table of America.[43] Though the project was started by Wheeler, his move to the London Museum meant that the main burden of direction fell upon his students, V.E. Nash Williams and J.N.L. Myers, and his wife Mrs T.V. Wheeler, who directed the final eight months.[44] The site was then handed over to the Office of Works for preservation as a national monument. The excavation of the Caerleon amphitheatre was thorough, virtually total and was published by the Wheelers very rapidly in 1928.[45] The site remains one of only two completely excavated and displayed amphitheatres in Britain.

Indirectly the Caerleon work led to the discovery of the other legionary amphitheatre – that of Chester. Lost to sight and unknown to history, the only evidence to suggest that an amphitheatre had existed here was the discovery in 1738 of a slate relief depicting a gladiator of the *retiarius* or net-fighter class (*94*).[46] In 1929 a local antiquary, W.J. 'Walrus' Williams was approached

35

by some workmen, who had found Roman pottery and coins while working on the installation of a new heating system in the Ursuline Convent School at Dee House. Accompanying the men to the site, Williams was shown a curving, buttressed stone wall and was immediately reminded of the Caerleon amphitheatre, the excavation of which he had visited. Williams wrote a very short paper, which very simply stated that Chester's amphitheatre had been discovered.[47] The discovery was not before time, as the City Corporation had plans to straighten the road that, retrospect shows, curved around the northern side of the amphitheatre, a curve which had been a feature of the town plan since the first map was made by John Speed in 1610 (*107*).[48] Between 1931 and 1934 excavations undertaken by Professors R. Newstead and J.P. Droop confirmed the identification of the amphitheatre and established its northern limit.[49]

Chester was not the first 'new' amphitheatre to be found during the pre-Second World War decades, though it was certainly the most celebrated. The supposed amphitheatre at Caerwent was discovered during excavations within the Roman town in 1904.[50] It lies within the town walls and has been controversial since its discovery, with other possible interpretations attached to it. Very uncontroversial, on the other hand, is the amphitheatre at Chichester. In 1934, believing that a Roman town of such size and importance would have an amphitheatre, a Mr Carlyon-Britton examined the outskirts of the town, and discovered a possible location. In 1935 Miss G. White commenced excavation, and the amphitheatre of *Noviomagus* was confirmed.[51]

During 1933-4 the Verulamium theatre was totally excavated by Kathleen Kenyon, prior to its consolidation and display as a public monument.[52] The work established the structural sequence and phasing for the building, and demonstrated that in its first phase the *orchestra* was an uninterrupted oval, far more like an amphitheatre arena. It was concluded that the building served a dual function as both a theatre and an amphitheatre, and the term 'Gallo-Roman theatre' was coined, recognising the presence of many structures of this type in Gaul. An unusual book by Anthony Lowther[53] attempted to interpret the theatre through factually based imagined vignettes of episodes in its history. The first of these is the opening of the theatre. Stage performances are described, and:

> eventually it comes to an end, to the relief of many, for whom the items now to follow are the only ones of interest. The wrestling, bear baiting, acrobatic feats and so forth are what they have come to see, and they have been full of impatience while all this 'play-acting stuff' has been going on …

A wild-beast show is then prefaced by a wrestling match between Progon, the 'Lion of Leptis' and Telchus 'the Batavian Hercules'!

DISCOVERY AND EXPLORATION

In the 1940s to 1970s amphitheatre studies in Britain were chiefly advanced by a major campaign of excavation in Chester. Other discoveries were made, however. In 1951 a housing development in Carmarthen was the context for the identification of a possible amphitheatre site by the Borough Surveyor, G.L. Ovens.[54] His perspicacity ensured that it was not overbuilt,[55] and in 1968 excavation confirmed the identification of the amphitheatre. Less satisfactory was the claim that an earthwork at Winterslow on Salisbury Plain, previously thought to have been a long barrow, was a rural amphitheatre following excavation in 1959.[56] A post-war rescue excavation in Canterbury revealed a theatre. Though the second phase was of Classical, semi-circular form, the primary phase, of which very little survived, may have been of the same Gallo-Roman form as that at Verulamium.[57] An entirely new type of amphitheatre-related structure was found in 1970 during excavations on the site of a Neronian fort at 'the Lunt', Baginton, near Coventry. Within the Roman fort was a circular, palisaded timber structure, which was variously interpreted as a *gyrus* for the exercise and training of horses, a *vivarium* for the keeping of animals, or even a prison-camp.[58]

At Chester the discovery of the amphitheatre had been a local and national *cause célébre* in the 1930s, not least due to the proposed road scheme. The Chester Archaeological Society mobilised support for the preservation of the amphitheatre, or at least to avoid the construction of the road through the centre of the monument, a development that would, even if it did not destroy the amphitheatre, at the very least compromise its coherence and legibility. Support was strong and came from high places, including the Chief Inspector of Ancient Monuments, Sir Charles Peers, Mortimer Wheeler and even the Prime Minister of the day, Ramsay MacDonald. The Society launched an appeal to save the amphitheatre, raising £5000. In 1933 consent for the road scheme was revoked and in 1934 the Chester Society purchased, for £4000, the large Georgian townhouse known as St John's House, which occupied the north-west quadrant of the amphitheatre. The building was leased to the County Council and through rent, grant aid and other sources a considerable fund towards excavation was amassed. The City Corporation purchased properties on the site to allow limited road improvements and the Ministry of Works committed to begin excavation when these were complete.[59] Excavation of the northern half of the amphitheatre was directed by the then curator of the Grosvenor Museum, later General Secretary of the Society of Antiquaries of London, F. Hugh Thompson. Thompson began with exploratory trenching in 1957-9 and continued until 1970, with the major seasons taking place between 1965 and 1969 (*15*). By 1972 the monument had been consolidated and opened to the public as a free-access site. The publication of the work took place in 1975,[60] when the report appeared in the same volume of *Archaeologia* as Bradley's final report on Maumbury Rings. The appearance of this

15 Excavations in progress at Chester in the 1960s. *Chester City Council/English Heritage*

volume was a seminal event in the study of British amphitheatres, as it contained, remarkably, the final reports on two of the only three such monuments to have been excavated on a large scale (the other being Caerleon, which had been published 47 years previously!). At the same time as the Chester project, a research excavation was finally begun at Cirencester in 1962. The project was initiated by John Wacher and continued by Alan McWhirr in 1966. Trenches were dug on the banks and the main north-east entrance was virtually completely excavated, however this site too suffered from a long delay in publication with the final report, written by Neil Holbrook, only appearing in 1998.[61]

In 1930, a book on the *Archaeology of Roman Britain* by R.G. Collingwood and Sir Ian Richmond appeared for the first time. The 1969 revised edition[62] adds little to the discussion of amphitheatres provided in the original. The illustration of amphitheatre plans, the first time comparative plans on the same scale were published (*16*), shows only two excavated examples – Caerleon and Chester – and four earthworks – Tomen-y-Mur, Maumbury Rings, Aldborough, and Cirencester. As Chester was still under excavation at the time of revision, it is not surprising that the version of the plan is that based upon the excavations of the 1930s. The main contribution of this book, however, was to make a firm distinction between the military amphitheatres, or *ludi*, and the civil sites, amphitheatres proper. The distinction was functional. Amphitheatres were predominantly for the types of Roman games we associate with the word. The *ludi* on the other hand were provided for military drill and weapons training, though they may have had a subsidiary function as show venues. This volume is the first place where Tomen-y-Mur is adopted into the list, defined as an auxiliary *ludus*. Charterhouse-on-Mendip is cited as doubtful not only as to interpretation but as to category. Was it a *ludus* for troops guarding the important lead mines? As well as the sites illustrated, civilian amphitheatres were recognised

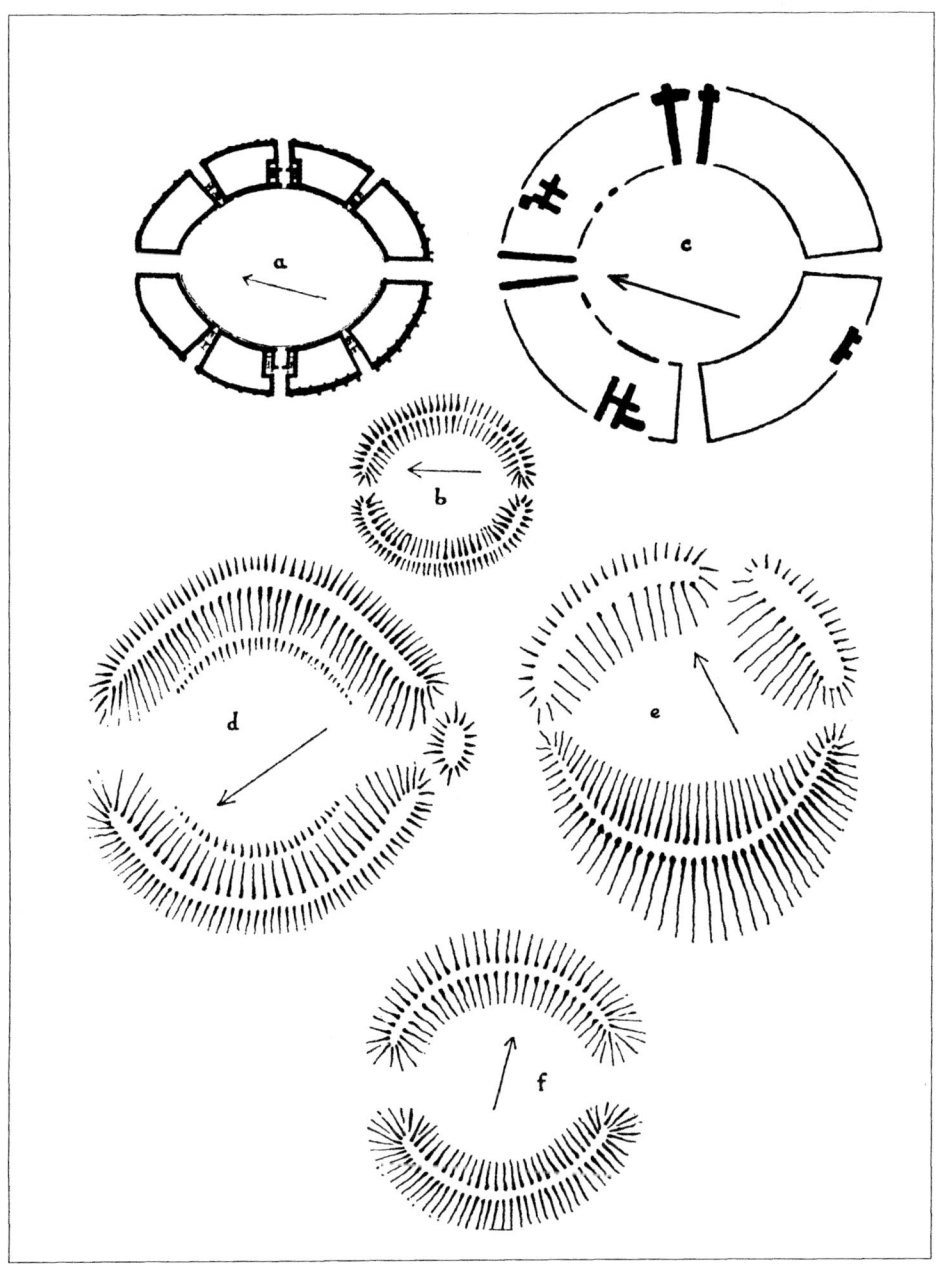

16 The first set of drawings of British amphitheatres to a common scale ever produced, from Collingwood and Richmond's 1969 edition of *The Archaeology of Roman Britain*. Illustrated are (from top left) Caerleon, Chester, Tomen-y-Mur, Dorchester, Aldborough, Cirencester

at Chichester, Silchester, Caerwent and at Richborough, where the size of the amphitheatre encouraged the conclusion that it served the town and was not a *ludus* for the fourth-century Saxon Shore fort on the site. Apart from the addition of the new discoveries at Chester and Chichester the list is strikingly similar to that compiled by Allcroft 60 years before (*13*).

Since the 1724 identification by William Stukeley of wooded earthworks surrounding a pond as the amphitheatre of Silchester, the site was accepted as one of the three that appeared on every early list (the others being Cirencester and Dorchester). Until the late twentieth century it remained untouched by the spade, having been excluded from the permissions granted to the Society of Antiquaries of London for excavation at Silchester.[63] In 1979 the amphitheatre was taken into state guardianship and excavations were begun at the request of the Inspectorate of Ancient Monuments, directed by Prof. Michael Fulford of the University of Reading. Reading that one of the aims of the work was to determine whether it actually *was* an amphitheatre, as well as to gather evidence for its structure and its chronology, reminds us that this interpretation was still in some doubt over two centuries after it had been advanced. The discovery of well-preserved masonry arena walls and entrance passages led to an expansion of the scope of the work, which now included the excavation of structural elements for consolidation and display.[64] Excavation continued seasonally for seven years, 1979-85, and its rapid publication in 1989 provided British amphitheatre studies with a model, modern case study,[65] allowing David Bomgardner in his review of the volume to suggest some ways forward for British amphitheatre studies.[66] It can fairly be argued that the appearance of the Silchester monograph and its critical response in review literature mark the beginning of a new and modern chapter in the study of the British amphitheatres. Fulford's publication provided the first in-depth discussion of all aspects of the British amphitheatres and their context, the first map of the location of amphitheatre sites and also an indication of the level of confidence of their interpretation (*13*). The map includes three new sites. Just two years before work started at Silchester, in 1977, aerial photography during the exceptionally hot and dry summer had identified a potential amphitheatre outside the walls of the Roman town of *Venta Icenorum*, Caistor St Edmund, near Norwich.[67] At Frilford, Oxon, a rural sanctuary site was thought to consist of a temple and a circular 'rotunda'. The temple was dated to the later third to early fourth century.[68] Survey work, particularly aerial photography, located a stone-walled *temenos* boundary and a ploughed-out structure interpreted as an amphitheatre, which has been examined by means of aerial, geophysical and field survey and small-scale excavation since the 1980s.[69] The discovery of the amphitheatre of the provincial capital, *Londinium*, in 1987, however, was in a wholly different league.

DISCOVERY AND EXPLORATION

17 Excavations in progress on the London amphitheatre during the 1980s. *Museum of London Archaeology Service*

The London amphitheatre (*17*) was discovered in the heart of the historic City of London, beneath the medieval Guildhall and its yard. The redevelopment of the Guildhall Art Gallery on the eastern side of Guildhall Yard required a routine archaeological investigation to be made of the site. It soon became apparent that the various fragmentary Roman walls were part of the eastern entrance to the amphitheatre. With great good fortune, the development had been sited over what was possibly the most recognisable part of the building. This was a totally unexpected find and caused a great deal of press interest. The development was suspended pending a public enquiry and the site was scheduled as a protected ancient monument. A revised development scheme was granted consent on the condition that full, proper excavation of the site took place, and that the amphitheatre was preserved. Excavation resumed under the direction of Nick Bateman of the Museum of London Archaeological Service and continued until 1996. Following an extended interim report in 1997, the final report on the excavations was published in 2008.[70] The entrance to the amphitheatre was preserved and is the centrepiece of an underground museum dedicated to the building. The outline of the amphitheatre is laid out in the paving of Guildhall Yard, around the church of St Lawrence Jewry. Bateman took advantage of the opportunity afforded by the publication of the final report to put the London amphitheatre into context, producing a further list of sites and a distribution map, which included both amphitheatres and theatres[71] (*13*), again showing to what degree the interpretation could be relied upon. Again new sites were now available, both in the north, with the identification of amphitheatres at Catterick and Newstead. In 1995, excavations in advance of development on the racecourse at Catterick in North Yorkshire were at first hailed as having revealed an unknown amphitheatre – indeed the predecessor of the racecourse itself as a place of entertainment.[72] During the early 1990s the Roman fort site of Newstead in southern Scotland was the scene of a major research programme by the University of Bradford. In the course of this project the suggestion was made that a depression near the fort complex might have been a small amphitheatre.[73] Survey work followed and the results were confirmed by excavation in 1996. Catterick was uncertain at the time, and can now be dismissed, as it has been revealed as a Neolithic henge monument, but the Newstead site is almost certainly a small amphitheatre like that at Tomen-y-Mur.[74]

In the late 1990s and the early years of the twenty-first century the flurry of research on British amphitheatres has continued. In 1997 excavations near the important Roman fort of Inveresk recovered a curving timber-built structure, which was soon hailed as an amphitheatre, seemingly eclipsing Newstead's short reign as the most northerly in the Roman Empire.[75] There are major problems with this interpretation due to the scale of excavation. It is possible that the site is a species of *gyrus*, like that at Baginton, but it is probably not, strictly speaking, an amphitheatre. Finally we must return to Chester. As we have seen, following Thompson's excavations, in 1972, the northern half of the amphitheatre was laid out as a public monument. Between 1999 and 2001 small-scale trial excavations conducted by Keith Matthews of Chester Archaeology demonstrated that Thompson's conclusions as to the phasing of the building were not necessarily safe. At the same time, the construction of a civil court building impinging on the southern edge of the amphitheatre led to debate on the future preservation and presentation of the monument, and on the future of the eighteenth-century former convent school building known as Dee House which occupies the site of the southern half of the amphitheatre, held by a massive concrete retaining wall. In 2003 a joint project was conceived by English Heritage and Chester City Council to undertake large-scale research and recover new data to inform decision making. This project included an extensive programme of non-invasive work on the multi-period urban landscape, and a large-scale research excavation directed jointly by Dan Garner for Chester City Council and Tony Wilmott for English Heritage (*18*).

DISCOVERY AND EXPLORATION

18 Excavations on the Chester amphitheatre in 2005. *Chester City Council/English Heritage*

This work concentrated on a portion of the *cavea* previously examined by Thompson, showing that the excavations of the 1960s were far from total, and also examined areas of the *cavea* and arena not previously excavated. These excavations in 2004-6 comprehensively overturned Thompson's conclusions, and have resulted not only in exciting new data on the construction, use and status of the building, but on the pre-Roman archaeology of the site and the use of the amphitheatre and its site in the post-Roman centuries.[76] During the new Chester Amphitheatre Project two further new departures occurred. The first was the publication by Roy Wilding of the first book devoted to the amphitheatres of Britain,[77] consisting of a brief introduction, gazetteer and summary of the sites, though the selection of sites was somewhat uncritical, with surprising omissions and inclusions. The second event was an international conference on amphitheatre studies, bringing together scholars from around the world to discuss amphitheatres across the Empire and to truly contextualise the amphitheatres of Roman Britain.[78]

4

TYPE, DISTRIBUTION AND CONTEXT

> Tacitus tells us so early as the time of Agricola in Titus, his reign, they began to introduce luxury among the Britons; for he exhorted them privately and publicly assisted them, to build temples, and places of public resort, and fine houses; and by degrees they came to those excitements to debauchery, portico's baths and the like, of which we frequently find ruins. Therefore we may suppose that amphitheatres were not forgotten.[1]

The concept of a north-west/south-east divide in the nature of Roman Britain is a familiar one, and work on the preparation of the Ordnance Survey's updated Map of Roman Britain, together with a review of the distribution of specifically Roman monument, settlement and building types, confirms this long-established idea.[2] Though the pattern is not simple and there are exceptions and areas of overlap, the divide is generally centred on a line dividing the Highland and Lowland areas of Britain between the River Tees in the north-east and the River Exe in the south-west. The area to the south and east contains substantial towns and a Romanised landscape of more or less urban settlements large and small, villages, villas, rural temples and shines. To the north and west, the province was extensively militarised, containing many permanent and short-lived military installations, including the frontiers of Hadrian's Wall and the Antonine Wall, legionary fortresses and auxiliary forts. This area contains few Romanised settlements other than the *vici*, the civilian settlements which grew up around fort sites, and the towns that did exist were smaller than those further south. Amphitheatres and amphitheatre-like structures existed to entertain people established in settlements and so it is only to be expected that these structures reflect the type of settlement that they served. Sure enough, though these buildings are distributed across Britain (*19, 20*) from the southernmost at Chichester to the most northerly at Inveresk and from the easternmost at

TYPE, DISTRIBUTION AND CONTEXT

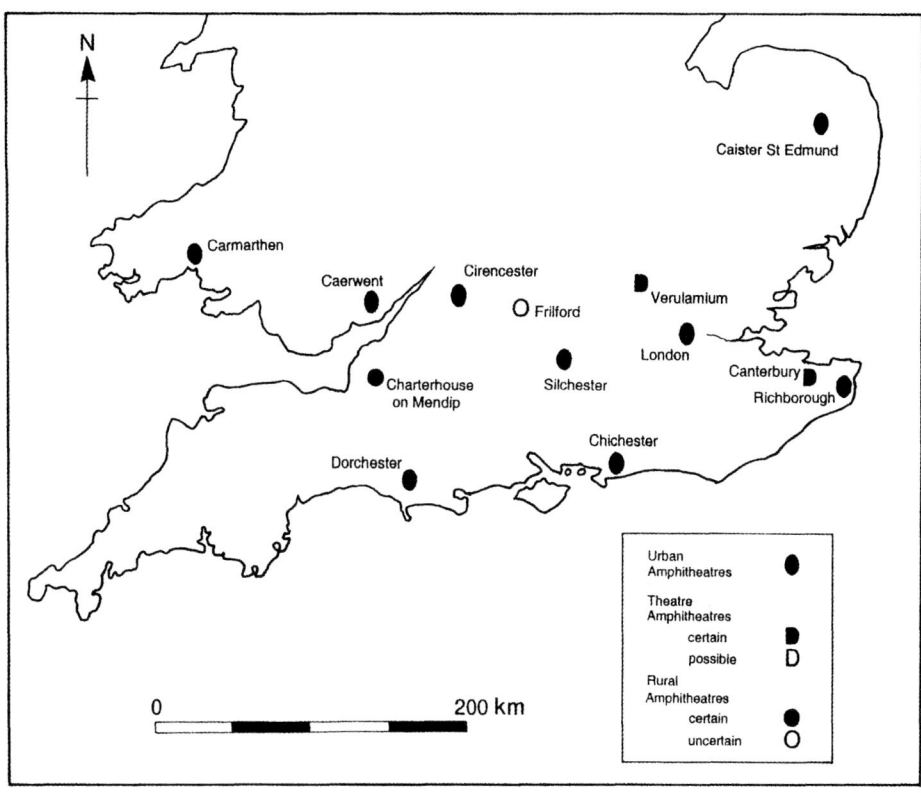

19 Location map showing the amphitheatre sites of the south and east. Chris Evans

Richborough to the most westerly example at Carmarthen, there is a major difference in typology between what we can still refer to as the 'civil' and the 'military' zones of the province.

Attempts to establish a typology of British amphitheatres in the past have tended to pre-judge functional differences between the structures in question, resulting in a circular argument. This is particularly true of the distinction drawn between military and civilian amphitheatres. This separation may have originated with Stukeley's use of the term 'castrensian amphitheatre' at Richborough,[3] the site of a highly visible late Roman fort. More recently it has been emphasised by the modern use of the word *ludus* (pl. *ludi*) for the military type, leading to the assertion that amphitheatres located at fort sites were purely for use as training and parade facilities,[4] whereas civilian amphitheatres were the venues for *munera* and *venationes*. The definition of *ludus* is, in fact, simply a training facility. In his table of definitions of amphitheatre terms Thompson sounded the necessary warning against the assumption that *ludi* and military amphitheatres were one and the same thing:

45

Ludus (gladiatorius): a (gladiatorial) training school sometimes (it is claimed) in the form of an amphitheatre.⁵

The distinction between military and civil is occasionally accompanied by a kind of squeamishness, suggesting that a military amphitheatre such as that at Chester hosted nothing more sinister than a kind of Edinburgh military tattoo. A more reasonable interpretation is that amphitheatres at forts were multifunctional, allowing gladiatorial and wild beast shows, and also displays of military skills and prowess.⁶

My preference in this book is to divide the British amphitheatres by the type of community they served. As we will see below, and in more detail in the next chapter, this works surprisingly well in terms of structural typologies as well. Other amphitheatre-type structures such as the theatres at Verulamium and Canterbury, and the *gyrus/vivarium* at the Lunt then form separate categories.

The classification is as follows:

Urban amphitheatres:	Shorthand for 'amphitheatres associated with towns'.
Urban amphitheatres (exceptions):	The amphitheatres at Richborough and Caerwent which are either, in the first case, possibly not urban, or in the second, possibly not an amphitheatre.
Rural amphitheatres:	Rare in Britain, and the least satisfactory of my classifications. Amphitheatres associated with rural villages, cult sites, or industrial centres.
Theatre-amphitheatres:	'Romano-Celtic' theatres which may have had a dual purpose, and which have only been found in towns in Britain.
Legionary amphitheatres:	Amphitheatres located adjacent to legionary fortresses.
Auxiliary amphitheatres:	Amphitheatres located adjacent to auxiliary forts.
Gyrus/vivaria:	Circular or oval structures with 'arenas' enclosed by a palisade or wall, but with either no facilities or minimal facilities for seating. Situated at auxiliary fort sites.

TYPE, DISTRIBUTION AND CONTEXT

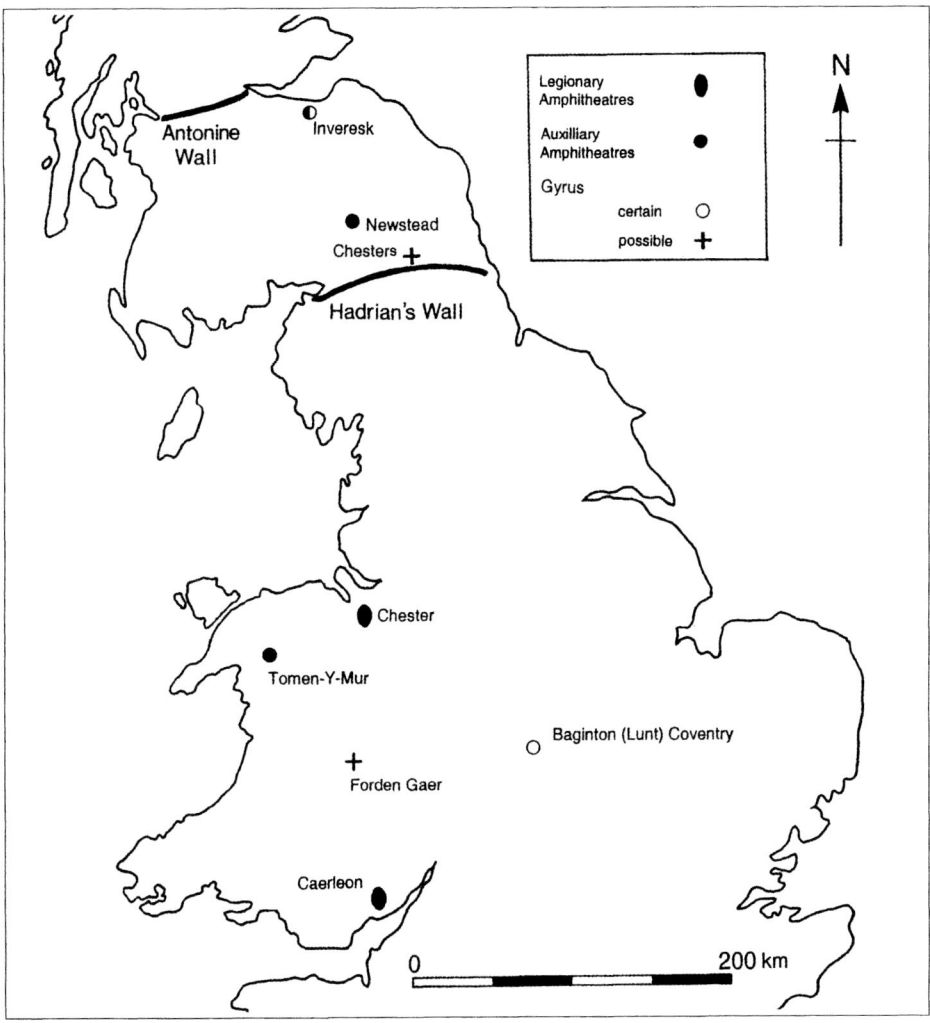

20 Location map showing the amphitheatre sites of the north and west. *Chris Evans*

Classification by settlement type implies a distribution, of course. The first three categories (including the urban exceptions) are concentrated in the south and east, with outliers in South Wales, and the last three in the north and west (*19, 20*).

URBAN AMPHITHEATRES

The class of urban amphitheatre is the most numerous, with nine examples. Apart from London and Richborough, all urban amphitheatres are located in towns of the class we call *civitas* capitals. None of the towns of the senior official rank, the so-called *coloniae*, had amphitheatres. The *coloniae* were towns planted in the province by Imperial authority. On the whole they took little regard of existing populations or political structures. They were essentially settlements of veterans from the legions, all of whom were Roman citizens prior to enlistment. The custom of giving land allotments to soldiers on retirement originated in the late years of the Republic and was one of the problems which contributed to the fall of that system. During the early Principate, when large numbers of veterans were discharged they would generally be allotted land,[7] usually, by the time of the invasion of Britain in AD 43, on the imperially owned sites of legionary fortresses in provinces recently conquered. Three such *coloniae* were founded in Britain during the first century; Colchester in AD 49, Lincoln in AD 90-6, and Gloucester in AD 96-8. The fortresses were taken over, their streets and buildings providing the basis for urban growth. They have been characterised as converted army camps.[8] Part of the role of these towns is often thought to have been to stimulate a desire for things Roman and for the Roman lifestyle among the new provincials,[9] though this may have been very much a secondary objective. The lack of that most Roman of structures, an amphitheatre, at the *coloniae* is an indication in itself that these towns were not primarily to promulgate *Romanitas* by example.

The only one of these early *coloniae* to have truly flourished was Colchester. It was situated next to the major Iron Age centre of Camolodunum, and may have been developed as the main focus or capital of the province. It appears to have been the centre of the Imperial cult, as the temple of the divine Claudius was built here. It was well provided with Roman styles of building, with the temple itself and a *basilica*,[10] and also had places of entertainment in the form of a theatre and a circus,[11] but no amphitheatre appears to have been built there. Despite this, the presence of arena iconography on many objects from Colchester may indicate that *munera* took place there, possibly in the context of the Imperial cult, and possibly in the theatre located in the precinct of the temple of Claudius. This would perhaps be consistent with the similar cult centre at *Lugdunum* in Gaul (p. 19), which did boast an amphitheatre.

The *civitas* capitals were, as the name suggests, the administrative centres of political units known as *civitates*, which in Britain were largely formed from the pre-existing tribes. The tribal aristocracy became the class of landowning *decuriones* who formed the town *ordo*, or senate, from which council and magistrates were drawn by election and which was responsible to the provincial government for the collection of taxes.[12] Most of the *civitas* capitals were founded on sites that had been occupied by conquest forts, though these forts had themselves often been sited near existing tribal centres. In some cases the actual physical centre moved from one location to another (as at Cirencester and Dorchester), probably as the result of Roman roads linking fort sites rather than existing population centres.

In other places (as at Silchester and to a degree, Chichester)[13] existing centres became the Roman towns.[14] This also occurred at Verulamium, where the town, though perhaps an early *civitas* capital, was also the only British example of the second official rank of towns, a *municipium*. Other *civitas* capitals further north and west, such as Caerwent and Carmarthen, perhaps developed in larger part from Roman forts and the civilian settlements (*vici*) around them, after the unit which had occupied the fort moved northwards out of tribal territory.

London does not fit any of these established models of town development. It certainly began early, with occupation starting *c*.AD 50, and developed rapidly. Not only was development rapid, it seems also to have been planned. Geographically it was situated on two low hills separated by a stream valley (the Walbrook) on the gravel river terrace on the north side of the River Thames. It lay at the lowest practicable bridging point of the river and on a fine harbour capable of receiving seagoing vessels and cargoes. Though the bridge and the beginnings of the road system, which spread out from London, would have required official intervention, the rapid growth of the town seems to have been due largely to trade. By AD 60-1, Tacitus could describe it as an 'important commercial centre, flocking with traders'.[15] In the pre-Roman period the site was unimportant and lay in a politically neutral location, and this allowed a purely Roman community to be established on neutral ground. The early planning of the city reflects this, with a rudimentary street grid in existence even before the Boudiccan revolt. Following this event the provincial administration may have moved from Colchester to London. It is possible that the office of the *Procurator*, the chief financial officer of the province was in London before this date. The combination of a major centralised administrative centre and a booming commercial port allowed London to develop early the suite of Roman buildings which might be expected of such a place[16] including a *forum, basilica* and temple complex on the top of Cornhill, which was probably built *c*.AD 75-85,[17] and the first timber-built amphitheatre (p. 93), which was still earlier, being dated by dendrochronology to AD 70-1.[18]

Given the nature of early London and its probable foundation by people from the Roman Empire beyond the new province, it is unsurprising that one of the earliest British amphitheatres should appear here. Many of the inhabitants were perhaps accustomed to Roman entertainments and therefore saw this facility as an important requirement of the new city. The amphitheatre might well have been built as part of an architectural reflection of a society or group identity that perceived itself as different to the rest of the province, perhaps in terms of its possession of Roman citizenship and foreign origins, a community, or set of communities intent on establishing familiar institutions for their new settlement.[19] The movement of the administration to London may also partly explain why Colchester did not have an amphitheatre and London did. This might also account for stamps on some of the timbers from the first amphitheatre, which suggest that the timber came from an official supply[20] and that the amphitheatre may have been built as an Imperial state initiative. A couple of points should be made on the site of the amphitheatre. It is often said that amphitheatres were built 'outside the walls' of Roman towns in Britain. This is not generally the case, as most amphitheatres pre-date the provision of defences. It is true rather to say that amphitheatres were built on the fringes of towns, on the edge of the occupied area. The fact that the London amphitheatre lies within the later walls has caused confusion; it was, in fact sited on the edge of the occupied area early in the development of a city that was to continue to grow around it. A further aspect of the site to provoke discussion has been the proximity of the amphitheatre to the Roman fort at Cripplegate, which lies immediately to the north-west. The relationship of the amphitheatre to the corner of the fort recalls that of legionary amphitheatres to their forts, allowing at least the speculation that it was a military establishment.[21] The fort was built in stone *c.*AD 120, at a similar date to the stone rebuild of the amphitheatre. Troops were certainly seconded to London before this, as shown by one of the Vindolanda writing tablets, dating to AD 90, and it is possible that there was a timber-built predecessor to the stone fort, though evidence for this is yet to come to light. At present it is not necessary to assert that the London amphitheatre might have been a military enterprise, though some element of military involvement may have taken place (p. 93).[22]

After the *civitas* capitals were established, their development differed in terms of style and rapidity. One very marked difference is in the acquisition of public buildings, including amphitheatres. It is important to stress that such facilities were generally not provided from taxation income, as Roman taxes were used for a fairly limited set of purposes with 50 per cent of total income used to fund the army alone during the first century AD.[23] Despite this, Imperial subventions were sometimes available for public works, as may be reflected by the provision of a Gallic type of *forum* and *basilica* at Verulamium, the dedicatory inscription of which gives the imperial titles, and the name and designation of the governor Gn Julius Agricola.[24] A driving force for the provision of public buildings throughout the Roman Empire was the tendency for the moneyed political elite to provide public facilities, games and feasts. This might be seen, in the context of competition for public office – a way of influencing the electorate in favour of an individual who desired the sort of magistracy that could itself be personally lucrative – as a civic duty by an office holder, or simply derive from a sense of civic pride.[25] The provision of public buildings or amenities such as roads, temples, aqueducts, public squares, fountains or amphitheatres, would be celebrated with a dedicatory inscription. It has been shown that in Britain this impulse towards munificence

21 Inscription from Brough-on-Humber (*Petuaria*) recording the donation of a theatre *proscaenium* by the *aedile*, Januarius

was muted,[26] and what has been called the 'epigraphic habit' – the practice of erecting celebratory inscriptions – failed to gain a real foothold in the province. In Britain there are a very small number of civic benefactions made by individuals and these were mainly for religious structures. The only one known for a place of entertainment is the oft-cited gift of a new stage building (*proscaenium*) for a theatre at Brough-on-Humber (*Petuaria*) in AD 140-4 by the magistrate (*aedile*) M Ulpius Januarius (21).[27] More frequent are benefactions made corporately by a *civitas*, an example being the *forum* at Wroxeter (*Viroconium Cornoviorum*), dedicated by the *civitas Cornoviorum*.[28] This pattern of collective benefactions is also shown in *Gallia Belgica* and other northern provinces. The reason for the lack of individual donations may be simply that the tribal leaders who formed the *ordo* had no need to compete for power, as they already possessed it through an oligarchic system. The oligarchy as a group would invest in the creation of basic Roman facilities without the wasteful extravagance often seen resulting from individual or family competition in the Mediterranean provinces.

The construction of an amphitheatre, even one built of earth and timber such as the earliest British examples, would have been an expensive and highly labour-intensive operation. To give some idea of the scale of labour and implied cost, it has been estimated that at Dorchester it would have been necessary to excavate from the arena and entrances some 7000m³ of chalk rubble, weighing some 12,500 tonnes and to deploy this material in the seating banks.[29] This is to say nothing of building the banks properly, building the timberwork around the arena and in the entrances, or putting in any timber seating. Such an operation would perhaps be more likely to be provided through corporate rather than individual enterprise or euergetism, and the fact that the urban amphitheatres were largely earthwork constructions might suggest that imperial help was not a part of their funding. At the heart of the Empire amphitheatres were provided through both types of donation. At Pompeii the amphitheatre was constructed in 70 BC at the personal expense of the *duumviri*, Quinctius Valgus and Marcus Porcius, the land and building being donated to the *colonia* in perpetuity,[30] and that at Alba Fucens by Tiberius' notorious Praetorian Prefect, Macro.[31] The great imperial amphitheatre at Pozzuoli (*22*) on the other hand was provided corporately by the *colonia Flavia Augusta Puteolana* at its own expense (*pecunia sua*).[32]

In the *civitas* capitals, then, it is probable that the amphitheatres were provided through corporate civic effort. Most were of simple earthwork construction and it may be significant to note the similarity between the building techniques involved in amphitheatres of this type and the tradition of the building of large-scale earthwork structures on a communal basis in Britain, from the henge monuments of the Neolithic to the hillforts of the Iron Age. We can, perhaps, see here the adaptation of this tradition to the new Roman reality.

It is still possible that they were built with a view to the staging of *spectacula*, to be funded later either by corporate or individual munificence. Games would certainly be less of a drain on the individual purse than the building of such a facility. The addition to original earth and timber amphitheatres of stone arena walls, entrances with vaults etc., which took place in London, Silchester and possibly Cirencester, would allow a second bite of the philanthropic cherry, either corporate or individual. For instance at Feurs, the *civitas* capital of the Segusiavi in central Gaul, an inscription commemorates Ti Claudius Capito, who rebuilt in stone the theatre which Lupus son of Anthus had originally built in wood.[33]

Apart from London, the two earliest urban amphitheatres were those of Silchester (p. 97) and Dorchester (p. 103). The first timber amphitheatre at Silchester (*Calleva Atrebatum*) was probably built in the third quarter of the first century, between AD 55 and 75.[34] This early date is not surprising, as Silchester was a precocious town, its acquisition of a timber *forum* around AD 55-65 and an amphitheatre at about the same time demonstrating an indigenous hunger for Romanisation in this part of the former client kingdom of Cogidubnus.[35] Dorchester (*Durnovaria*) has been seen as a slightly ambiguous case. The town is the capital of the *civitas* of the Durotriges, whose hillforts put up a stiff resistance to Rome. In this respect they present a stark contrast to the Atrebates of Silchester. It is currently thought that a fort preceded the town and the foundation of the *civitas* was part of a Flavian expansion, perhaps beginning with timber buildings around *c*.AD 60.[36] Though it has been suggested in the past that the amphitheatre might have been associated with an early fort, the tiny amount of dating evidence can be interpreted to suggest

22 Substructures beneath the arena of the Pozzuoli amphitheatre in Italy. This amphitheatre was erected through corporate civic beneficence

that the relationship of the town and the amphitheatre may not be problematic after all,[37] with both founded in the early Flavian period, that is to say around AD 70, and the amphitheatre being an early structure in the history of the town, as at Silchester. The possibility has even been raised that the Dorchester amphitheatre may not, in point of fact, have been built until the early second century.[38]

At Silchester certainly and at Dorchester probably, amphitheatres were constructed at the time that their associated towns were initiated, but this does not seem to have been so at Chichester. Two building inscriptions from Chichester (*Noviomagus Regensum*) show Roman buildings erected before the legal foundation of the *civitas*,[39] though it is possible that these were at the instance of the client king Cogidubnus – one certainly was, as it names him. On current evidence the town seems to have been initiated in the early Flavian period.[40] If so, there was a lapse in time before the amphitheatre (p. 108) was built. Though the excavator considered a date *c*.AD 70-90,[41] the pottery in the seating bank suggests a later date, possibly during the reign of Trajan in the early years of the second century. This would be supported by the fact that the arena wall was built of stone from the first, with no timber precursor as far as may be seen. A similar sequence may be adduced at Cirencester (*Corinium Dobunnorum*), with a Flavian town foundation[42] and an amphitheatre (p. 110) provided after AD 104-9,[43] though the first amphitheatre may have been at least partly timber built. Of the amphitheatres at *civitas* capitals, the last of the known examples to have been built seems to have been Carmarthen (*Moridunum Demetarum*). Little is known of the town, and the amphitheatre (p. 115) may be symptomatic of its advancement to *civitas* capital status, around AD 120.[44]

From this point on, different amphitheatres had different structural histories. The stone amphitheatre in London was constructed *c*.AD 125, possibly again as an official enterprise, and a second timber phase at Silchester was constructed in the second quarter of the second century, at the same time as the second, entirely stone-built amphitheatre was erected at Cirencester. Cirencester saw further major work in the later second century. At Silchester there may have been a period during which the amphitheatre was either disused, or not well maintained, as there is pollen evidence that the area of the north entrance was colonised by oak and ferns during the later second century, prior to a full-scale rebuilding in stone in the early third.[45] Interestingly a similar sequence may have occurred at Dorchester, where a build-up of soil was followed by a renewed timber gateway between the mid-third and mid-fourth century.[46]

Where evidence exists, it is clear that the urban amphitheatres went out of use during the later years of the Roman period. The late third century has been suggested for Chichester and Cirencester, the late third to early fourth for Silchester and Dorchester, perhaps the early to mid-fourth for London.

	Flavian (AD 69-96)	Trajanic (AD 96-117)	Hadrianic (AD 117-36)	Later 2nd cent AD	3rd cent AD	4th cent AD
SILCHESTER	Timber Phase 1: c.AD 55-75		Timber phase 2		Stone Phase	Disuse: c.350
LONDON	Phase 1: c.AD 70-1		Phase 2: stone built			Disuse: c.350
DORCHESTER	Construction c.Mid-Flavian				New entrance	Disuse: c.350
CIRENCESTER		Phase 1: after c.104-7	Phase 2	Phase 3		Disuse: c.340-50
CHICHESTER		Construction: c.Flavian/Trajanic				Disuse: early 4th century
CARMARTHEN			Construction c.AD 125			

23 Comparative dating table of British urban amphitheatres

The supposed amphitheatre at Caerwent (*Venta Silurum*) is an anomaly (p. 109), as it would seem to have been built in the third or fourth centuries. It was built within the walls of the town and overlay early buildings. The only remnant of this building was an 'arena' wall and a fragment of what may have been an outer wall. It is, of course, possible that this was not an amphitheatre at all.

The case of Richborough (*Rutupiae*) is an intriguing one. Whether or not Richborough was, as often claimed, the scene of the landing of Roman forces for the conquest in AD 43,[47] it was at least a major early port. Until recently it has been best known as the location of a late military fort on the third-century Saxon Shore system, and before that the location of a huge, free-standing triumphal arch which probably commemorated the conquest. Richborough was at the very least, a symbolic entrance point to Britain, as which it appears in Classical literature.[48] Geophysical survey in recent years has shown that Richborough was also a substantial town, which appears to have grown rapidly during and immediately after the conquest, reaching its height in the later first and early second century (the arch was built c.AD 85) after which it suffered a long decline.[49] A major contribution to this decline was almost certainly the rise of London as a major trading centre. Though the town flourished in the late first and early second century, it subsequently declined and shrank. During the mid-third and fourth centuries the heart of the town was replaced by one of the forts of the Saxon Shore system. When the amphitheatre was excavated during the nineteenth century, its masonry was compared to that of the Saxon Shore forts, and coins from the site were mostly fourth century in date.[50] Recent geophysical survey around the amphitheatre shows buildings of the town running right up its outer edge,[51] but the survey also seems to indicate that these buildings pre-date the amphitheatre, which may have been constructed over their remains. Only further excavation can elucidate this important relationship, but it is at least possible that Richborough's amphitheatre was after all a military structure associated not with the town, but with the Saxon Shore fort which was also built over the town's earlier, demolished, buildings.

As we will see in the next chapter, the architecture of the urban amphitheatres remained simple. They were predominantly earth banks with provision for spectators on the inside and with the arena walled, at first in timber and later in stone. We will see that capacities were relatively modest, and that the one feature that would have allowed greater capacities and formal seating and entrances, namely the provision of an outer wall, did not generally happen. It seems possible that the *civitates* which built amphitheatres saw them as essential trappings of *Romanitas* in the early years, but the amphitheatre as a cultural institution failed to take root among the British *civitates*.[52]

RURAL AMPHITHEATRES

In many ways this is the most unsatisfactory of my categories. The only certain example is that of Charterhouse-on-Mendip, where the amphitheatre, now located on a high-point in the Mendip hills, served an area of lead mining, established soon after the Roman conquest of Britain. It is possible that this amphitheatre was provided with the military supervisory garrison in mind and that it had more in common in function with the auxiliary amphitheatres discussed below. Amphitheatres in rural locations have been claimed in three other locations in Britain. Two of these, at Winterslow, Wiltshire (p. 132) and Woodctts, Dorset (p. 134), can be rejected as misinterpretations, probably of prehistoric earthworks. As excavation and research continue, the excavators of the third example, identified at Frilford in Oxfordshire, are increasingly unconvinced with the identification of the building (p. 130). If it is an amphitheatre, it is a very odd one, and is a unique type of site in Britain, an amphitheatre associated with a rural shrine.[53] Such sites are found in Gaul, though it is more usual there for rural shrines to be associated with theatres, or theatre-amphitheatre type buildings.[54] An example of this kind of settlement in Britain is at Gosbeck's Farm, near Colchester, where a classical theatre served a major rural sanctuary.[55]

THEATRE-AMPHITHEATRES

This class of structure is represented by the very well-known theatre of Verulamium (p. 123) (*colour plate 14*), and probably by the theatre at Canterbury (*Durovernum Cantiacorum*), though only a tiny fragment of this building has been excavated (p. 127). The terminology for these structures has varied through time. Kathleen Kenyon first used the term 'Gallo-Roman theatre' after the excavation of the Verulamium theatre and the French scholar Grenier later coined 'theatre-amphitheatre'.[56] J.-C.

Golvin, in his great work on the Roman amphitheatre, has a category of Gallo-Roman 'mixed edifices',[57] which divide into two types. The semi-amphitheatres, like the structures at Lutetia and Lillebonne, have full oval arenas, with a *cavea* on only one side. The stage is then placed across the centre of the short axis (5). Theatre-amphitheatres, as defined by Golvin, have a virtually full oval *cavea*, broken on one side by the insertion of a stage. Verulamium is one such, there is one at Lixus in Mauretania, and the rest are in the Gallic provinces, for example at Drevant, Sanxay and Valognes.[58] The buildings would have been financed in the same way as the urban amphitheatres, indeed the theatre at *Petuaria*, whose *proscaenium* was funded by the *aedile*, Januarius, may well have been of this type.

As the name suggests, theatre-amphitheatres were in all probability dual-function structures with the capacity to put on both theatrical and amphitheatrical events, although it is also possible that in their Gallic form they catered to specific provincial forms of entertainment (p. 19). It may be significant that at towns with theatres (Verulamium, Canterbury, Colchester, Brough-on Humber), no amphitheatres are known and vice-versa. Perhaps a single building for *spectacula* was considered sufficient for any town, leading to the conclusion that similar entertainments took place in both kinds of building. In other provinces theatres and amphitheatres were often interchangeable, whether as successive buildings or single multi-functional buildings. Thus at Sofia (*Serdika*) in modern Bulgaria a theatre was replaced on the same site by an amphitheatre[59] and at Augst (*Augusta Raurica*), in modern Switzerland, a Flavian theatre was replaced *c.*AD 100 by an amphitheatre, which was in turn succeeded *c.*AD 150 by another theatre associated with a monumental temple. All of these changes were related to changes in a religious precinct, of which the theatres and amphitheatre were an integral part.[60] This association of theatre and sanctuary is seen in Britain at Verulamium, Colchester and at Gosbecks Farm.

LEGIONARY AMPHITHEATRES

The two most impressive amphitheatre buildings in Britain are those at the legionary fortresses at Chester and Caerleon. Unlike the urban amphitheatres, both of these have stone outer walls. The second amphitheatre at Chester has no parallel in Britain, with external architectural decoration and internal vaulted stairways. The reason for this is not hard to find: they were built by the specialist builders and engineers of the legions and had Imperial and military resources behind them. Even in their primary phases, these buildings were more impressive and better built than their urban counterparts. The contrast strongly suggests that the urban structures were not, in fact, built under Imperial *aegis* and by military engineers, an argument previously made by several writers with regard to early urban public works.[61]

The legions were the backbone of the Roman army. Heavy infantry units, each 5-6000 strong, they included in their ranks all manner of specialists. Above all, every soldier was a Roman citizen.

It is appropriate here to attempt to lay to rest the idea that these amphitheatres were intended exclusively for training. Collingwood and Richmond (p. 37) attempted to distinguish between amphitheatres and *ludi* by claiming that in the latter the area of the arena was noticeably larger in relation to the surrounding seating. Golvin has shown that there is considerable overlap between arena sizes, and that this criterion cannot be considered to be valid.[62] It has been argued that the expression 'military amphitheatres' should be used, if at all, only for amphitheatres near forts and used by soldiers.[63] Le Roux has dismissed any idea of amphitheatres near forts being conflated with the functions of exercise buildings, training grounds or parade grounds, and the proximity of the parade ground at Caerleon to the amphitheatre suggested to Boon that the two had different functions.[64] Perhaps troops were drawn up on the parade ground in preparation to filing into their seats in the amphitheatre.

At the time of the building of the amphitheatres, *c*.AD 80 for Caerleon and perhaps less than a decade later for Chester, the legions were manned by citizens from outside Britain. In AD 43, at the time of the Claudian conquest, 80 per cent of the small sample of legionaries whose origins we know were from Italy, by the end of the century this number reduces to 20 per cent.[65] The non-Italians were drawn predominantly from the provinces of Gaul, Spain, the Danube and the Balkans. These men were sufficiently Roman to be accustomed to and probably enthusiastic for the entertainments offered at the amphitheatre. The soldiers would have shared the entertainment tastes of the populace[66] of the highly Romanised provinces from which they came. Recent work has rightly seen the Roman army not merely as an institution, but as an Empire-wide community,[67] somewhat apart and distinct from the myriads of different cultures and communities among which it was stationed, though taking much from those communities, and becoming more diverse as time went on. As a newly conquered province with legions whose personnel were drawn from elsewhere, this sense of a distinct community must have been strong among the first-century British legions. The army 'through dress, display, and use of space … selectively emphasised their distinctness from the surrounding civilian society'.[68] Part of this expression of identity seems to have been the construction of a style of amphitheatre which reflected the attitudes and tastes of what were, after all, the largest communities of Roman citizens in the province. These amphitheatres were '*primarily* designed to mount the range of spectacular blood sports which so fascinated the population of the Roman

Empire'.⁶⁹ We have already briefly considered the role of the amphitheatre in reinforcing loyalty to the emperor and in stressing and reinforcing concepts of military *virtus* among the legionaries (p. 19). The nature of the audience – soldiers accustomed to weapons-training – may have given rise to a different kind of spectacle. It is possible that military exhibition bouts replaced expensive gladiatorial shows, with the latter on high days and holidays. We should not think of the audience as wholly military, as it is likely that the civil populace of the towns which grew outside the forts, the legionary *canabae*, also attended. A taste for arena shows thus acquired has been seen as the reason for the addition of a second, civil amphitheatre to an original military amphitheatre in the legionary forts and towns of Carnuntum and Aquincum on the Danube.⁷⁰

It is probable that the structures, placed as they were close to frontiers, had a subsidiary function to 'shock and awe' native frontier populations with a vision of Roman engineering abilities. The Chester amphitheatre, for example, built on an eminence over the River Dee, was well placed to dominate both the road in from North Wales and incoming shipping from the Irish Sea.

The third permanent legionary fortress in Britain, York, might perhaps be expected to have had an amphitheatre, particularly as the legionary *canabae* was elevated to the rank of *colonia*. A particular context for an amphitheatre is the period during the early years of the third century when the Emperor Septimius Severus was based in York (he died there in AD 208) and perhaps there is one awaiting discovery (remembering that Chester's amphitheatre was not found until 1929, and that in Sofia, Bulgaria, not until 2004).⁷¹ A possible site immediately to the east of the legionary fortress has been suggested on the basis of an apparent elliptical space on early maps, and an inscribed bone slip bearing a text relevant to gladiators (p. 166) has been found in an inhumation burial.⁷²

AUXILIARY AMPHITHEATRES

Like the legionary amphitheatres these would have been built under military authority. The vast majority of the military sites of Roman Britain are the forts of auxiliary units. These troops were deployed in units known as *cohortes* (infantry and mixed units) and *alae* (cavalry). Originally recruited from conquered areas of the Empire, the names of the units usually included an ethnic name. After the first generation in Britain, however, recruitment would have been from within the province. The auxiliaries were non-citizens, but acquired Roman citizenship on retirement after 25 years of service. It was Collingwood and Richmond⁷³ who, in distinguishing between civil amphitheatres and military *ludi*, identified the oval earthwork at the auxiliary fort of Tomen-y-Mur, Gwynedd (p. 153), as an auxiliary amphitheatre, the counterpart to the structures known at the legionary forts (*16*). They were, in fact, the first to take up the 1888 suggestion that the earthwork was an amphitheatre.[74] The subsequent discovery of an amphitheatre near the fort of Newstead (*Trimontium*), Roxburghshire,[75] made the Tomen-y-Mur identification still more likely, not to mention that of the small amphitheatre at Charterhouse-on-Mendip which may have been associated with military control of the lead mines. Although Tomen-y-Mur was the only strictly auxiliary amphitheatre to have been identified in Britain, amphitheatre-like earthworks outside auxiliary forts on the Roman frontiers (*limes*) in Germany have long been so interpreted, specifically at the sites of Dambach, on the Raetian *limes*, and Zugmantel, on the *limes* of Upper Germany.[76] Without excavation these identifications remained doubtful, however, until a totally unexpected discovery at another fort, that at Künzing in Bavaria, in 2003.[77]

There is no doubt at all that this structure, which has now been totally excavated, was an amphitheatre (*24*) and that it was provided for a fort constructed in the late first century. The garrison of the fort, *cohors III Thracum c.R. equitata*, was an auxiliary unit consisting of both cavalry and infantry with a nominal strength of 500 men, similar in size to the garrison of the fort at Wallsend on Hadrian's Wall. Though Tomen-y-Mur and Charterhouse-on-Mendip are smaller, there is a very close similarity between the sizes of the amphitheatres at Künzing, Dambach and Newstead. At

24 Excavations at the amphitheatre at Künzing, Bavaria. *Bayerisches Landesamt für Denkmalpflege, K. Leidorf, L7344/008 8822-28*

Zugmantel two amphitheatres have been found, and it has been suggested that these were built for specific events, such as official visits. This argument may be relevant to Scarth's observation of two amphitheatres at Charterhouse-on Mendip.

GYRUS/VIVARIA

This category is only represented in Britain, or for that matter in the Roman Empire, by the extraordinary circular structure at the Lunt fort near Baginton, Coventry (p. 155). It consists of a levelled, circular 'arena' surrounded by a timber palisade. It has been suggested that similar structures may have been located at the auxiliary fort of Forden Gaer (*Levobrinta*) in Montgomeryshire,[78] a tenuous identification, which should be treated with considerable caution, and at Chesters on Hadrian's Wall. The fenced structure which was partly excavated at the fort of Inveresk, Midlothian (p. 156) might also conceivably be one of these.[79] Interpretation of the Baginton structure has not moved beyond that put forward by the excavator.[80] The term *gyrus* he derives from the Greek writer Xenophon,[81] who used the term to refer to a training ring used for the schooling of horses and their riders. The palisaded entrance to the ring has suggested the control of wild or untrained animals approaching the ring. The term *vivarium* means a place where animals are kept; there was a *vivarium* for the animals held prior to exhibition in the amphitheatre outside the *porta Praenestina* in Rome.[82] It has been suggested that the Lunt structure was used as a holding pen for animals destined for the amphitheatre. In support of this idea references to military hunters have been quoted. Titius Severus, centurion of Legion VI *Victrix* set up an altar to Diana when he had 'enclosed the *vivarium*' at Cologne.[83] This is appropriate as Diana was goddess of the hunt and also had an important role among the deities of the amphitheatre (p. 180). Most famous is the inscription from Bonn of the centurion of Legion I *Minervia* who boasts of catching 50 bears for the arena in a six-month period.[84] Quoting the same sources, the auxiliary amphitheatre at Zugmantel has also been claimed as a *vivarium*.[85]

It seems unlikely that the plain open area of the Lunt structure was a holding facility for animals for the arena. It would seem wholly unsuited to the purpose, unless the animals were socialised or tame. Capture of large carnivores in particular would require their confinement for a time in narrow dark boxes in order to quiet them. To be released into an open arena would require care and patience to avoid the animals injuring themselves, each other, or their keepers.[86] The shape of the ring and the idea that wild animals were controlled through the palisaded entrance brings to mind a corral or a horse-breaking ring. Bateman's idea that the *gyrus* might, in fact, have been a *ludus* for the training of recruits is also worth considering.[87]

5

PLANNING, CONSTRUCTION AND ARCHITECTURE

> An amphitheatre is properly a double theatre, or two theatres joined together. A theatre is a semicircle, wherein are the seats of the spectators, the apparatus of the actors, or scenes, filling up the diameter. ... Now two such as these joined together, throwing away the scenic part, constituted an amphitheatre; taking its name from circular vision ... the faces of all the people being directed to the centre of its excentricity.[1]

Until relatively recently no comparative essay on the planning and architecture of the British amphitheatres would have been remotely possible. The publication of major excavation reports for Caerleon, Maumbury Rings, Chester, Silchester and Cirencester, and the interim report on the London amphitheatre, all but the first of which have been published since 1975, make this more feasible. This chapter will attempt to assess the planning, architecture and reconstruction of amphitheatres in Britain based upon our limited excavated and structural evidence. The main sections concern the two categories where we have a degree of comparative excavated and structural data: the urban and legionary sites. A final note looks at the potential of the auxiliary sites. The details of the theatre-amphitheatres at Verulamium and Canterbury and the rural sites are discussed in the individual site descriptions in the following two chapters.

URBAN AMPHITHEATRES

All of the urban amphitheatres are constructed with an arena hollowed out into either a hillside or the ground. Some are built into valleys or existing hollows. In all cases the material for the banks was acquired by hollowing out the arena. This had all kinds of advantages. With an arena floor well below ground level, there was no need to build up the surrounding seating banks to form a high *cavea*. The material from the arena could, moreover, be deposited to form the banks; although there is occasionally evidence that this was insufficient and that material had to be imported from elsewhere. In the typology of amphitheatre structures created by J.-C. Golvin,[2] they are all variants of Type 1: amphitheatres with the *cavea* supported on a continuous bank. In no case is there evidence for an outer wall of stone for these structures, implied in Golvin's Type 1b, though for two (London and Carmarthen) there is the suggestion of a timber outer wall built with framed timber seating, which would place these structures into Golvin's Type 1a.

Planning and layout
The first task was to lay the shape of the amphitheatre out on the ground. A great deal has been written about the design and planning of amphitheatres,[3] and there is no doubt that in some cases sophisticated survey methods were used. Study has shown that some arenas are elliptical, others are oval, and different techniques are needed to draw these two shapes. Very few British urban amphitheatres allow us to reconstruct the way the Roman surveyors worked out the plans. In order to do so it is necessary to have very accurate knowledge of the measurements used and this exercise can only be carried out conventionally where the whole structure, or at least the whole arena, is available to measure.[4] This precondition exists only for the various phases at Silchester, and for Dorchester. In London a very small area of the amphitheatre has been excavated, but mathematical modelling has enabled researchers to arrive at a persuasive argument for the layout method used.[5]

The first phase arena at Silchester was, within a small tolerance, circular. No simpler layout could be imagined. Surveying could simply involve placing a central post with a rope at the required length of radius (average 21.4m). Fulford has attempted to translate the dimensions of the amphitheatre into the two types of Roman foot measure,[6] the *Pes Monetalis* (*pM*=296mm) and the *Pes Drusianus* (*pD*=332mm) with unsatisfactory results, however, with the arena measuring overall 129.5 x 127.1*pD* it is at least conceivable that a diameter of a notional 130*pD* was intended. At Dorchester the plan was only slightly more sophisticated.[7] The size was dictated by the pre-existing henge monument which was reused to build the amphitheatre (p. 105), however the builders of the amphitheatre were not satisfied with the circular shape which their Neolithic predecessors had bequeathed to them and wanted a more oval shape for their arena. To this end they seem to have used a layout based not upon a single circle, but three intersecting circles of a diameter of 24.4m. The diameter of the central circle gave the short axis of the arena, two further circles, each with a centre on the long axis, created the shape which would elongate the arena to north and south by a distance of 4.7m, creating a 'stretched circle'.[8] The simple circular layout at Silchester suggests that the builders understood the nature and purpose of the amphitheatre, but not how to create the correct shape. It reinforces the notion that this was the rapid construction of a society anxious to adopt the appearance of Roman ways, but not yet fully equipped to do so (p. 152). At Dorchester the intention to create a more 'Roman' arena shape, despite already having a circular earthwork to work from, confirms, perhaps, that the building was later than Silchester (p. 153). It has occasionally been assumed that amphitheatres were laid out by military surveyors; no such interpretation is needed for either of these.

In the subsequent phases at Silchester the arena became more of an oval or elliptical shape. Although this means that greater surveying knowledge was available, we certainly do not need to invoke the military to explain this. The layout was still relatively simple. The planning of the Dorchester and Silchester amphitheatres actually demonstrates an almost textbook progression of layout techniques from the circular to the oval/elliptical. In fact an ellipse is difficult to create, as it is a shape whose curvature changes with size. The curves need to be calculated for every example. An oval, on the other hand, is based upon a series of circles. It is constructed from segmental arcs, or parts of the circumferences of a series of intersecting circles, where these circles share the same tangent. The first Silchester timber amphitheatre was a single circle, and when this was turned into an oval for the second timber amphitheatre, it seems that two circles centred on the east–west axis were used, in order to slim down the width and turn this into the short axis. Dorchester appears to have been based upon three circles (a most unusual technique, possibly used because the shape of the site was already dictated) and the stone amphitheatre at Silchester was based upon four circles. In fact the simplest oval can be constructed using the arcs of four circles, drawn from four centres, which are paired equidistantly on the main axes (25).[9] This is the technique used to generate the oval arena at Silchester.[10] By multiplying centres and arcs, an oval shape closer to an ellipse can be formed, and it has recently been shown that this was the technique used for the Colosseum itself.[11] Interestingly, Stukeley came up with a scheme for Dorchester very like that published by Bradley.[12] He too worked from the arcs of two circles with centres upon the long axis and took the radius from the centre point as establishing the side curves. He called this a four-centre scheme, though it is more properly a four-arc plan. As the site had not been excavated, Stukeley's plan fitted the earthwork, rather than the timbers of the arena wall, very well, so is slightly more elongated at the narrow extremities.

The London amphitheatre appears to have been planned rather differently.[13] Mathematical analysis of the curves of the excavated portion of the building

PLANNING, CONSTRUCTION AND ARCHITECTURE

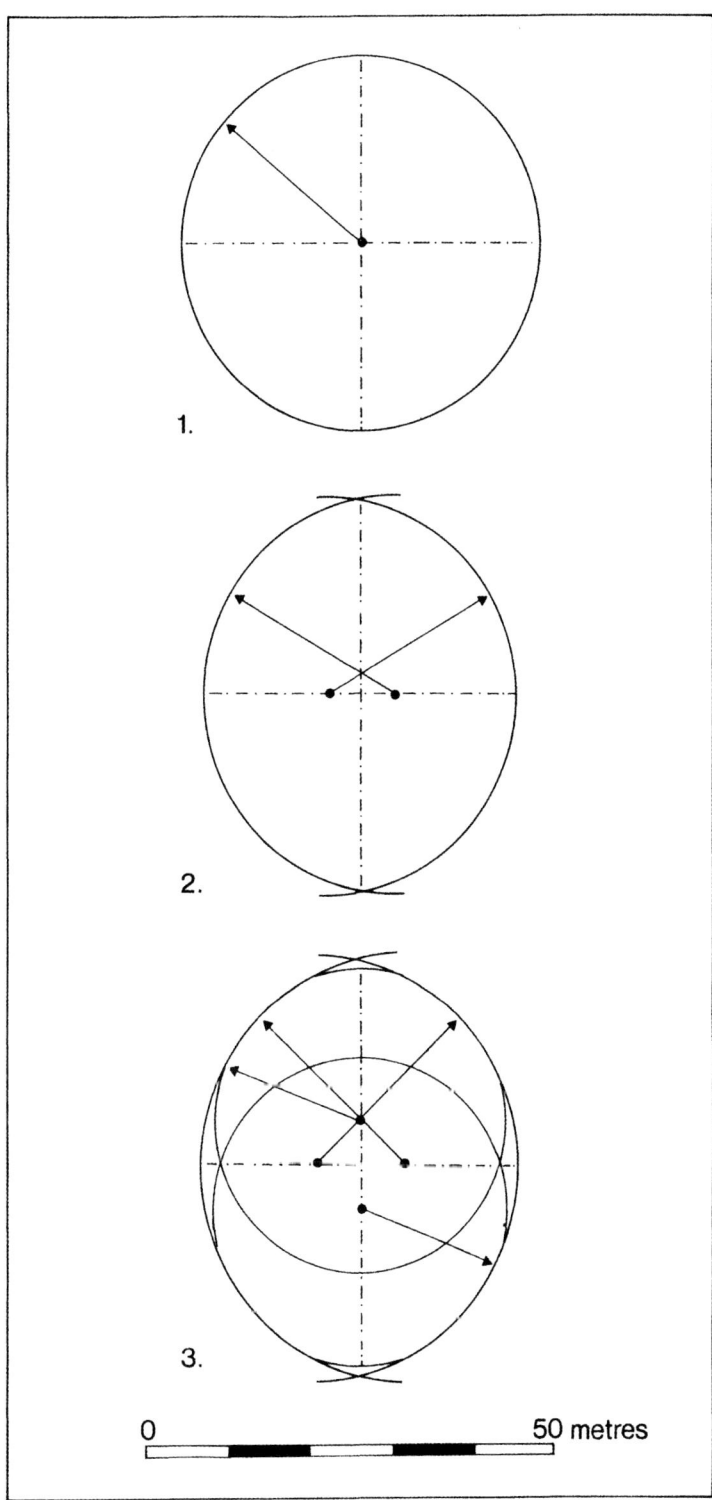

25 Reconstruction of the planning schemes for the amphitheatres at Silchester, (top to bottom, timber phase 1, timber phase 2, stone phase), showing progression from a circle to a two-centre layout to a four-centre oval. *Chris Evans*

has allowed an algorithm to be created which will allow the calculation of the parameters of the elliptical shapes of partially excavated amphitheatres. This analysis suggests the use either of a true ellipse in the planning of the London amphitheatre, or alternatively, a system of arcs derived from eight centres.

Once the shape of the amphitheatre had been laid out construction could begin. In all of the urban amphitheatres, the initial survey would almost certainly have been limited to the arena wall and the entrances. The rear of the *cavea*, if built as an earthwork, would have been measured back off the edge of the arena wall in order to provide a rough guide for the deposition of the spoil excavated from the entrances and arena. One can imagine that this rear line might have been altered during construction according to the properties of the excavated soil. Different materials could be piled with differently angled faces to the earthwork, depending on factors such as compaction and potential to slump. The inner face of the earthwork also needed to be carefully angled to allow a graded auditorium. In its first phase, Silchester had a bank of 15-17 degrees, upon which were broad terraces. This was later steepened to 25 degrees, a slope which appears to be more-or-less standard for these structures. An aspect of planning must have been an estimate of how deep the arena had to be in order to provide the correct bank height. This could to some extent be made up as excavation continued, though the ultimate need to have a flat arena surface meant that some pre-planning was a must in order to avoid the kind of partial over-digging which did, in fact, occur at Silchester.[14]

The arena required a wall around it to retain both the sides of the hole, which it effectively was, and the foot of the artificial bank raised around this hole. The entrance passages giving access to the arena were also dug out as ramps and the sides of these passages also had to be revetted. These arena and entrance structures were provided in timber at three sites, London, Silchester and Dorchester. At Cirencester the original entrances were revetted with drystone walls. The arena wall was represented by a cobble foundation, which could have taken either a timber or a stone structure.[15] Chichester, Carmarthen and Richborough were stone from the start, while Caerwent is a special case. At London and Silchester the original timber structures were later replaced in stone.

Timber structures

The supposed timber amphitheatre at Chester[16] has been disproved by recent excavation[17] and even if the interpretation of this structure had been correct it would have been radically different from all of the urban amphitheatres, except that at London. The timber amphitheatre structures available for study are therefore those at London, Silchester and Dorchester.

PLANNING, CONSTRUCTION AND ARCHITECTURE

26 Support post for seating framework at London, with plank levelling beneath. *Museum of London Archaeology Service*

All three amphitheatres used timber for the arena walls. In London, squared posts were placed in a construction trench around the base of the cut. Both here and on the *cavea*, timber posts were preserved (*26*). These posts presumably supported timber shuttering on the arena side, to present a continuous, even wall. At Silchester, in its first timber phase, a similar structure had squared posts in individual post-pits rather than a running construction trench, but in the second timber phase, in which the arena was changed in shape from circular to oval, post-in-trench construction was adopted (*27*). The reconstructed *gyrus* at the Lunt gives an excellent impression of the probable appearance of such arenas (*colour plate 20*). It is unlikely that a simple palisade would have been sufficient to prevent the arena sides and banks from slipping, so some form of tie-back into the bank material would have been needed. Evidence for this has only been found at Dorchester,[18] but has been suggested at Silchester and London.[19] Dorchester also had a timber arena wall consisting of posts set in a trench (*14*), but here there was an additional factor, as there were two timber slots for a double wall. The two walls were 910mm apart, allowing a practicable narrow passage around the entire circumference of the arena. This feature was probably a service passage and its existence bespeaks knowledge of amphitheatre architecture. Although such passages exist in no other British amphitheatre, they are extremely common elsewhere, usually in stone buildings. To name but a few, they appear in the Italian amphitheatres of Paestum (*28*) and Pompeii, the newly discovered amphitheatre at Leon in Spain, at Maktar in North Africa and, in timber, at Xanten-Birten in Germany.[20] If open to the sky, this passage might have been used as a refuge for participants in the games, rather like the screens used in modern Spanish and Provençal bullfights; if covered like the stone passages elsewhere, it could have been used to service the arena. This could not happen, however, unless doors were provided. Any doors would have had to open outwards, or they would block the corridor, and there is no evidence of arrangements of posts that have marked such openings.

27 North entrance at Silchester as excavated, showing the foundation pits for posts supporting the sides of the entrance and the arena wall in the first timber phase, the drain in the entrance and the post-in-trench construction of the second timber phase arena wall, and the final stone structure. *Society for the Promotion of Roman Studies and Prof. Michael Fulford*

28 The inside of the Paestum amphitheatre showing the service corridor around the arena

PLANNING, CONSTRUCTION AND ARCHITECTURE

Above 29a Sill of timber gate into the arena in London. *Museum of London Archaeology Service*

Below 29b Reconstruction drawing of the gate. *Museum of London Archaeology Service*

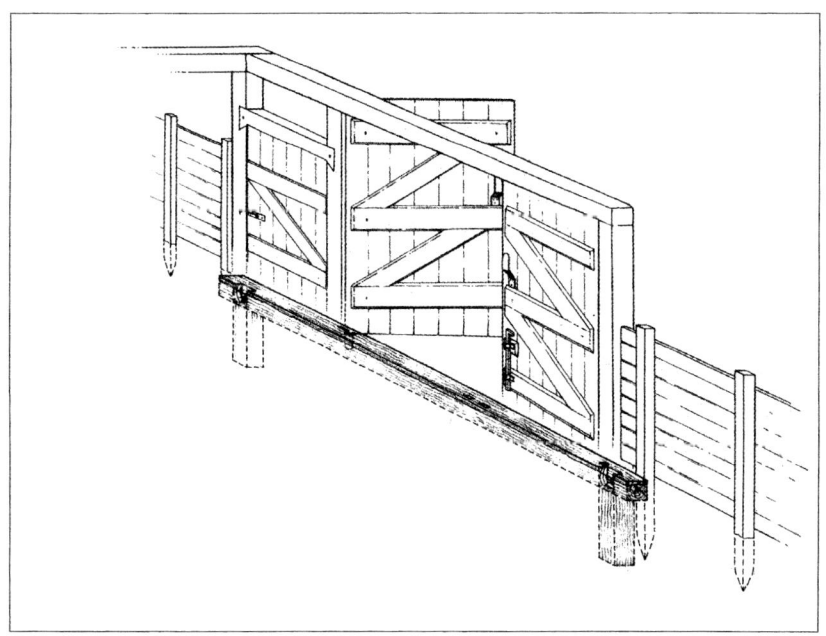

Entrances in these amphitheatres were simple passages. At Silchester there were opposed entrances, one each end of the long axis, and the same is assumed in London, though Dorchester, unusually, had only one entrance, utilising the single entrance of the henge monument from which it was formed. These entrances led into the arena only, with no evidence of any access from the entrance passages to the *cavea*. In all three sites the hollowed-out entrance passages were lined with timber posts set in individual post-holes. It is assumed that the posts retained shuttering against the sides of the passage walls and may have supported bridging timbers, which would have carried the seating over the entrances. In London, at the junction of the entrance passage and the arena wall two large post-holes in the arena wall line flanked a horizontal tie-beam, and these formed the frame for a timber gate opening into the arena (*29*). A similar arrangement was found at both Silchester and at Dorchester, where the horizontal beams were represented by timber slots. At Dorchester the two ends of the service passage opened onto the entrance passage outside the gate into the arena (*60*).

Although Dorchester had only one entrance (on the northern side), on the south, east and west sides, on the lines of the major axes, three recesses were cut back into the chalk and lined with timber. These created three small 'rooms', which could presumably have been accessed from the service corridor. Posts in the corners of these recesses may have supported some form of superstructure above. At least one similar recess opened from the arena on the west side of the Silchester amphitheatre.[21]

Stone structures
In the stone-built amphitheatres, the arena walls averaged 1.3m thick. This was entirely adequate to act as a retaining wall to the sides of the arena. At Richborough and London the walls were very well faced with alternating layers of stone and tile. There is evidence from Chichester, Cirencester and London to show that the arena walls were plastered and painted. This is frequently encountered. Most arena walls so decorated were simple, but others, like that at Pompeii, had elaborate scenes depicting combat (*92*).[22] There is no evidence that the British examples featured anything more elaborate than painting imitating marble panelling. In London coping stones were found within the arena. These were probably used to finish the top of the arena wall. They were half-round in section and at the top of the curve holes were provided for iron railings, which were secured into the stones with lead. One similar coping stone has been found at Silchester.[23]

Before discussing the layout of entrances, which has implications for the nature of the superstructure and seating, we should discuss other structures set around the arena. Recesses opposing each other at each end of the short axes

PLANNING, CONSTRUCTION AND ARCHITECTURE

30 North recess opening from the arena in the stone phase amphitheatre at Silchester

have been noted in the timber amphitheatre at Dorchester. Similar niches were provided in the stone phase at Silchester (*30*). These were apsidal in plan, and may have been roofed with semi-domes, however their function remains unknown. It was suggested by St George Gray that the recesses at Dorchester were used to house cult statues or altars.[24] As these recesses were rendered invisible by the service passage, this is unlikely, though it remains a possibility at Silchester. If so they may have been shrines to Nemesis, or Nemesea[25] (p. 178), and this is further indicated in the stone phase at Silchester, as one of these niches contained a stone base, possibly for an altar.

At both London and Cirencester, the only excavated entrances were at one end of the long axis. Each were flanked by rectangular, stone-built chambers which were supplied with two doorways, one communicating with the arena and one with the entrance passage (*colour plate 8*). At Cirencester in one of the gates into the arena there was a stone threshold, in which was cut a pivot hole for a gate, and striations on the door-sill suggest that the door comprised an iron grille. In London, a similar stone threshold was cut for timbers best interpreted as supports for a vertical-sliding trap-door (*31, 32*). In both cases it is hard to avoid the conclusion that these were *carceres*, or pens to accommodate animals prior to their entry into the arena. Animals could be taken down the entrance passages with perfect safety, as these did not communicate with the *cavea*. It is highly unlikely that carnivorous or dangerous animals were driven into the *carceres*, though experience of bull-running and fighting suggests that bulls might have been. Anything more potentially dangerous, such as bears, would probably have been carried in in travelling crates, which would have allowed them to be released into the *carceres* without contact with their handlers.[26]

Left 31 The entrance to the *carcer* adjacent to the main entrance of the London amphitheatre. Note the mortices for the support beams of the trapdoor door traces. *Museum of London Archaeology Service*

Right 32 Reconstruction of the *carcer* with sliding door at the London amphitheatre. *Museum of London Archaeology Service*

At London and Silchester (*33*) the side walls to the entrances were simply straight retaining walls with no sign of any support for a superstructure and the entrance passages were thus probably open to the sky (*34*). Cirencester was clearly a more ambitious structure,[27] however, as here a series of three pairs of stone imposts set one at each end and one in the centre of the passage must have acted as supports for a barrel vault which carried seating over the entrance passage (*35*). At the point where the passage met the arena was a pair of stone jambs and a threshold, which retained slots for the drop-bolts of a single timber gate. Behind these jambs, at the arena end of the passage, lateral flights of stone steps led to left and right to allow spectators passing down the passage to enter their seats in the *cavea*. Unlike at London, the *carceres* flanking this entrance were secondary structures, being built into the stairwells when the stairs went out of use in a later phase (p. 116).

PLANNING, CONSTRUCTION AND ARCHITECTURE

33 South entrance to the arena at Silchester

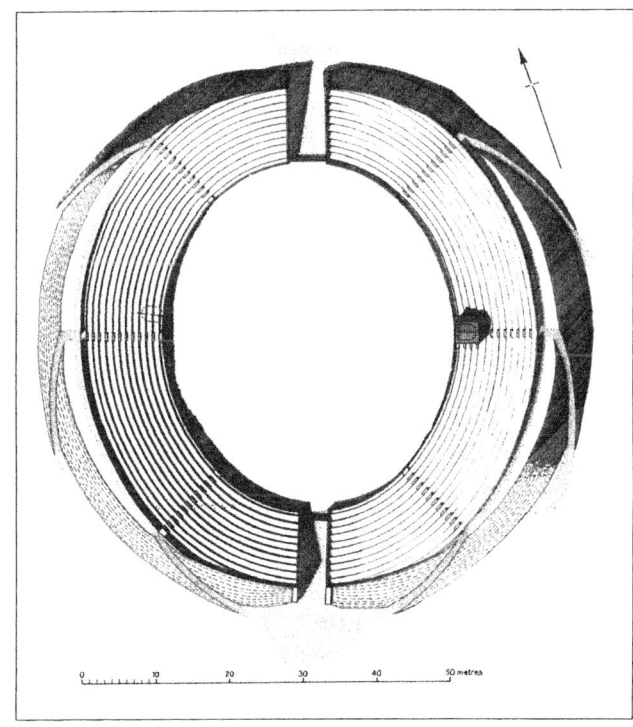

34 Reconstruction drawing of the stone amphitheatre at Silchester, showing the entrance passages open to the sky. *Society for the Promotion of Roman Studies and Prof. Michael Fulford*

THE ROMAN AMPHITHEATRE IN BRITAIN

35 Pier base within the entrance passage at Cirencester, showing that the passage was probably vaulted. *Cotswold Archaeology*

Cavea and seating

The form of the *cavea* of British amphitheatres and the way in which seating was arranged and constructed is problematic for two reasons. Firstly, most excavations of British amphitheatres have concentrated not upon the *cavea*, but on the arena and entrances, and secondly the evidence that survives for seating can be scanty and confusing. As we have seen, the *cavea* were constructed using the material excavated from the arena. At Dorchester the volume excavated from the arena and entrances seems to have been adequate to create the banks, as they survive. At Silchester extra spoil was required from elsewhere to make up the full bank height.[28] In the case of most of our other urban amphitheatres too little excavation has taken place to allow this kind of judgement to be made. Certainly in most cases the sites chosen for the amphitheatre were selected because there were pre-existing hollows, which could be remodelled to form the arena and *cavea*. At Cirencester a former quarry was used, at London a stream valley and at Dorchester a prehistoric henge. At Silchester, Chichester and Carmarthen the sites chosen all sloped to varying degrees, meaning that at least one side was sufficiently high to require less building-up than the other. In the case of Carmarthen the construction of the north side of the *cavea* into a steep hillside would have provided nowhere near enough material to build up the south *cavea* to the same height. It is extraordinary how little attention has been devoted to the outer faces of these earthwork amphitheatres. Only at Silchester has this problem been seriously addressed, though only through a single cross-section, which showed that in its first phase there was a rear retaining wall of stacked turfs *(36)*. This form of construction is resilient and long-lasting, as can be seen from its use in so many Roman military works, including fort ramparts and the northern

PLANNING, CONSTRUCTION AND ARCHITECTURE

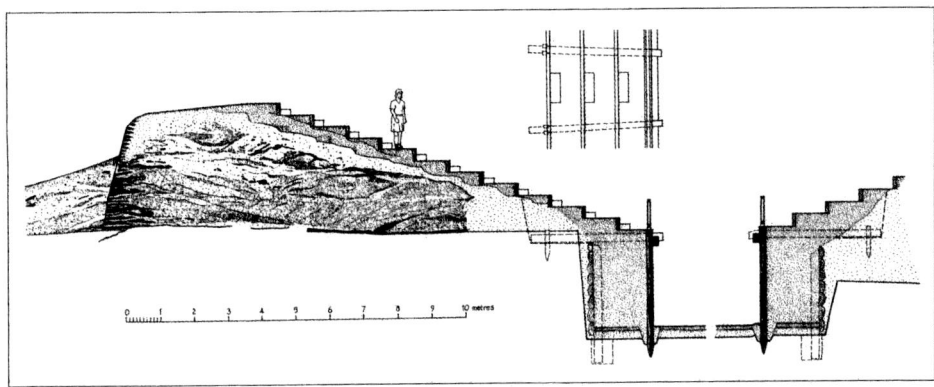

36 Section of the Silchester amphitheatre in the second timber phase to show the turf revetment of the rear of the *cavea*, the two phases of terraces for standing spectators, and the bank at the rear of the *cavea*, possibly a remnant of an external stair. *Society for the Promotion of Roman Studies and Prof. Michael Fulford*

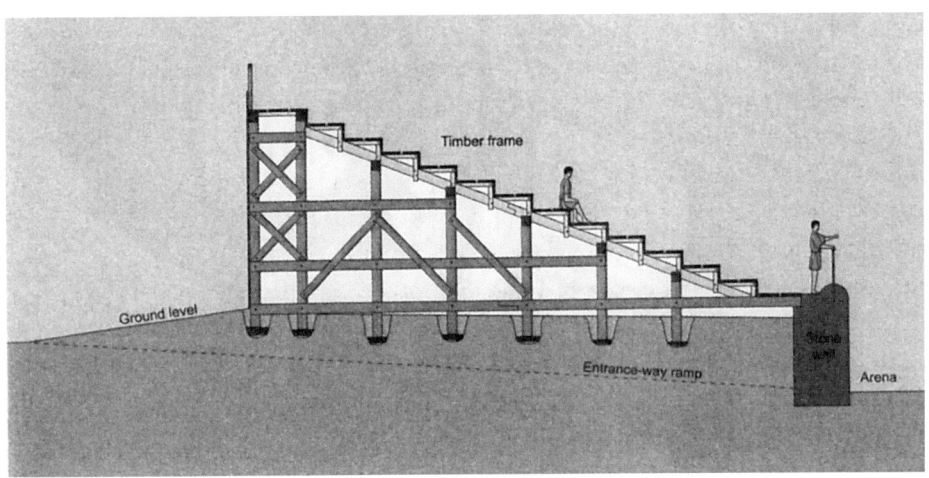

37 Sectional reconstruction of the possible appearance of the timber seating framework at London. *Museum of London Archaeology Service*

frontier walls built by Hadrian and Antoninus Pius. The bank at Dorchester was built of chalk rubble, which would have been stable in itself, as would the limestone quarry waste which formed the banks at Cirencester.

London is a special case, where the bank in the first timber phase consisted of only 200mm depth of material over the natural surface into which the arena was cut. Even in the later phase the maximum height of the bank was only 1.00m.[29] This may be due to the fact that the natural soils on the site, light brickearth and gravel, would not readily lend themselves to the construction of large earthworks.

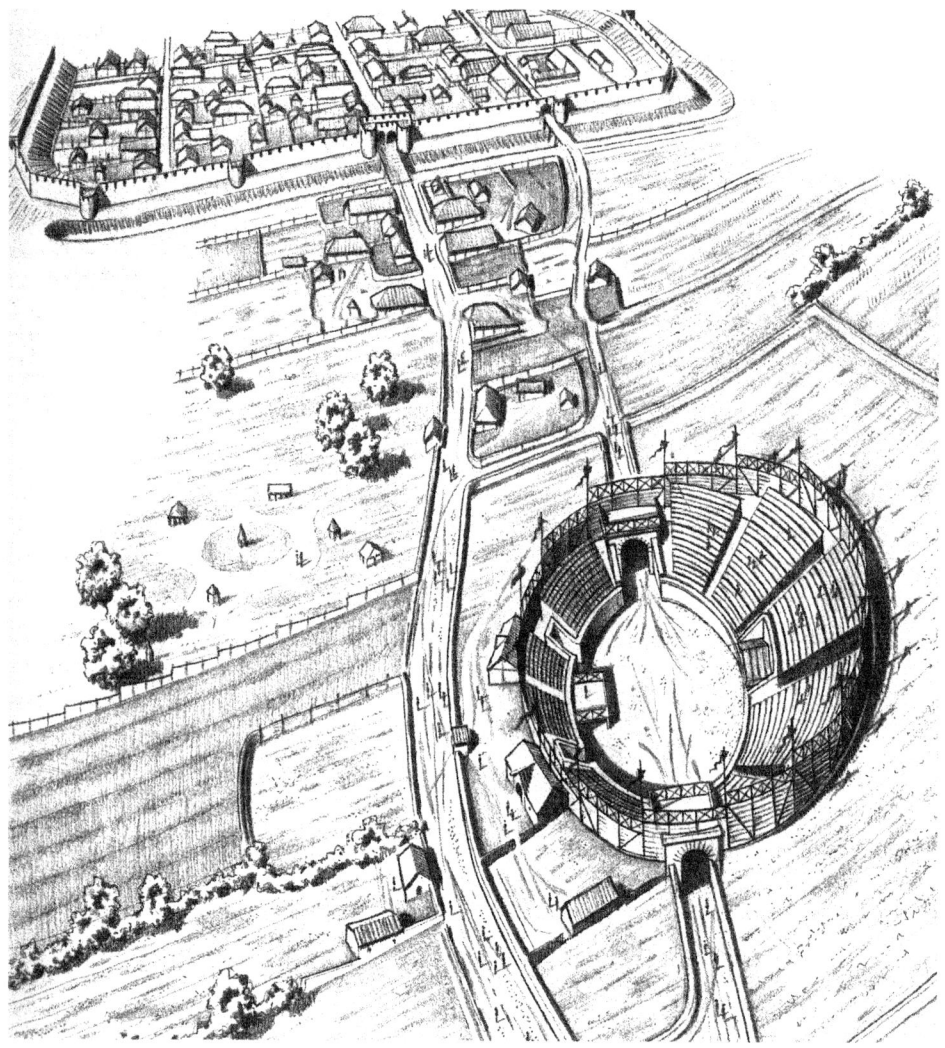

38 Artist's impression of the appearance of the amphitheatre at Carmarthen. *Society for the Promotion of Roman Studies*

Here it is likely that the seating was a virtually free-standing timber structure during both phases, and post-holes have been found which may have been part of the supporting framework for this. Such a structure might have had a boarded outer face, which would have effectively been an outer wall, and in the absence of contrary evidence this appears in reconstructions (*37, colour plate 1*). The same solution has been suggested for the south *cavea* at Carmarthen (*38*).

Access to the *cavea* in these amphitheatres has not been much discussed. At London and Carmarthen there is no evidence whatsoever, except for the fact

PLANNING, CONSTRUCTION AND ARCHITECTURE

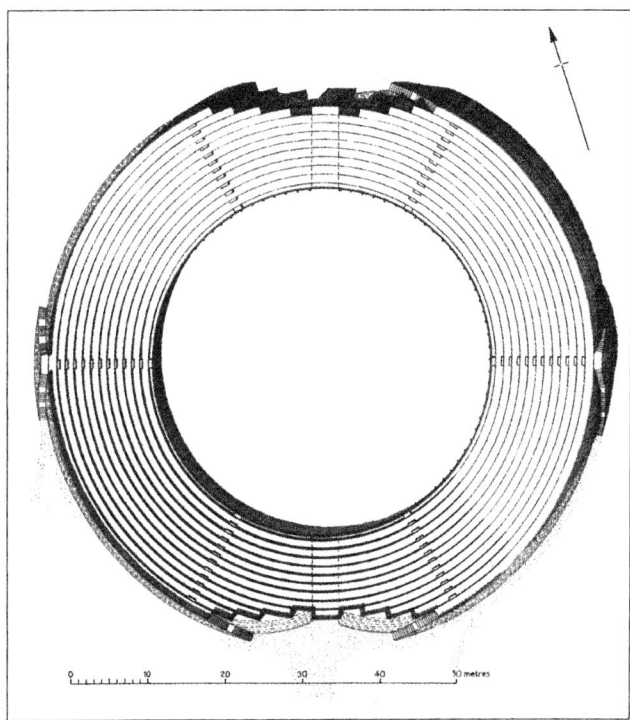

39 Reconstruction drawing of the first timber phase at Silchester, showing bridged entrance passages and external stairs. *Society for the Promotion of Roman Studies and Prof. Michael Fulford*

that at London we can be sure that there were no steps from the entrance passage in either phase (such steps have, misleadingly, been reconstructed on site at Carmarthen). At Cirencester the first phase was provided with stairs leading up from the entrance passages, but later these were replaced with *carceres* and the entrances must have been moved elsewhere. At Dorchester, where no evidence at all was found, it was suggested that the seats were reached over the back of the raised banks of the *cavea*,[30] and at Silchester in the first phase, an earthen bank built up against the rear of the *cavea* has led to the idea that external ramps or stairs were provided (*36, 39*). It has been suggested that formal stairs were used in the first phase, but that the establishment of 'desire routes' would have compromised this pattern[31] by the time of the second timber amphitheatre. In the end, when the second amphitheatre was built it is 'assumed that access for spectators would have been via tracks worn into or formed out of the rear of the bank and following the "desire lines" established over many years of use'. The vision of a picturesque free-for-all, as some 3000 spectators swarmed into their seats (or double this number into standing positions) over a muddy bank, seems utterly chaotic (if attractive) and very much at odds with the order that the careful planning of entrance patterns in the greater amphitheatres implies, although, in the absence of any evidence at all, alternatives are hard to find.

An important question for both considerations of access and of the capacity of the amphitheatres is the relationship of the *cavea* with the entrances. At Cirencester the presence of stone vaulting over the entrances must suggest that there were structures over these entrances and that the seating was extended over the vaults. In the timber amphitheatres this is a more controversial judgement. At the front of the *cavea*, between the parapet formed by the top of the arena wall and the front row of seats (*podium*), a walkway was often provided. At Dorchester this may have been on top of the closed-in timber service corridor, or further back. This walkway may have been carried over the main entrance passage to allow communication between the two halves of the *cavea*, though seating spanning this passage may be considered unlikely.[32] In his reconstructions of Silchester's amphitheatres, Nigel Sunter considered that the paired timbers in the entrances of the first phase could have supported a continuation of the *cavea* over the entrance passage (*39*), though this was not continued into the succeeding remodellings (*34*). Reconstructions of the London building have suggested the continuation of seating over the outer half of the entrance passages (*colour plate 1*).

The most important aspect of the *cavea* – the seating arrangements – remains a problem. Stukeley thought at Dorchester in the eighteenth century, 'viewing the sides very curiously, when the sun shone upon them with a proper light and shade, that I could see the very marks of the poles that lay upon the slopes whereon the benches were fastened'.[33] Similarly at Silchester, Richard Gough recorded 'five rows of seats above one another at the distance of six feet on the slope'.[34] At both sites these may alternatively have been cattle tracks.

At three sites, Silchester, Cirencester and Carmarthen, evidence for structures built directly on the earth or stone banks of the *cavea* has been recorded. In the primary bank at Silchester a series of seven terraces were preserved in the top surface. An overlying layer, which served to heighten the bank at a later phase, also showed evidence of terracing. Terraces were 60-150mm high and 550mm-1.1m wide, with some stratigraphic evidence for timbers retaining the terrace edges.[35] At Carmarthen the banks again preserved evidence for terraces.[36] In this case there had been stepped timber frames, with the spaces between the timbers packed with gravel to form terraces 762mm wide. At Cirencester there was clear evidence that the banks were constructed as a series of terraces created by pressing flat stones into the bank make-up, with the bank material retained by drystone walls (*40*). Sixteen such terraces, up to 900mm wide, were identified. These features have now been seen at all three excavated urban amphitheatres in which any such evidence has survived, and may also be inferred at Chichester (p. 110). It begins to seem almost a generality. They are surely not strictly speaking seats, being too broad and shallow. They are tiered terraces, which would allow standing spectators to see over the heads of those standing in front of them, in

PLANNING, CONSTRUCTION AND ARCHITECTURE

40 The arena wall and tiered stone terraces at Cirencester. *Cotswold Archaeology*

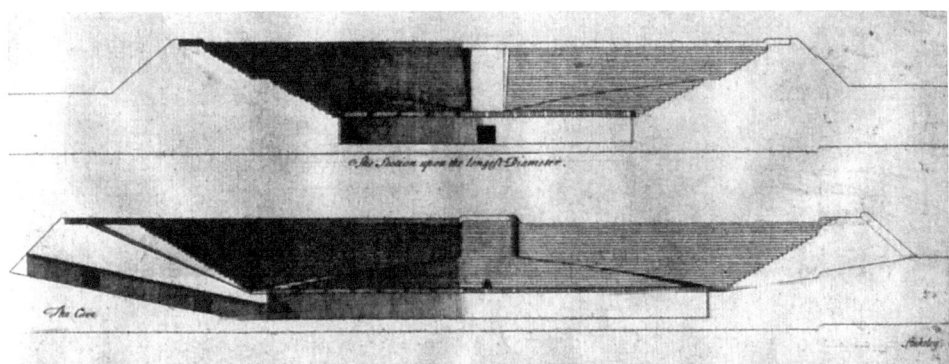

41 Reconstruction of seating at Dorchester, by William Stukeley (1723)

the manner of British football stadia before the Hillsborough disaster of 1989 and the consequent introduction of all-seater stadia. In his review of the Silchester report, George Boon drew particular attention to the fact that the spectators appear to have stood in these amphitheatres.[37] It is possible that some brought their own seats, perhaps the presiding magistrates used folding chairs, but the terraces were far more suited to standing spectators.

Attempts have often been made to calculate the audience seating capacity of amphitheatres. As ever, it was Stukeley who made the first attempt for Dorchester (*41*):

> If we allow a foot and a half for each person sitting, and the number of seats, as I have delineated it, 24; then one side of the building spread *in plano* will form a conic frustum 440 feet long at top 280 at bottom; taking the medium number 360, multiplying it by 24 gives us 8,540 feet; from which take of a fourth part, to reduce it to single places of a foot and a half, there remain 6,480 places on one half of the amphitheatre; double this for the other side and you produce 12, 960 single places for spectators.[38]

In this scheme Stukeley takes account of the fact that the upper terrace would take many more spectators than the lower, because the outer circumference at the back is very much greater than the circumference in the front rows around the arena. Although he does not take into account the depth of the seats, if we do this for him and estimate a depth of 2ft, the total area Stukeley implies for a single seated spectator would be 432in^2, which equals 0.278m^2. This is almost identical to the estimate used to calculate capacities by modern authorities like Golvin and Bomgardner,[39] at 0.28m^2. Based on these kinds of calculations estimates have been attempted for some British amphitheatres. Thus for London seating areas of from 3036m^2 to 4943m^2 have been estimated, giving capacities of between 6800 and 11,000.[40] If the audience was seated, Cirencester could take some 8000, or 11,500 if the rear 11 terraces were occupied by standing spectators.[41] At Silchester, in Phase 1, if the spectators stood two deep on each terrace, the capacity could have been 7250, half this if seated.[42] These calculations can only ever be estimates, though are useful in giving an impression of possible numbers. There are many variables, like the number and size of seating or standing terraces, which allow a wide range of estimated figures.

There is no doubt that magistrates, the sponsors and *editors* of the amphitheatre shows, together with important citizens, would have been provided with special facilities – the equivalent of the emperor's box in the Colosseum. Though there is little direct evidence for such boxes or tribunals, we can make tentative suggestions. Firstly, they would have been placed in the positions which would allow the best view of the arena. This would have been in the front, at ringside, at the widest part of the arena, in other words on the line of the short axis. This was the position of the niches or recesses in the arena walls at both Silchester and Dorchester. It can be fairly confidently argued that the timber posts within the recesses at Dorchester and in the two timber phases at Silchester, as well as the vaulted roofs of the recesses in the stone phase at Silchester acted as supports for tribunals (*42*). The south gate in London appears to have been elaborate, and it may be that the twin passage walls also supported a box structure at podium level.

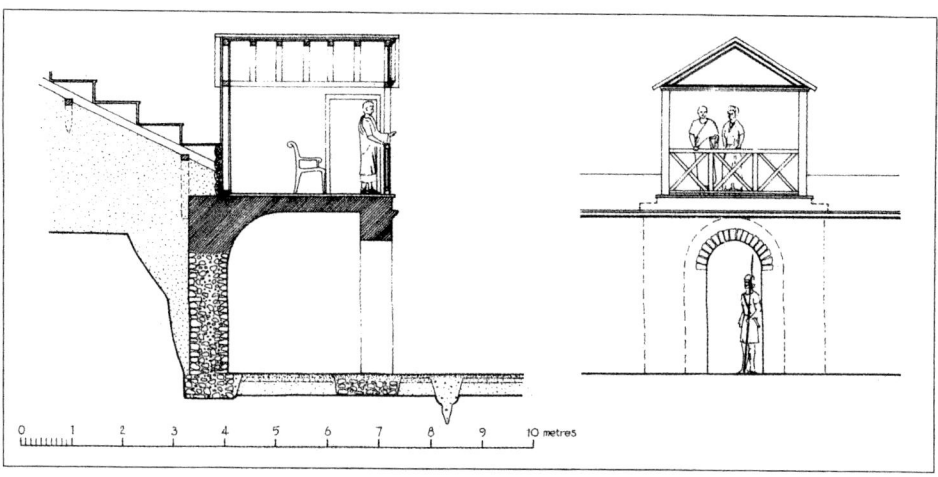

42 Conjectural reconstruction of a tribunal supported above one of the arena-side recesses at Silchester. Society for the Promotion of Roman Studies and Prof. Michael Fulford

LEGIONARY AMPHITHEATRES

The legionary amphitheatres are very different from their urban equivalents, but they are also very different from each other. There are two sites, but effectively three amphitheatres, as while Caerleon retained the same basic shape, the first amphitheatre at Chester was replaced with a larger and more grandiose structure. The two buildings have one basic thing in common, namely the fact that they were provided with stone-built outer walls (Golvin Type 1b). This meant that the whole width of the *cavea* could be used for a rising tier of seats, whereas in amphitheatres built as earthworks, only half this width, the inner facing slope, could be used for spectators. Of the urban sites, only that at London, with its timber outer wall, could utilise the full *cavea* width in this way. The existence of an outer wall of either timber or stone also implies that entrances would have to be specific and controlled. There could be no creation of desire lines over an earthwork bank like those suggested for Silchester.

The legionary amphitheatres were, simply by virtue of having stone outer walls from the start, more ambitious than the contemporary earthwork urban structures. They were built by and for a force of Roman citizens, for a purpose entirely familiar and desirable to the legion. The fact that these amphitheatres were built by legionaries is shown by the presence of centurial stones – building stones recording the centuries responsible for parts of the work. A good example is the stone at Caerleon recording building by the century of Rufinus (*43*).

These buildings had in common with the urban amphitheatres the basic fact that the arenas were hollowed out of the ground and the spoil cast up to form

43 Centurial stone from the Caerleon amphitheatre commemorating building work by the century commanded by Rufinus. National Museum of Wales

the banks. Bank structure was less important, however, as each side of the bank was supported by a stone wall. This meant that the banks were not structural, but were in-fill, creating a solid mass between two walls.

Planning and layout

The surveying of these buildings would have been somewhat more advanced than for the earthwork examples, as the survey would have had to plan the position of both the outer and arena walls. At Chester, the first part to be built was the outer wall. This meant that the arena and outer wall had to be surveyed on the ground as concentric ovals. The same is probably true at Caerleon. This enabled the builders to excavate the arena and to simply throw the resulting spoil up against the inside face of the outer wall to begin the *cavea* construction. As in the urban amphitheatres, principal entrances consisted of ramps leading down a gradient towards the level of the arena, and these too had to be excavated, their spoil adding to the *cavea* mounds.

J.A. Wright worked out the method used to set out the shape of the arena[43] at Caerleon. He concluded that the limitations of the site meant that the optimum size could only be achieved by first laying out the short, east–west axis. Caerleon is one of the few amphitheatres in Britain so completely excavated that this method can be described with accuracy (*44*). Three-quarters of the length of the short axis gave the radius of two lateral curves centred at focal points. The same measurement gave the point at which the curve ended. Two further focal points were used as centres for the curves at the narrow ends of the arena. This method thus generates an oval by means of two pairs of segmental arcs based upon four focal points.[44] Although Chester was not fully excavated, and the

PLANNING, CONSTRUCTION AND ARCHITECTURE

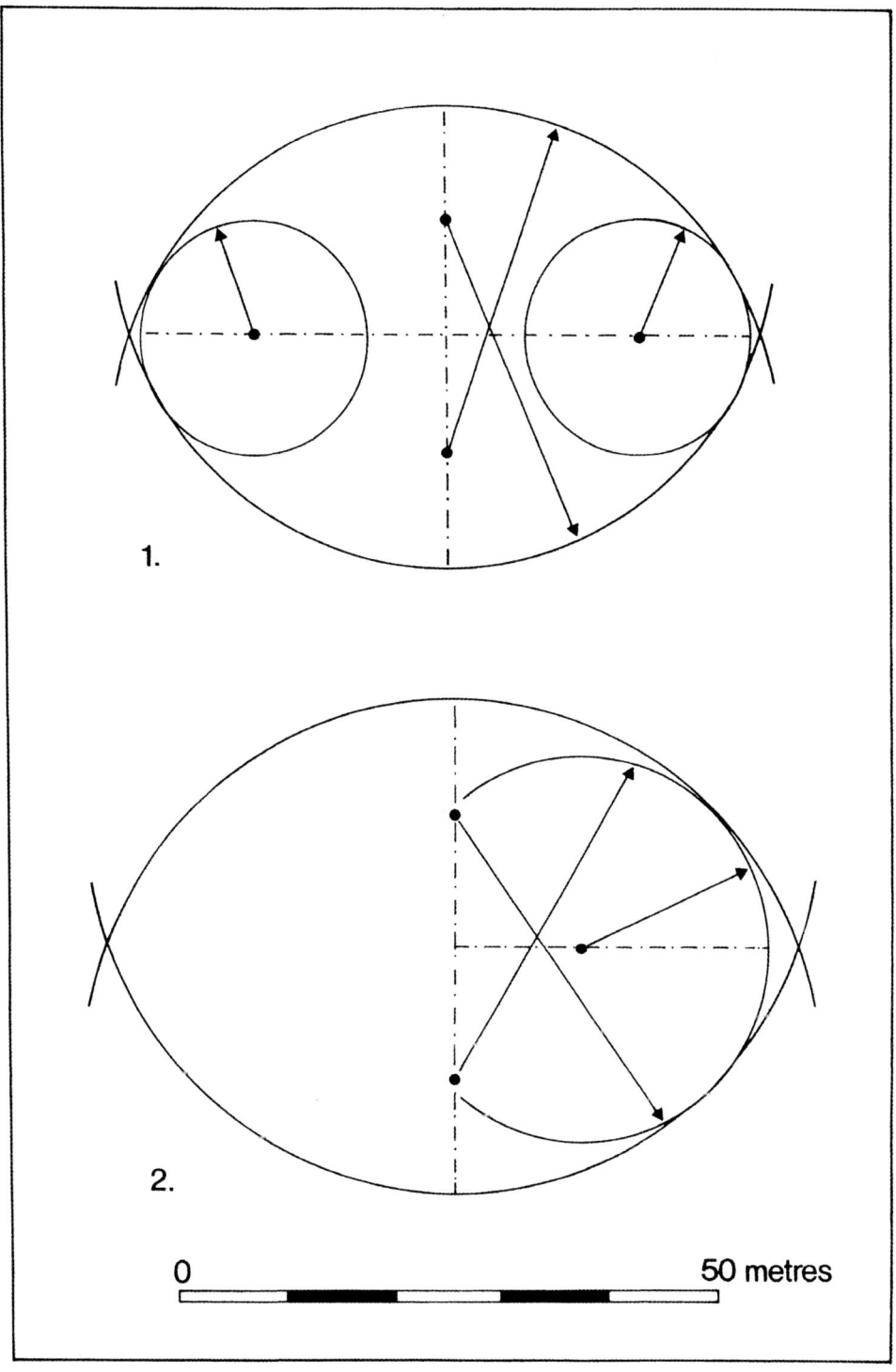

44 Reconstruction of the planning schemes for the amphitheatres at Caerleon (top) and Chester (bottom). Both are based upon four-centre ovals. *Chris Evans*

estimate of surveying methods advanced by the excavator was based upon a misunderstanding of the nature of the two phases of the building, it appears that an oval constructed from the arcs of circles drawn from four points was the means of surveying here as well.[45] This is one of many different techniques by which an oval or ellipsoid plan could be achieved. Indeed one survey of legionary amphitheatres on the Rhine and Danube frontiers shows that no solution to the problem was used twice.[46]

Stone walls and entrances

Caerleon and Chester 1 were built using a coursed rubble facing technique typical of Roman legionary work – the sort of masonry that the legionary builders later used to build Hadrian's Wall. The arena wall, outer wall and entrances were all faced in this way. The later Chester 2 had much better quality stone facing, but this was an exceptional building for Britain in many ways, as we will see. All three buildings were completely different in the way in which entrances were planned. This is a major difference, which may be a reflection of the differing experience of the legionary architects of the two legions. A preliminary look at the histories of the legions suggests that this does not reflect general experience gathered in former postings, and must relate to the knowledge and experience of individuals within the legion.

The entrances of Chester 1, which may have been built c.AD 90, seem to have consisted of four simple ramps into the arena from the opposite points of the long and short axes. These entrances were almost certainly vaulted, the vaults carrying seating over the entrance passages. Later developments obscured the early arrangements, but it is probable that the front seats were accessed from stairs situated at the arena end of the entrance passage. Shortly after construction the simple form was quickly altered. The seating arrangements were changed and the entrances were augmented by the addition of stone stairways against the rear face of the outer wall to allow access into the rear seats of the *cavea* over this wall. The size of the foundation of these stairs and the reconstruction of a practicable gradient allows an estimate for the outer wall height of some 4m (*colour plate 2*). By coincidence, the outer stairs at the amphitheatre of Paestum (*45*) in Italy are of a similar size to those at Chester, and the stairs and outer wall there survive to full height – 5m. It is probable that, in the case of Chester, the front seats were reached by stairs leading up from the sides of the four main entrances, and that tribunals or boxes were sited over the two opposing entrances on the short axis.

The Caerleon amphitheatre was probably built c.AD 80 and is therefore broadly contemporary with that at Chester. Though smaller than the Chester

PLANNING, CONSTRUCTION AND ARCHITECTURE

Right 45 External stair at the amphitheatre of Paestum, Italy

Below 46 Main north entrance passage wall at Caerleon, showing the piers provided to support vaulting

47 Entrance on the short axis at Caerleon, showing the main stair down into the chamber opening into the arena. Beneath the arch is the L-shaped stair leading to the tribunal above the chamber

amphitheatre, it seems to have been structurally more ambitious. At each end of the long axis were simple entrances leading into the arena only. These were certainly vaulted, as the side walls retain the piers which supported the vaults (*46*). The entrances on the short axis were complex, with stairways leading both to the *cavea* and apparently to a pair of boxes or tribunals, which were provided above side chambers at arena level, like the recesses at Silchester, but larger and rectangular in shape (*47*). These may well have functioned as *carceres*. Between each pair of major entrances were further entrances, which led into the *cavea*, emerging at the level of the *podium* at the top of the arena wall. All entrances, therefore, led to the front of the auditorium. The boxes or tribunals on the short axes had their independent access, while the bulk of the audience entered by way of ramps and stairs which led to the *podium*, from which they would have to ascend the *cavea* into the rear seats.

The second Chester amphitheatre was the largest and most elaborate such structure in Roman Britain (p. 136). Its outer wall was very much higher than that of the first building and it was therefore impossible to access the rear seats over the back wall. The front seat access remained via stairs from the arena end of the four main entrances, but rear seats were accessed by means of *vomitoria*, two between each pair of principal entrances (*colour plate 7*). These were vaulted stairways which ran straight upwards from external street level, to emerge at a high level in the face of the auditorium. The very presence and need for such entrances shows that the amphitheatre had a high outer wall, probably with a two-storey façade, and that the seating rake was steep. This mode of access, common on the continent, is found nowhere else in Britain. On the west side of the arena end of the main north entrance was a chamber. This opened into the arena and may originally have opened into the entrance passage as well. The discovery of an altar to Nemesis shows that it was used as a *Nemeseum*, but this may have been a secondary use. The chamber when built was most probably a *carcer*.

Cavea and seating

At Caerleon there is evidence for the provision of timber seating raised on the banks of the *cavea*. Post-holes found on the banks suggest that this seating was built off the bank and it is probable that the rear timbers were keyed into the top of the stone outer wall. With a timber seating scaffold, this would mean that the stone portion of the building would comprise a lower, service storey, with stone entrances, vaults, stairs and ramps, surmounted by an open timber structure. This is exactly the appearance of an amphitheatre built by Trajan's army in Dacia, which is depicted on Trajan's column (*48*), and this is the basis on which the reconstruction of the building has been made (*colour plate 4*).

48 Scene from Trajan's column showing a stone-built amphitheatre with timber superstructure

It is possible that the first amphitheatre at Chester looked somewhat similar, though the early renovation that resulted in the insertion of the external stair, also included a major renovation to the seating (*colour plate 2*). The change took place around AD 100 and this second phase of the first amphitheatre at Chester is the one of which we know the most. The embanked *cavea* was cut away, forming a flat terrace at the level of the top of the arena wall upon which prefabricated timber frames were installed to support a timber-framed seating scaffold (*colour plate 5*). The base-plates of this scaffold, with their diagonal and vertical upright members (*colour plate 6*) were held in place by the weight of a mass of coarse red sand and sandstone, which was derived from the deepening of the arena, and a new stone arena wall was built. It is probable that the top of the seating coincided with the top of the outer wall, so that this could be entered directly from the external stair. If the timber seats were built above the level of the top of the wall some sophisticated carpentry would be needed to create passages through the seating scaffold in the nature of the later *vomitoria*. We have already seen that purpose-built stairs allowed access to tribunals at Caerleon above the entrances on the short axes. The same was surely true at Chester and there is evidence to indicate such a structure at the eastern entrance to the building.

External treatment

There is evidence from both sites that the buildings were decorated, both architecturally and by painting. Both sites produced evidence for painted arena walls, though no ambitious decorative scheme can be suggested. At Caerleon, at least part of the building was rendered with plaster, picked out with false ashlar jointing in red paint.[47] The outer wall on the downhill slope was supported with buttresses. The spacing of these was carried on around the whole of the face of the outer wall in the form of shallow pilasters, no doubt to give a uniform decorative appearance. The second Chester amphitheatre was provided with buttresses or rather pilasters, flanking each of the 12 entrances and between each pair of entrances was a further stone base. Two of these, excavated in 2004, proved to have mortar pads on the top, semi-circular in shape and evidently intended to support half-round decorative columns (*49*). Work is continuing on the reconstruction of the appearance of the building,[48] but the use of half columns, paralleled on the continent (*50*), suggests the use of a blank arcade. The height of the building attested by the need for *vomitoria* further suggests that there were two stories of arcading.

PLANNING, CONSTRUCTION AND ARCHITECTURE

49 Stone pilaster base on the outer wall of the second amphitheatre at Chester. Note the semicircular mortar pad, and the fissures in the stone around the pad. *Chester City Council/English Heritage*

50 Semi-columns on the façade of the amphitheatre at Capua, Italy

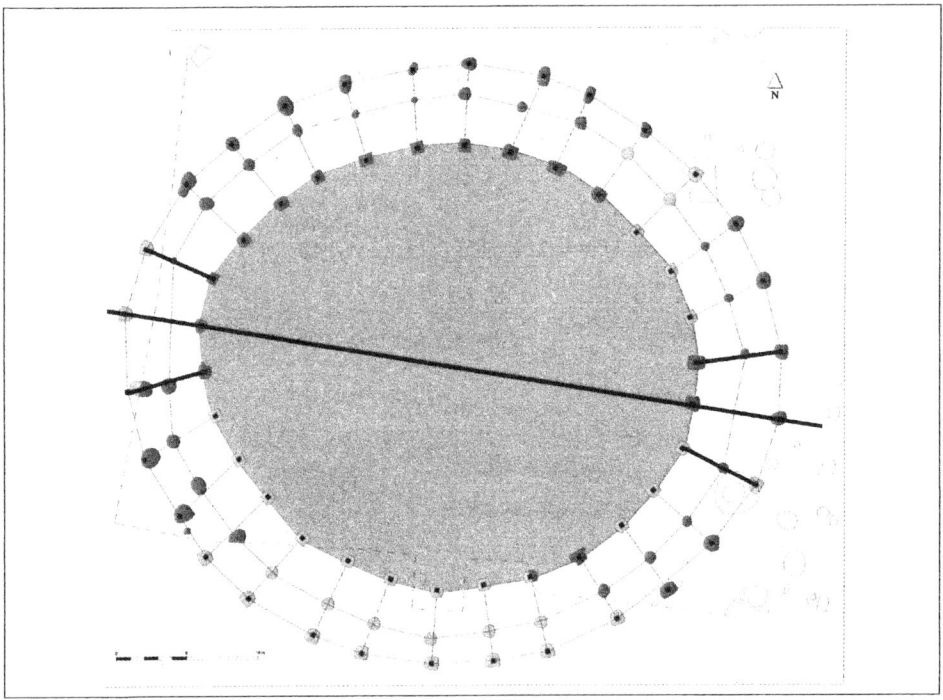

51 Plan of the auxiliary amphitheatre at Künzing, Bavaria. *Karl Schmotz*

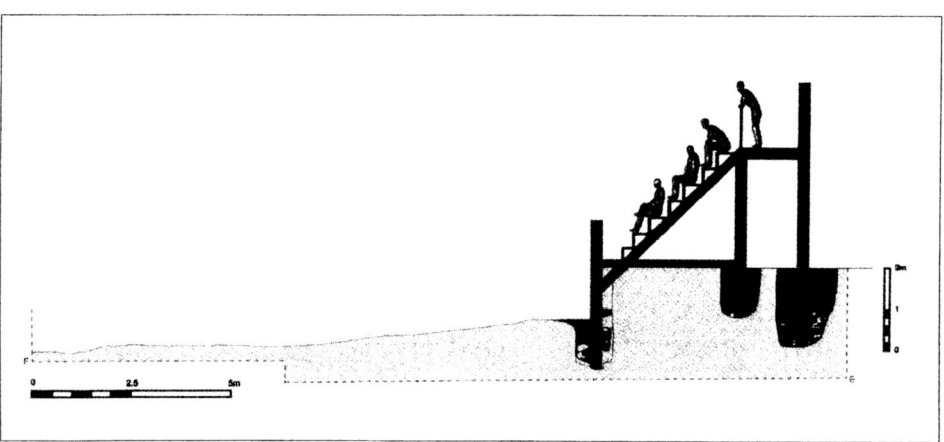

52 Reconstructed section of the timber-framed seating at Künzing, Bavaria. *Karl Schmotz*

AUXILIARY AMPHITHEATRES

Without excavation there is little that can be said on the structure of these buildings, beyond the fact that they seem to have been timber-revetted earthworks. Only Newstead has revealed any structural data and that concerns its probable timber arena wall. Tomen-y-Mur is unexcavated and Charterhouse-on-Mendip, which can perhaps stylistically be included among these sites, is inconclusive. The reconstruction of the only fully excavated auxiliary amphitheatre in the Empire, at Künzing, Bavaria, is of a fully framed structure with a back wall tied into the arena wall below timber-framed seating. The plan and reconstructed section are included here (*51, 52*) to give an idea of the kind of structure whose remains might yet be found in Britain.

6

THE SITES: THE SOUTH AND EAST

Therefore we may suppose that amphitheatres were not forgotten; and probably this was not later than that time, so near the southern coast (which among the Britons themselves was the most civilised): so rich and fine a country: for Titus, his father Vespasian, partly under Claudius and partly under Aulus Plautius his lieutenant, conquered all the parts hereabouts.[1]

The southern and eastern portion of Britain contains all of those structures listed in Chapter 4 as urban amphitheatres, rural amphitheatres and theatre-amphitheatres (*19*), and all of these are described in the summaries that follow. The final section covers sites whose identification as amphitheatres has been rejected. I have rejected the identification of the two sites of Woodcutts and Winterslow as amphitheatres, but I include them together with reasons for their rejection, as they have appeared recently in the literature of the subject.[2]

URBAN AMPHITHEATRES

The urban amphitheatres of the south are described in approximate chronological order of their first construction.

London (Londinium)
The London amphitheatre was discovered during excavations within the City in 1987, conducted in advance of the redevelopment of the Guildhall Art Gallery for the Corporation of London. Excavation began in earnest in 1992, continuing until 1996, and the southern entrance was discovered during a separate project in 1999.

THE SITES: THE SOUTH AND EAST

The site was, naturally, constrained by its urban position and the excavation took place within the footprint of the area to be developed. This area fortuitously covered the whole of the principal east entrance to the building, at the end of its long axis. The site of modern Guildhall Yard occupies the greater part of the amphitheatre with the medieval Guildhall on the northern side of the *cavea* and the church of St Lawrence Jewry virtually in the centre of the arena. The amphitheatre was built on the eastern flank of the western hill of Roman *Londinium*, in a shallow tributary valley of the Walbrook, the stream which ran between the two hills upon which the City was built. The site chosen for the amphitheatre lay on the fringes of the city, though later development was to grow up around it, including the fort at Cripplegate. The later city walls enclosed the building.

The site appears to have been chosen so that the natural depression could be enlarged and remodelled by digging out the arena to use the spoil as the base for the *cavea*. The alignment of the amphitheatre, which is orientated almost exactly due east-west, differs from that of the nearby street grid, though this may have been as much due to the natural constraints of the site as to a preference for this alignment. Two principal phases of construction were found during excavation, a primary timber phase and a phase of rebuilding in masonry. The following description is principally derived from an interim report on the excavations published by the excavator, Nick Bateman, in 1997, a popular summary by the same author and the full publication which appeared in 2008.[3]

It has recently been shown that the layout of the amphitheatre was based either on a surveyed ellipse, or on an oval derived from the arcs of eight circles.[4] In the first phase (53) the arena was excavated into the ground and the spoil from this operation piled around the arena to form the beginnings of the *cavea*. Only 200mm of spoil overlying the natural brickearth was found and the bank may never have been much higher than this. The height of the arena wall from the arena floor to the top of this bank would have been in the order of 2m. A number of deep post-pits and timber slots found in the surface of the bank may relate to the timber phase of the amphitheatre, the stone phase or both, but clearly represent the foundations for a timber framework supporting seating (37). Many more of these were found to the south of the main east entrance than to the north – perhaps the seating was not carried around the entire *cavea*.[5]

The structural evidence for the first, timber-built, phase comprised post-holes, beam-slots and also a large quantity of well-preserved timbers, which survived in the waterlogged ground. Full analysis of the timber structure, particularly with regard to the framework supporting the seating, is yet to be completed. Beginning with the arena, at the inner end of the excavated entrance, two large timber uprights some 300mm square were found on either side of a substantial buried tie-beam (29). This was evidently the gateway into the arena. The gateway opened

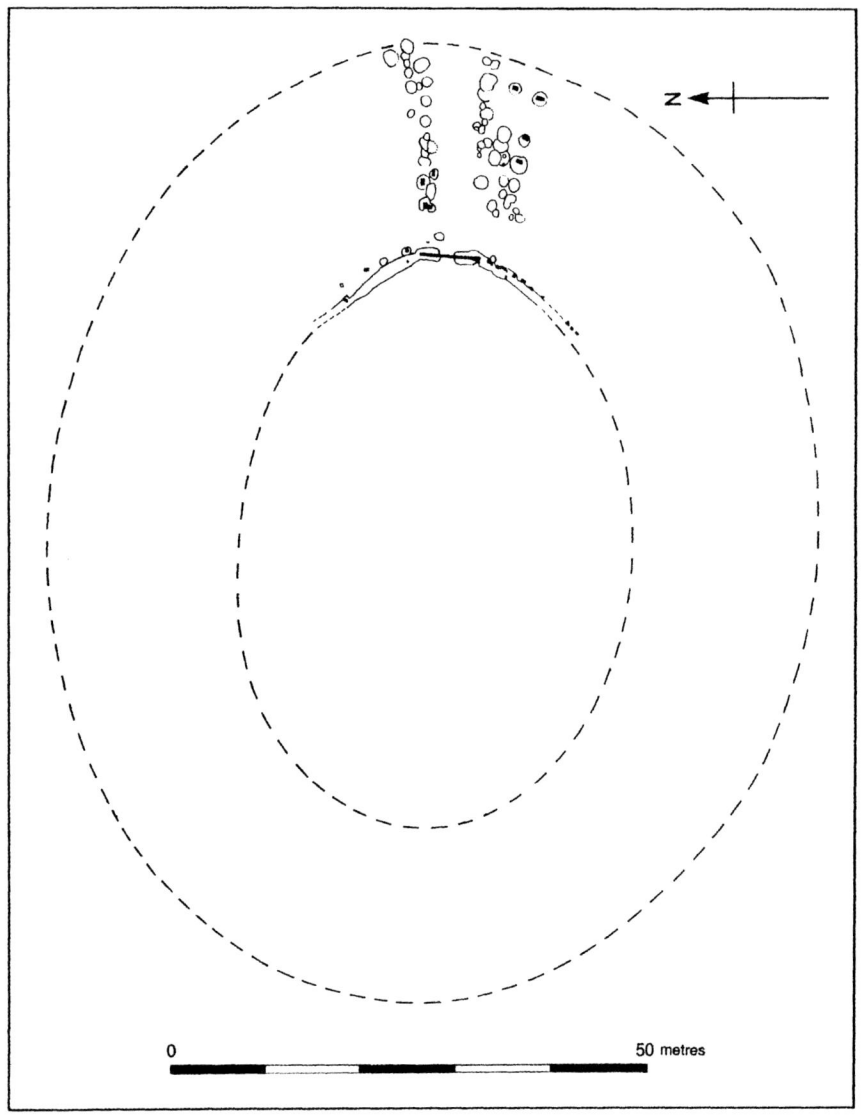

53 Plan of the first, timber, phase of the London amphitheatre. *Chris Evans, after Bateman 1997, 2000*

through a timber arena wall, the evidence for which consists of a series of squared timber uprights set in a construction trench, which described the shape of the end of the oval arena. These probably supported a wall of timber shuttering, though whether they were braced back into the bank they supported is unclear. The entrance was some 5m wide at the inner gate and at least 17m long. A clear line of posts and post-holes defined the line of the northern side-wall of the entrance.

THE SITES: THE SOUTH AND EAST

Like the arena wall, it is presumed that these uprights supported a system of timber shuttering which retained the sides of the entrance passage. On the south side the story is more complicated, as a series of intercutting post-holes suggests that these were replaced and the side-wall rebuilt or repaired on at least one occasion. Several of the surviving timbers provided the potential for dating through dendrochronology. Two pads from post-pits in the entrance gave dates of felling in the spring or summer of AD 70. Combined with other factors, such as the fact that no coins before the reign of Vespasian were found in the deposits relating to the amphitheatre, a date of AD 70-71 has been suggested for construction.[6]

The second phase (*54*) is dated archaeologically to around AD 125.[7] It began with the virtually complete removal of all significant timber uprights. It is possible that there had been some collapse of the banks, as both the arena and entrance passages were cut back into the *cavea*, presumably to provide clean, straight sections against which to build the stone retaining walls. These walls were 1.20m wide, and comprised 4-5 courses of squared Kentish ragstone rubble, alternating with double courses of brick; a construction technique common in Roman London. In some places the walls survived to a height of 1.5m and it is likely that the arena wall stood no higher than 2.5-2.7m. In the debris at the foot of the arena wall two coping stones were found, half-round in profile, with the lead-filled holes provided to support an iron grille or railing on the top. There were other cuts in the stones, which may have engaged with timber supports in the *cavea*. There was a small amount of evidence that the arena wall may have been faced, at least at the base, with *opus signinum*, and fragments of painted plaster hint at a painted arena wall.[8] The surface of the arena consisted of 50mm of rammed gravel mixed with a hard mortar, over which was a layer of fine silty-sand some 30m thick. Similar successions of hard and soft material characterised subsequent re-surfacings, which raised the level of the arena floor by some 600mm during the life of the building. Several rebuilds or repairs of the arena and entrance passage walls also took place.

The arena end of the east entrance was flanked by two side-chambers, almost square, each with an internal area of 11m² (*colour plate 8*). Each had doorways communicating both with the arena and with the entrance passage. The thresholds into the passage were simple timber beams, but a large stone threshold lay in the arena entrance of the southern chamber. Sets of parallel mortises on each side of the threshold are interpreted as provision for a vertically sliding timber trapdoor allowing beasts to be released from the chamber (*31, 32*), which would thus be interpreted as a *carcer*.[9] The threshold from the northern chamber into the arena did not survive. The entrance passage itself was 7m wide at the arena wall, splaying slightly towards its outer end. Squared timbers were laid across the passage to act as thresholds at various times, one retaining an iron fitting which was probably the pivot for a timber gate. The southern entrance

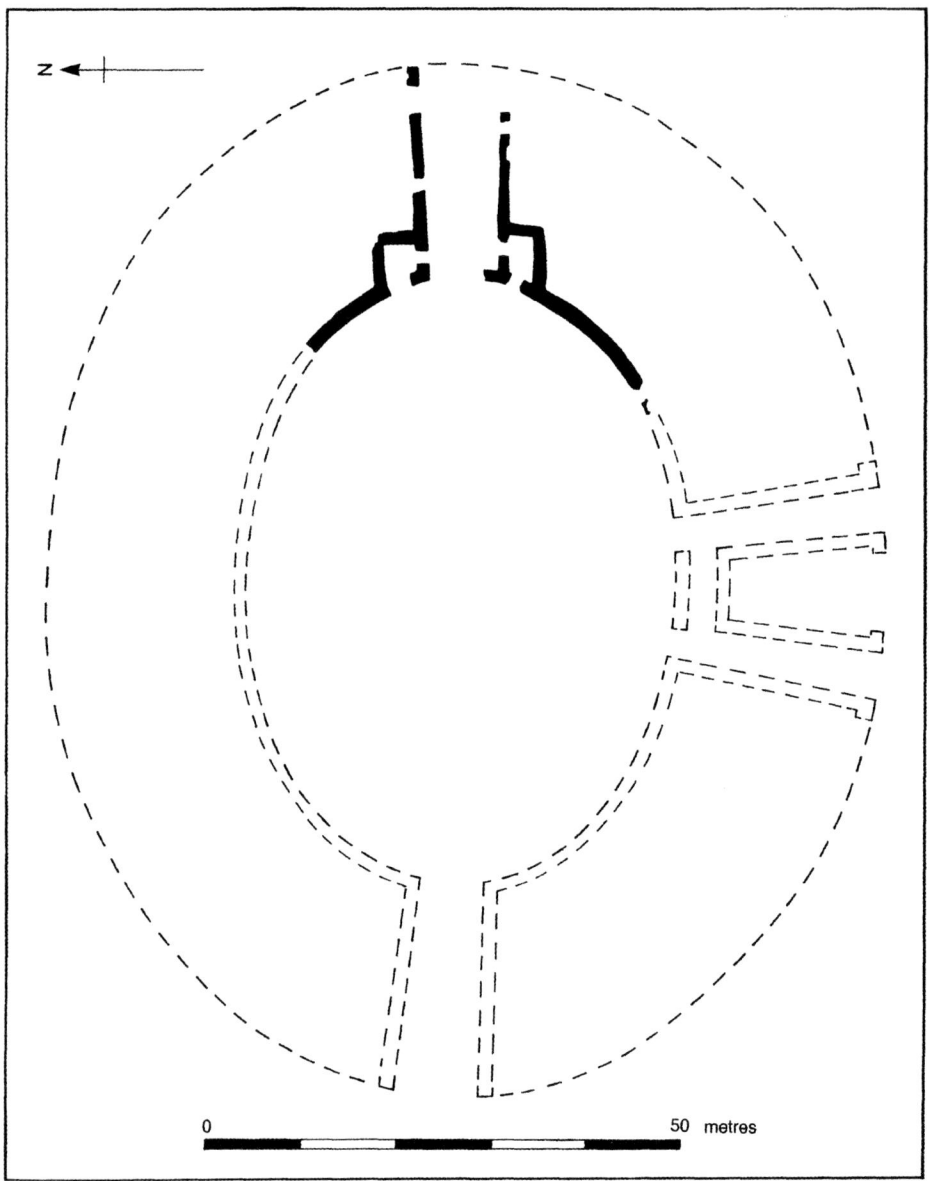

54 Plan of the second, stone, phase of the London amphitheatre. *Chris Evans, after Bateman 1997, 2000*

probably comprised two entrance passages running beneath the seating to a single chamber just behind the arena wall on the short axis of the building. It is likely that from this entrance and its northern counterpart, it would have been possible to access the *cavea* by means of a short stair, and that a tribunal was built above the chamber which unified the entrance (*colour plate 1*).

There was no trace of an outer wall to the amphitheatre and it is very difficult to suggest exactly where the outer limit of the building lay at any given time. Excavations have revealed a variety of types of feature, of differing dates, occupying the areas where the outer limit of the building might be expected. If the seating rake was 25 degrees and the *cavea* 21m deep, this would imply an external elevation of 9.8m. A rear wall of timber would be necessary, and would be built as part of the system of framed seating (*37, colour plate 1*).

The site chosen for the amphitheatre made drainage essential, both to canalise the stream that ran through the valley occupied by the amphitheatre and also to carry away run-off water in the sunken arena. The principal elements of the drainage were an axial drain along the main axis of the arena and perimeter drains around the inside of the perimeter walls. At different times these drains took different forms. Some were unrevetted gullies, others either timber-lined or fully carpentered drains complete with silt-traps (*colour plate 9*). Other perimeter drains were stone and tile lined, or loose-filled soakaway drains. The directions in which the drains ran, once outside the amphitheatre, were constantly re-routed according to the drainage regimes in the city beyond. The axial drain, which ran down the centre of the eastern entrance passage, effectively divided the passage into two zones which were differently treated and which may have had different functions. There was no evidence that this was ever a public entrance; it communicated only with the arena and the side chambers. To the south of the drain was a solid ragstone-cobbled floor, whereas to the north the floor was a patchy earth and gravel surface, but was higher than the floor to the south.

The later history of the amphitheatre is one of consistent maintenance of drains with a date after AD 243 for the timbers in the latest rebuild of the central drain. The silt deposits which signal the disuse of the site contain coins from *c*.AD 340-80, which may indicate that the amphitheatre went out of use in the early to mid-fourth century. The robbing of the masonry took place after *c*.AD 367. Like much of the rest of Roman London, the area of the amphitheatre was deserted in the fifth century and was unoccupied until the eleventh century, when late Saxon buildings were constructed in the former arena. Excavation of the south entrance in 1999 revealed a heavily truncated Roman wall, and that the clay bank of the amphitheatre was cut by an inhumation burial, followed by the medieval entrance road to the Guildhall Yard.[10]

Silchester (Calleva Atrebatum)

The amphitheatre at Silchester was first identified by Stukeley, who wrote of it that:

It is in bulk, in shape, and at all points the same as that of Dorchester, but not built of so solid materials; for it is chiefly sand and gravel; it stands upon a sloping piece of ground. … The whole area or arena within it is now covered with water … it is a most noble and beautiful concave, but intirely grown over with thorn bushes, holly, briars, broom, furze, oak and ash trees &c. and has from time immemorial been a yard for cattle and a watering-pond.[11]

Stukeley's engraving of the amphitheatre (*8*) is very inaccurate and much influenced by his work at Dorchester. He included a circular walkway halfway up the *cavea*, which is obviously based upon his interpretation of the ramps at Dorchester built for guns during the English Civil War. The site has been much discussed and described, but was not excavated until it was taken into state guardianship in 1979. The excavations were at first concerned with demonstrating whether or not the structure was, in fact, an amphitheatre, and to get information about phasing and structure. Ultimately the work was extended to allow the masonry walls and banks to be consolidated and laid out as a publicly accessible monument.

Silchester is the single most extensively excavated and best published amphitheatre in Britain,[12] and is the best understood of the urban group. It developed in three phases, the first two of timber construction, and the third built in stone. The excavation was fully published by Professor Michael Fulford in 1989, in an influential report which set the standard for future publication of the British amphitheatres and which can be regarded as the beginning of the modern phase of such studies.

The site of the amphitheatre lay to the north-east of the occupied area, and was later excluded from the walled circuit when earthwork defences were built in the second century. Phase I[13] was a simple structure, the basis of which was the excavation of the arena to sufficient depth to provide material for the banks (*55*). The amphitheatre stood on sloping ground and the level arena was 2.38-2.97m below the old ground surface. At one point over-digging took place and needed to be levelled up. The banks were 14m wide and were revetted at the back by stacked turfs. They consisted of dumped gravel, turf and clay, and the excavation recovered detailed information on how the bank was built. The material from the arena would have produced only half the volume of the banks and a large amount of extra material had to be imported. On the top of the primary bank, running down the face of the *cavea* towards the arena was a band of clay which lay at 15-17 degrees of slope, and in which evidence for seven terraces was recorded. These were 60-115mm in height and 550mm-1.10m deep, with the lowest step 1-4m above the natural ground surface (*34*). It has been estimated that if the amphitheatre audience stood on these terraces a capacity of 7250 might be achieved, with 3640 if seated.

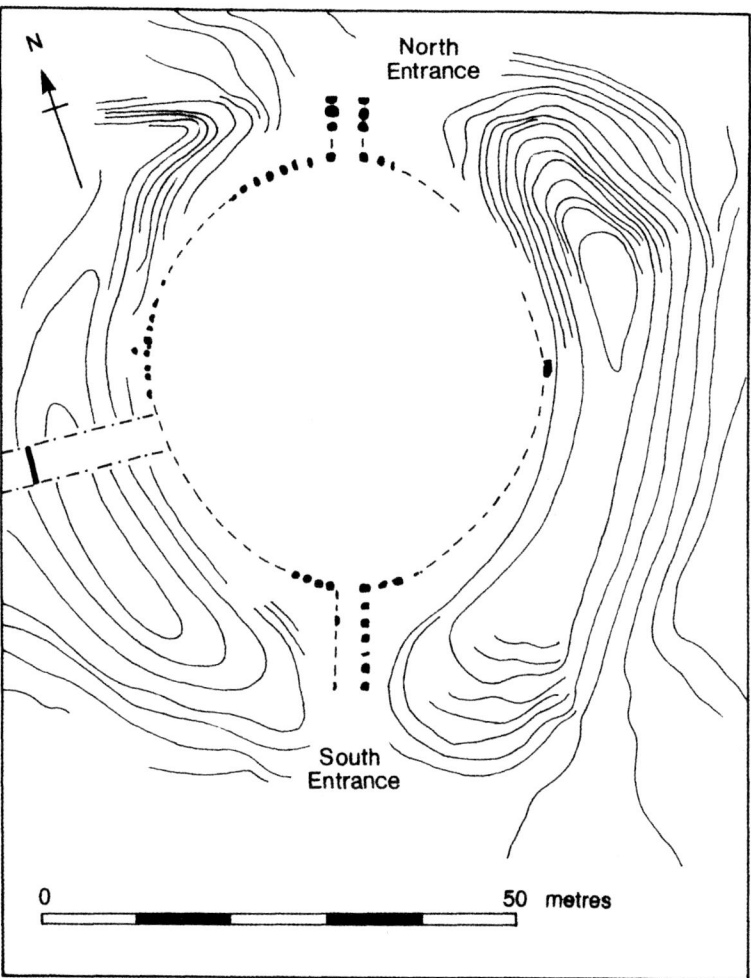

55 Plan of the first timber phase of the Silchester amphitheatre. *Chris Evans, after Fulford 1989*

Around the edge of the arena, which measured 43 x 42.2m, and was thus virtually circular, were a series of timber posts set in individual post-pits. Within these pits the shadows of squared posts measuring some 240-260mm square were found. The posts were spaced 1.25-1.3m apart and were sunk 850mm-1m into the ground. It is thought that the timbers were clad with timber shuttering which acted to retain the cut and the banks above, and formed an upright arena wall. It is unlikely that these upright timbers would be sufficient in themselves to support the weight of the banks, and there is evidence that horizontal beams, embedded in the bank material, were also provided to support and reinforce the uprights.

Entrances were provided at the north and south sides of the arena (27). The entrance passages were flanked with squared timbers set in post-pits, though these were larger, at 320-340mm square, than those surrounding the arena. The south entrance passage was 10.35m in length, as the width of the *cavea* banks was reduced at the entrances. It was lined with seven pairs of posts, including one at the outer face of the bank and one pair on the line of the arena wall. This pair seems to have supported a timber gate into the arena and a slot in the ground between these uprights originally held a timber threshold. As the entrance ramp sloped downwards from outside, this gate would necessarily have opened into the arena. The gate and entrance passage were 3.3m in width and would have been lined with timber shuttering supported by the posts, and it has been considered possible that the paired posts were of sufficient strength to carry the terracing over the entrance passages. The north entrance appears to have been a mirror image of the south, except for the fact that a drain ran down its centre. On the east and west sides of the arena there was some evidence that small timber-lined recesses were provided, as forerunners to those provided in the later stone phase.

There was no sign of any provision for access to the *cavea* from the entrances. There was, however, evidence for at least one built-up bank constructed in turf, gravel and soil, against the rear of the turf revetment to the *cavea*. In the published reconstruction, six ramps or stairs engaged against the face of the rear wall were reconstructed on the basis of this evidence (*39*).[14]

The somewhat limited archaeological dating evidence suggests that Phase 1 was built c.AD 55-75. This lasted up to a century, with the refurbishment and remodelling of Phase 2 occurring in the mid-second century. This archaeological dating was consistent with the working life of the Phase 1 oak posts, as scientifically determined during the post-excavation process. It was found that posts of the scantling used in Phase 1 would have an expected life of some 120 years.[15] This suggests that Phase 2 was built as a response to the decay of Phase 1.

Phase 2, also of timber construction, featured a complete remodelling of the arena, creating an oval rather than a circle (p. 65), by the simple expedient of laying out arcs from two centres on the east-west axis, to bring in the sides of the *cavea*, narrowing the arena and making this the short axis (*56*). The arena now measured 44.4 x 37.5m. The northern and southern ends of the arena were lengthened, encroaching on the Phase 1 entrances, with a new retaining wall outside the line of the primary timber posts. The east and west sides were narrowed to form a short axis, with the new wall lying within the primary posts. The arena wall was different from that of the first phase, consisting of smaller timbers measuring in the order of 200mm square, this time set into a continuous post-trench. No evidence survived for the relationship of the arena wall with the *cavea*, as this was cut away by the insertion of the stone arena walls of the following phase. The south entrance was remodelled, as the Phase 1 posts were replaced. The north entrance, however, was drastically narrowed, from around 3.6m to 700mm. It is possible that a small chamber was built to one side of

THE SITES: THE SOUTH AND EAST

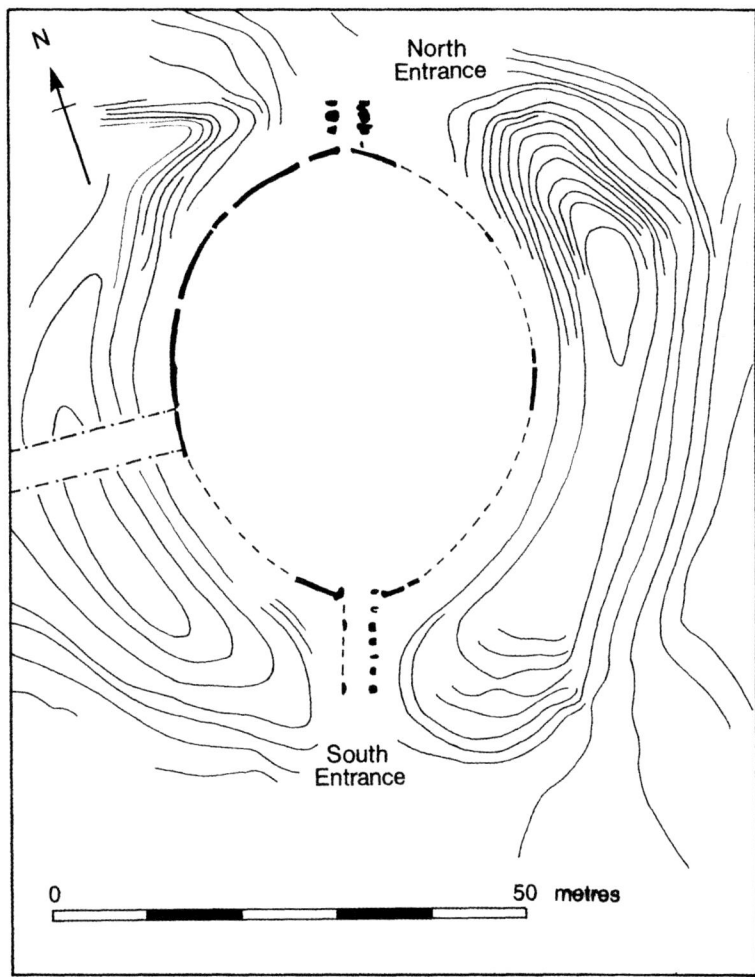

56 Plan of the second timber phase of the Silchester amphitheatre. *Chris Evans, after Fulford 1989*

the entrance passage. This may have been a *carcer*, open to the passage and the arena, though the evidence for this was sparse. It is unlikely that the terracing continued over the entrance passages in this phase, and the *cavea* would thus have comprised a pair of unconnected, half-moon-shaped, auditoria.

Phase 3 was the fully developed, stone-built amphitheatre (*57, colour plate 10*). Archaeological dating indicates a date in the mid-third century, *c.*AD 250. The arena shape was adjusted again, this time becoming closer to oval, at 45.5 x 39.2m. The arena was now surrounded by a stone wall, constructed using the variety of naturally available local stone, including flint, greensand and brown ironstone, which created a distinctive string-course. This string-coursing did not occur in the entrances and the recesses on each side of the arena, and was probably intended to be decorative. The arena wall is calculated to have been

THE ROMAN AMPHITHEATRE IN BRITAIN

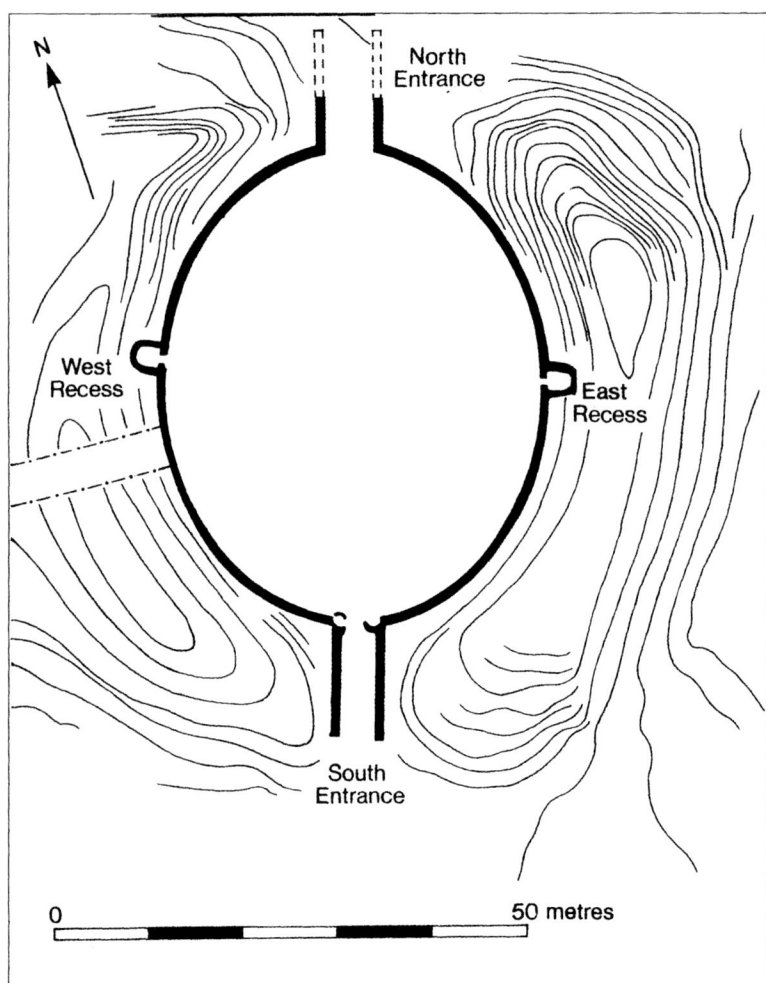

57 Plan of the stone phase of the Silchester amphitheatre. *Chris Evans, after Fulford 1989*

2.75m high, possibly with another metre added if it was provided with a parapet or railing. A half-round coping stone found nearby may have come from such a parapet. At the foot of the arena wall were a series of small triangular drains or weep-holes. There was no sign of any painted plaster or other decoration beyond the string-course. At either end of the short axis (actually slightly offset, though this would not have been apparent to the eye) was a pair of stone-lined recesses. These measured 2.1m wide and 2.6m deep with entrances 1m wide. In the eastern recess a worn greensand plinth was found, which has been interpreted as a possible altar base.[16] The curve of the back of this recess, which stands 2.2m high, suggests that these were roofed with semi-vaults (*30*). These may have served as shrines, or possibly as *carceres*. Around the arena shallow gullies and soak-aways acted as drainage.

THE SITES: THE SOUTH AND EAST

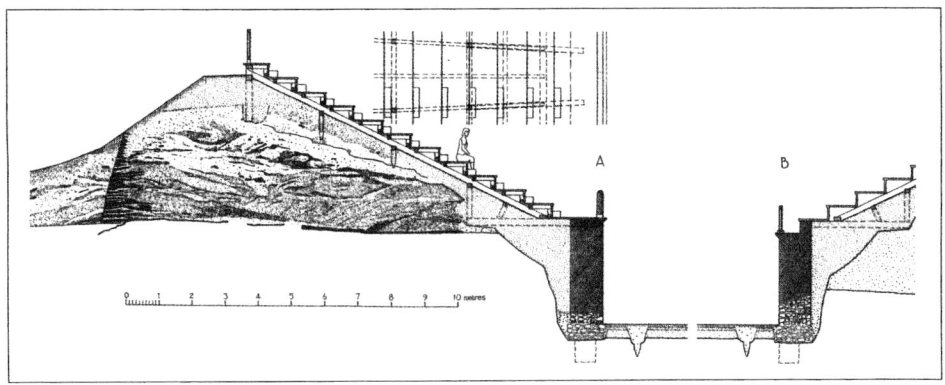

58 Section through the banks of the Silchester amphitheatre in the stone phase. Society for the Promotion of Roman Studies and Prof. Michael Fulford

The south entrance was 12m long and 3.8m wide between stone-built passage walls. Two large timber gate-posts were provided at the arena end of the passage. The north entrance was similar and was provided with an outlet drain in the floor. There was no architectural evidence to suggest that the entrance passages were vaulted to allow the terracing to be carried over them. Indeed the reconstruction by Nigel Sunter suggests that this was not the case (*34*). The *cavea* was heightened with more dumped material, probably partly deriving from the excavation of the foundation trenches for the stone walls. There is some evidence that the terraces were replaced with timber seating.[17] If so there would have been only 10-12 rows allowing an audience capacity of some 3000 (*58*). Access to the *cavea* appears to have been by means of worn desire-tracks over the back of the earthwork bank.

In later refurbishments the level of the arena floor was deliberately raised by the use of dumps of sand, clay and gravel. A ring drain was cut through this material. It seems likely that this was a response to the poorly drained nature of the arena, which was a pond in Stukeley's day and even following consolidation and drainage works in the 1990s is still often very wet. Dating evidence suggests the use, at least intermittently, of the amphitheatre up to the mid-fourth century.

Dorchester (Durnovaria)

The site of the Dorchester amphitheatre, known as Maumbury Rings, lies 500m to the south-west of Dorchester, alongside the Roman road leading to the south coast. It may have been the site mentioned by John Aubrey (p. 22), but was at any rate known to antiquarians from as early as the seventeenth century, having been

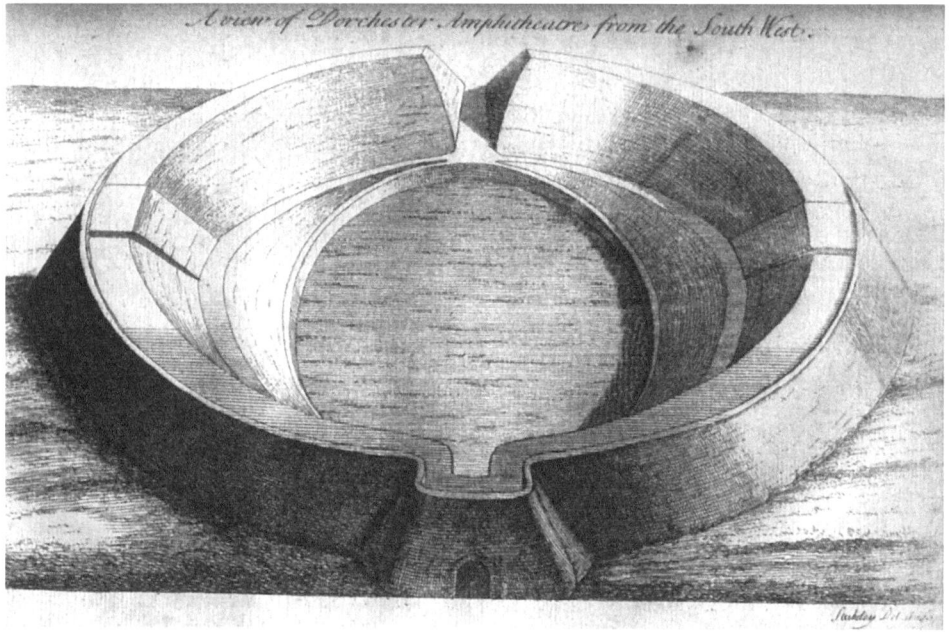

59 William Stukeley's reconstruction drawing of the Dorchester amphitheatre. *Stukeley 1732*

called to attention by no less an authority than Sir Christopher Wren,[18] and, as already mentioned, was described with great detail and enthusiasm by William Stukeley[19] (p. 22; *59, colour plate 11*). It was used as a site of public execution until 1760, recording numbers of spectators up to 10,000 for the execution of Mary Channing in 1706. During the present Queen's visit to Dorchester in 1952 it remained the only location in the vicinity capable of holding a large concourse of people from all over the county.[20]

During the nineteenth century the views on the identity of the monument divided into two schools of thought, one being that it was the town amphitheatre for *Durnovaria*, the other that it was a ritual site of the pre-Roman period. Both conjectures proved to be correct.[21] Trenching on the visible north entrance to the site in 1879[22] was followed by a major campaign of excavations on the site between 1908 and 1913. Funds were raised by public subscription, and an excavation committee was formed representing the British Archaeological Association and the Dorchester Field Club. The work was undertaken by H. St George Gray, however Gray was not able to publish the work, and a final report awaited the work of Richard Bradley, published in 1975.[23]

Perhaps the most important fact concerning Maumbury Rings is that the amphitheatre deliberately utilised a Neolithic henge monument,[24] remodelling and altering it to a significant degree. The importance of this is to show that such reuse did take place and to suggest that the idea of the conversion of similar prehistoric monuments elsewhere, to provide the venues for spectacles, is not necessarily far-fetched. The bank of the henge was raised around a virtually circular area. The material from which the bank was built probably came from an encircling ditch, which was dug inside the bank, and in the bottom of which deeper individual shafts were cut. The ditch was largely removed when the Roman arena was excavated to a lower level than its base, but the shafts defined a central, circular area some 52m in diameter.[25]

The Roman remodelling of the henge was undertaken on a grand scale (*60*). The arena shape was laid out using a layout based upon three intersecting circles of a diameter of 24.4m (p. 64). The circular central area of the henge, which had been level with the ground outside except for the encircling ditch, was hollowed out into the solid chalk to a depth of 3m to provide the typical sunken arena and (according to Bradley's estimate) 6494m^3 of chalk rubble deployed in the new seating banks, burying the Neolithic banks completely. The arena was oval in shape, with axes of 58.2m and 48.6m. It therefore removed large parts of the Neolithic ditch, and also would have required the removal of some of the prehistoric mounds. The Neolithic single, northern, entrance to the henge was replaced by a ramp, 27m in length, which sloped down from exterior ground level to that of the arena. Where there were soft spots in the arena floor, over the Neolithic features, the floor was consolidated with rammed chalk, and the entire floor was then covered with sand. It appears that in the first phase three recesses were then cut in the chalk wall of the arena; one opposite the main entrance on the south end of the long axis, the other two in the centres of the east and west sides. The main northern entrance was a sheer-sided, flat-bottomed trench cut into solid chalk. The base sloped at about 1:21, but levelled out before the arena was reached. The ramp, which was about 7m in width, ran northwards beyond the limit of the bank, probably to maintain a shallow slope. There was no sign that the sides of the passage were shuttered or protected in any way, despite the fact that the exposed chalk face would have been subject to degradation. This may imply that the passage was covered, though no provision for this was noticed, apart from timber structures at the arena end of the passage. This consisted of five (probably originally six, paired across the entrance) post-pits each almost a metre in depth, which had held timber uprights 300mm square. The pair of pits nearest the arena flanked a shallow slot. It seems likely that the inner posts retained a gate, possibly a double gate, 4.3m wide and opening inwards, with the slot between the posts retaining a tie beam, which may also have provided a stop for the gate(s) to close against. The other posts would have taken at least a bridge across the entrance passage, though they may also have been part of a structure provided to carry seating over the passage. The limited extent of the

THE ROMAN AMPHITHEATRE IN BRITAIN

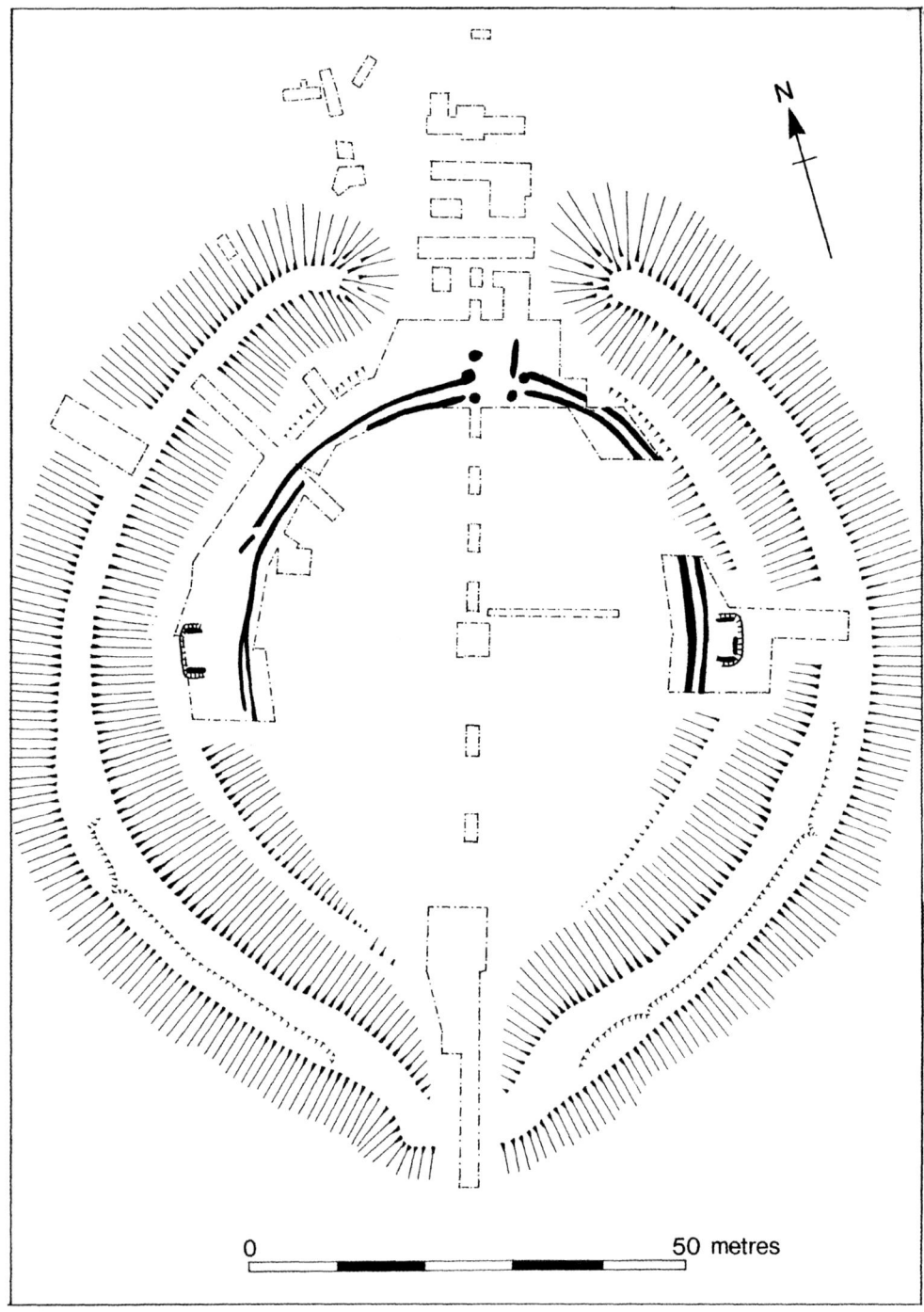

60 Plan of the Dorchester amphitheatre showing excavation area. *Chris Evans, after Bradley 1975*

excavation, and the fact of the disturbance of the entrance when the monument was modified during the English Civil War, make it possible that other supports for such a structure were missed. There was no sign of any outer wall around the rear of the earthen *cavea*, either in stone or in timber.

Around the arena was a pair of parallel trenches within which were timber posts (*14*). At the entrance these trenches ended at the outer and middle pairs of large posts respectively. Apart from at the main entrance, these ran around the entire arena. There were variations in the way in which timbers were placed in the trenches, but uprights were normally at a distance of 910mm apart and were between 180 and 300mm square, mostly at the larger end of the range. To the west of the entrance the outer timbers were reinforced with more posts. In this area there was evidence for beams that ran back into the seating bank. These beams were substantial, measuring 300mm square and 2.1m long. It was suggested that these could have tied the timber cladding of the arena wall back into the bank,[26] or that they supported a structure at a higher level. It is equally possible that these beams tied back into the bank a structure formed by the timbers in both parallel post-trenches. It is likely that this was a timber-built service corridor, paralleling those seen in so many continental amphitheatres. If so, this corridor would have only been some 910mm wide – probably the minimum width at which such a feature might function. The way in which this passage might have functioned with the recesses is unclear, but at the entrance it could certainly have been accessed to right or left without going through the gate leading into the arena. The southern recess, which contained stone and tile rubble, is a problem in interpretation. The recesses have been interpreted as preparation or changing rooms in order to explain their relationship with the service corridor. Post-holes and timber-slots within the eastern and western recesses may well have supported structures within the *cavea*, and it is possible that these were tribunals in which important individuals could be seated at events.

Subsequent developments are difficult to appreciate in detail, and those features that can be shown to be secondary cannot be seen as part of a single later design, possibly because there never was such a design, and the amphitheatre was simply maintained through a considerable period, or possibly because the extent and quality of the excavation was insufficient to recover such a scheme. The main secondary feature was the southern entrance. This mirrored the north entrance, but was cut through and across the filling of the southern recess. No structural elements were recorded.

Dating evidence recovered from excavation suggests a date of construction in the early Flavian period. It was suggested that three inhumation burials, and a cemetery around the amphitheatre might indicate abandonment around the reign of Hadrian,[27] however there is no evidence that these burials were later than the construction of the amphitheatre. There may have been a period of desertion or disuse, resulting in a build-up of soil deposits within the north entrance. This was followed by the building of a new timber gate, possibly between AD 250 and 350.[28] There is no evidence to suggest necessarily that the amphitheatre had changed function and that this gate was installed to serve some other purpose than access to a functioning arena.

Chichester (Noviomagus Regensium)

In 1934, a Mr Carlyon-Britton began an examination of the outskirts of Chichester, in the belief that a Roman town of the size and importance of Chichester would have been supplied with an amphitheatre. In 1935 a potential location was shown to Miss G. White, who commenced excavation. The site lies outside the line of the city walls to the south-east, 230m from the point at which Stane Street leaves the City through the east gate, to run along the north bank of the River Lavant. The amphitheatre lies to the south of the river, which separates it from the main road and the city itself. Access to the amphitheatre was thus probably across a bridge on a side road branching off Stane Street.

The amphitheatre (*61*) now appears as a slight earthwork 1.7m high. The circuit of the seating banks is complete except where destroyed by housing development on the south-west side. The north–south axis is some 70m from crest to crest, the east–west axis being 58m. The bank is very spread, especially on the northern side, and there are signs that the site was ploughed in medieval times. Some bank material seems to have been obtained from two quarries on the north-west and south-east sides, as well as from the arena. On the south and east sides are traces of ramps leading up to the crest, which may be modern in origin as a field gate stood here in the past.

The method adopted to establish whether the site was an amphitheatre was to cut four trenches across the inner side of the bank to establish whether there was an arena wall. A further two trenches were cut in the arena itself and two more in the bank. The following account is a summary of the published excavation report.[29]

The arena was an oval area measuring 56.3 x 45.72m. It was hollowed out to a depth of 1.2m in order to lower its level and to provide material for the encircling banks. The excavated hollow and seating banks were retained with a wall 1.2m in width built on a foundation of rammed gravel and flints. The wall was of flint and mortar construction and the evidence of material that had collapsed into the arena from the wall showed that it had originally been

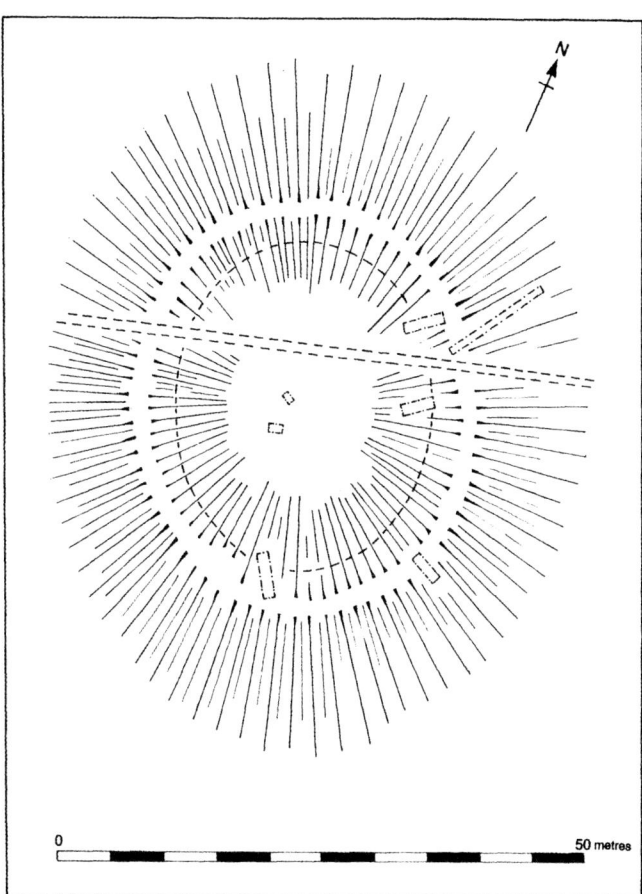

61 Plan of the Chichester amphitheatre showing excavation trenches. *Chris Evans, after White 1936*

plastered and painted in colours which included light and dark red, pink, purple, orange, yellow, green and grey. The banks consisted of layers of redeposited 'loam' and natural gravel won from the excavation of the arena. An outer stone wall was sought in vain and it appears that no such wall was provided. In a trench sited at the southern narrow end of the arena, masonry was found further back into the thickness of the seating bank than was anticipated. It is very likely that this trench encountered the remains of a stone gate passage, probably one of two sited at the narrow ends of the oval. After the arena wall was robbed, the banks slumped into the arena. The slumped gravel contained a large number of iron nails, hinting that timber seating had been provided on the banks. This presents an interesting parallel to Carmarthen, where a large number of nails formed part of the evidence for timber terracing, rather than seating. The arena floor appears to have been created using a 75mm deep layer of rammed gravel over the natural marl and gravel substrate.

The arena floor was laid over a small pit, which contained burnt material, bone and first- to second-century pottery. This indicates that there was earlier Roman activity prior to the building of the amphitheatre (there was also evidence for early Iron Age occupation on the site). The excavator suggested that the amphitheatre was built *c*.AD 70-90, though the material from the Roman pit and the fact that first- to second-century pottery was also found within the seating bank material suggests a rather broader date, possibly sometime in the late-Flavian or Trajanic period. Pottery on the arena floor included, at the latest, third-century material, implying that the amphitheatre was abandoned during this century.[30] At the foot of the bank, on the north-east side, was a complete late third- to fourth-century colour-coated beaker, empty and covered with a fragment of roof tile, which may have been part of a stray burial. The available evidence is sparse, however, and it would be unwise to draw any firm conclusion on the longevity of the amphitheatre without further work.

Cirencester (Corinium Dobunnorum)

The Cirencester amphitheatre (*colour plate 12*) lies some 160m south-west of the line of the defences of the Roman town. It survives as a pair of prominent grass-covered banks 32-40m in width and around 8m high, flanking an elliptical or oval arena, with the two entrances at the narrow ends of the ellipse (north-east and south-west) clearly visible. The structure is locally known as the Bull Ring, possibly because it was used during the seventeenth century for bull baiting.[31]

It was first identified as an amphitheatre by the local historian Samuel Rudder who described it as:

> an elliptical form ... Round it is a mound or wall of earth, thrown up to the height of about twenty feet, sloped up on the inside with so much exactness as to manifest the hand of care and design: and I am of the opinion, that there were originally rows of seats or steps, one below the other, from top to bottom, but time has much defaced them. There are two avenues to this area (east and west), and on the north side also is another straight approach, between two stone walls lately discovered by people digging for stone.[32]

In 1800 he stated that:

> This is so exactly coincident with the amphitheatre of the ancients, that if it be not a Roman work (and the materials of which it is composed furnish no reasonable doubt against such conjecture), it was evidently intended for public spectacles.[33]

Rudder's ideas were followed by later writers.

In 1824, the first excavations took place, when the Rev. John Skinner of Camerton, a prolific antiquary and diarist, undertook a small excavation, helped by 'one of the stable boys, with a spade'.[34] Skinner was searching for the stone seats which had been postulated by Rudder, but found none, concluding that the amphitheatre was not Roman, but a native British structure used for religious gatherings under a Roman aegis. Other unrecorded excavations were recalled during the British Archaeological Association visit to Cirencester in 1869.[35] At some time earlier, Buckman had excavated a section, found pottery and some coins, and concluded that the earthwork was indeed an amphitheatre. A section through the banks cut in 1868 by T.C. Brown again found no traces of stone seating,[36] but this did not change his view of the function of the earthwork. He suggested that the seating must have been of timber. As we have seen (p. 29) the visit caused some debate as to whether the Bull Ring was or was not an amphitheatre.

No organised excavations took place until 1962, when John Wacher began work, which was continued by Alan McWhirr in 1966. The excavation report was published by Neil Holbrook in 1998.[37] A series of trenches were excavated in the main north-east entrance, amounting to a virtually complete excavation of the area. A long trench sectioned the southern bank, and an additional small trench was also cut in this bank. A large square trench was opened in the arena and four small trenches were cut across the arena wall.

The Phase 1 amphitheatre (*62*) was built in a disused quarry and the south-eastern part of the *cavea* was constructed against the quarry face. The banks, some 30m in width, were built using quarry waste, and the arena was surfaced and levelled with the same material. There was clear evidence that the banks were constructed as a series of terraces created by pressing flat stones into the bank make-up (*40*). The long trench across the bank demonstrated that it was terraced, with the mound material retained by drystone walls set into the surface of the bank. The line of this trench is currently plainly visible on site, where its in-filling has subsided or washed-out, and the terraces can be made out clearly under the thin turf cover within the trench edges. Sixteen such terraces, up to 900mm wide, were identified. Holbrook was of the opinion that these terraces would have supported timber-framed seating and that there was sufficient space for some 28 rows of seats. The terrace length adjacent to the arena was 72m, and the upper, outer terrace was 120m long. Given a seat width of 600mm, a seating capacity of 8000 was estimated. It fact it is difficult to see how a timber structure might be built on top of these terraces without the support which could be given by principal, ground-fast, supporting members, and it is more likely that we should see these as accommodating standing spectators, as deduced at Silchester and at Carmarthen. The rake of the terracing varies, from 25 degrees

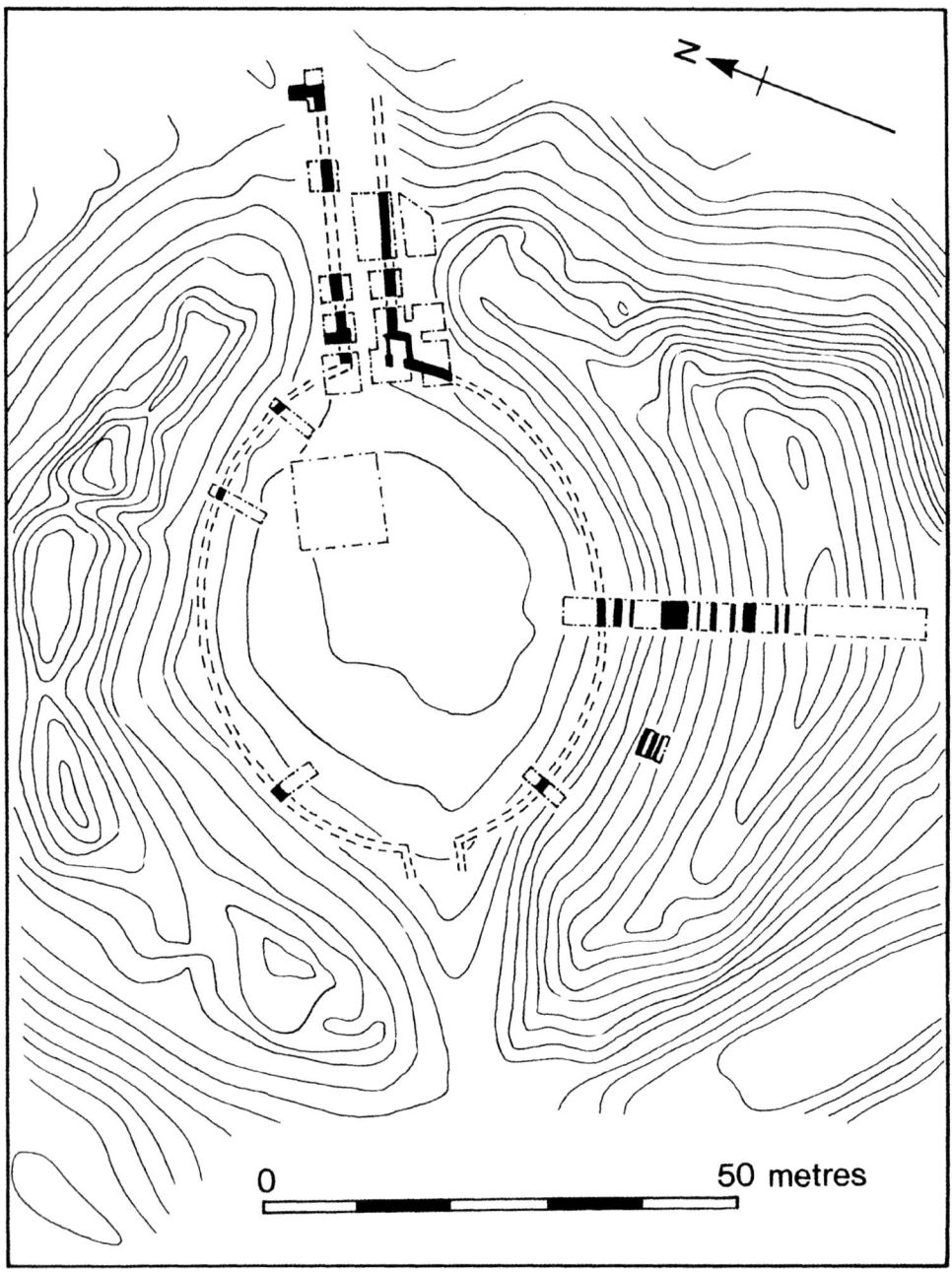

62 Plan of the Cirencester amphitheatre showing location of excavation trenches. Chris Evans, after Holbrook 1998

for the front seven terraces to 20 degrees for the rest; this is perfectly consistent with a standing crowd, standing two-deep upon the broader terraces. Holbrook

THE SITES: THE SOUTH AND EAST

made the suggestion that the rear terraces at least might have been for standing spectators, in which case more could be accommodated.[38] The upper terraces may have been carried over the entrances on some form of vaulting or timber framework, though any structural evidence for this has disappeared. Excavation has not been sufficiently extensive to determine the location of gangways, steps or entrances.

Despite the fact that the long trench was extended over 10m beyond the outer limit of the mound, no outer wall was found. It was suggested that such a wall may have been removed, and that the bank might have slumped across foundations or a stone-robbing trench,[39] though it is consistent with the form of most other British amphitheatres to assume that no such wall existed. The entrances and arena were much altered in later phases, however it seems that the north-east entrance for the first phase comprised a passage some 6.7m wide, revetted on each side by a simple drystone wall which retained the bulk of the seating bank. These walls were faced only on the passage side, and survived up to 17 courses high in places. The original arena wall was represented by a cobble foundation, though it was later entirely rebuilt. It could have been built of timber or of stone, but the evidence of quantities of white- and green-painted plaster in deposits within the arena suggests that the wall was plastered and painted. The dating evidence for the first phase of the amphitheatre is a coin of AD 104-7, within the reign of the Emperor Trajan, which gives a date after which the amphitheatre was built. The building probably lasted 50 years or less before it was rebuilt around the middle of the second century.

In Phase 2 the amphitheatre was completely rebuilt. The arena measured approximately 49 x 41m and the arena wall was rebuilt in masonry. It survived to a height of 1.37m, and it has been suggested that it could not have been higher than 1.8m above the latest arena surface on the basis of the relationship with the terracing. This seems worryingly low and may have been wrongly interpreted, though there may have been coping stones on the arena wall-top with railings set into them, as at London, Chester, Caerleon and possibly Silchester. The surface of the wall was plastered and painted in red with imitation marbling in black, yellow and white. There were traces of a quarter-round moulding at the foot of the wall and it is clear from fallen plaster debris that the arena wall was replastered and repainted many times.

The new north-west entrance passage was 4.45m wide, and six large stone imposts (three pairs of two) (35) now supported a barrel vault, which itself supported seating carried over the entrance passage. At the point where the passage met the arena was a gate. On each side of the gate was a stone gate-jamb. That on the north-west side of the entrance had a circular pivot hole-cut into the sill and a series of small slots which received drop-bolts when the gate was closed. This suggests that the gate was single. At the arena end of the passage, adjacent to the north-west gate-jamb, a lateral flight of stone steps, 2.8m wide (of which three survived), allowed spectators to access the front seats of the *cavea* from the passage. There was evidence for a similar set of steps on the opposite side of the entrance. An inward opening arena gate would have blocked these stairs, and it is therefore assumed that the gate opened outwards.

If the Phase 2 entrance passage ended at the third pair of imposts, then the outer 10.5m of the passage walls would simply have retained the seating bank on either side and would have been open to the sky. There is good archaeological evidence, however, that a fourth pair of imposts existed at the far outer corners of the passage.[40] If so, these would have supported a vaulted passage the full thickness of the banks, with imposts positioned every 9.3m.

Phase 3 of the amphitheatre saw the complete rebuild of the side walls of the entrance passage, perhaps following collapse due to pressure from the piled bank material. This suggestion is problematic, however, as the strength of a barrel vault should have counteracted such pressure. Whatever the reason for the rebuild, which appears to have taken place before the end of the second century, it incorporated a new feature: a pair of small chambers which flanked the entrance passage on the inner end. The south-eastern chamber measured 2.1 x 2.4m internally. It had a doorway into the arena (*63*) and also opened into the

63 Entrance into the *carcer* by the main entrance at the Cirencester amphitheatre. *Cotswold Archaeology*

entrance passage. The north-west chamber certainly opened into the arena, but it is unclear whether this also communicated with the passage. On the side of the doorway from the south-eastern chamber to the arena was a pivot hole for a gate, and striations on the door-sill suggest that the door comprised an iron grille. The chambers were placed in the former stairwells flanking the passage and would have been open to the sky unless roofed. It is highly likely that these chambers served as *carceres*.

Following this final rebuild, the amphitheatre seems to have remained broadly unchanged and continued in use to the late third century. The building may have fallen out of use and become dilapidated by AD 350-60, when the walls of the entrance passage were demolished and robbed of stone, which was removed for use elsewhere. When recommissioned in the mid-fourth century the amphitheatre was certainly not used for its original purpose (p. 185).

Carmarthen (Moridunum Demetarum)

The first published mention of Carmarthen's amphitheatre was by the Borough Surveyor, G.L. Ovens, in 1951,[41] evidence for it having been found during the development of a housing estate in 1947. Ovens' perspicacity ensured that the amphitheatre was not built over, apart from by encroaching gardens.[42] He recorded that the shape of the amphitheatre could be traced in the area north of Priory Street, and estimated its size at 64 x 50m with an arena measuring 24.5 x 16.5m. Preliminary excavations in 1968 confirmed the identification of the amphitheatre, showing that it had been built by cutting into a hillside, using the hillside as the north side of the *cavea* and the excavated material for the southern bank. The arena floor lay buried beneath 2m of silt.[43]

Larger-scale excavations took place in 1970.[44] The northern half of the *cavea* was formed by the excavation of a semi-circular hollow from the hillside (*64, colour plate 13*). Spoil from this excavation was deployed in the construction of a southern semi-circular *cavea*, which had been very much eroded. The overall dimensions were 91 x 67m and the arena measured *c.*50 x 30m. The arena was dug out in order to provide soil and rock for the construction of the *cavea*. The floor of the arena was surfaced with greenish sand above the natural shale. The arena wall was later totally robbed, possibly to build the nearby medieval priory. It was 1.3m wide and built of water-worn boulders set in clay.[45] The arena wall was fronted by a shallow channel 350mm wide and 80mm deep, which, despite the fact that it was not lined, was interpreted by the excavator as a drainage channel.[46] The hillside position of the amphitheatre seems to have required sophisticated provisions for drainage at a deeper level. Beneath the road levels of the eastern entrance, a rubble soakaway drain, 1.3m wide and 300mm deep, of

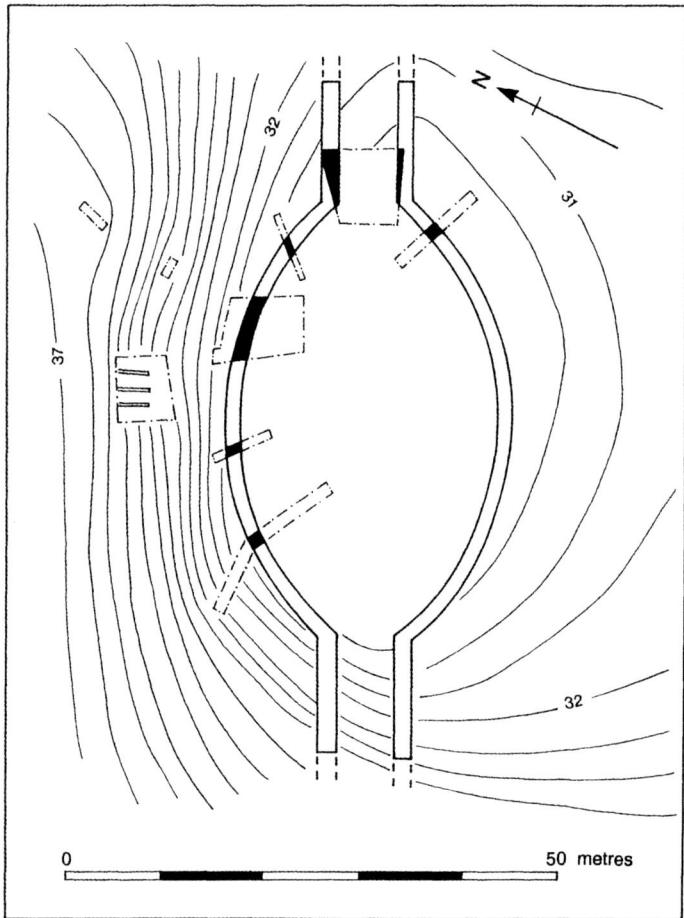

64 Plan of the Carmarthen amphitheatre. *Chris Evans, after Little 1971*

small, packed boulders, was found emerging from beneath the north *cavea* at a depth of 1.5m. It ran beneath the eastern end of the south *cavea*. A second similar feature, which terminated 1.5m beneath the arena floor 3m inside the northern arena wall, was traced up the north *cavea* a few centimetres below the level of the modern surface of the seating bank. The excavator suggested that this rubble drain was actually structural – intended to reinforce the artificially steepened slope and to divide the *cavea* into *cunei*, or wedge-shaped segments.

In the *cavea* there were traces of what appeared to be the original structure of timber-revetted terracing. Beam slots 250mm square were sunk into the natural shale running down the slope of the *cavea* at intervals of 1.3m. Across these were transverse timber members 250mm high and 50mm wide. The intervening spaces were packed with gravel and levelled to form what appear to be terraces measuring 762mm wide. Large quantities of iron nails found across the *cavea* presumably secured the timbers.

The north-east entrance showed evidence for long use, with three cobble surfaces, all containing Roman pottery, within a stone-built passage 6.1m wide. John Wacher[47] has considered that the size of the amphitheatre is the best evidence for the status of Carmarthen as the *civitas* capital of the Demetae, and that the slight evidence for construction in the first half of the second century may be a better indicator of the foundation date for the *civitas* than that provided by the street layout, which is *c*.AD 120 and follows the desertion of the fort which previously occupied the site.

A recent reconstruction of the amphitheatre[48] stresses that the northern, hillside-cut *cavea* would have potentially been considerably higher than the south-built *cavea*, which was built on flat ground. The material dug from the hillside was not augmented by spoil from a hollowed-out arena. It was suggested that the building might have been a theatre-amphitheatre, but this is not borne out because the south *cavea*, rather than a stage, does exist. The reconstruction drawing (*38*) suggests that the excavator was correct in thinking that the drain was part of a system of *cunei* in the south *cavea*, places a stage in the arena and postulates a timber-built outer wall and framed seating over the northern *cavea*. The addition of a stage with no apparent evidence, however, does not make a theatre-amphitheatre, and it is not clear how drainage from the hillside would function in the gaps between the *cunei*. However, the reconstruction is interesting and will provoke discussion of what is, after all, a very little explored and understood structure.

Caistor St Edmund (Venta Icenorum)

The Caistor amphitheatre was discovered through aerial photography in 1977 some 90m outside and to the south of the walls of the town of *Venta Icenorum*. It was first seen as a roughly circular bank approximately 14m wide and 60m in diameter.[49] Further analysis, including the examination of earlier photographs, suggested a deeply hollowed-out arena measuring approximately 38 x 32m surrounded by a bank 10m wide.[50] In the first photograph published, most of the north-east quadrant did not show and it was suggested that it may have eroded away. Subsequent close examination of the photographs showed a perimeter wall on the east side, but this was not evident on the west. From this it has been suggested either that only the arena is visible, or that the feature is a Romano-Celtic theatre, similar to that at Verulamium.[51] The only other work on the structure has been geophysical survey. In 1995, the clear outline of an amphitheatre appeared, revealing the arena at 40 x 33m, with a main entrance at the southern end[52] (*65*). Further survey of the area to the south of the defences showed early ditches clearly, but only as a faint image beneath the amphitheatre.[53]

THE ROMAN AMPHITHEATRE IN BRITAIN

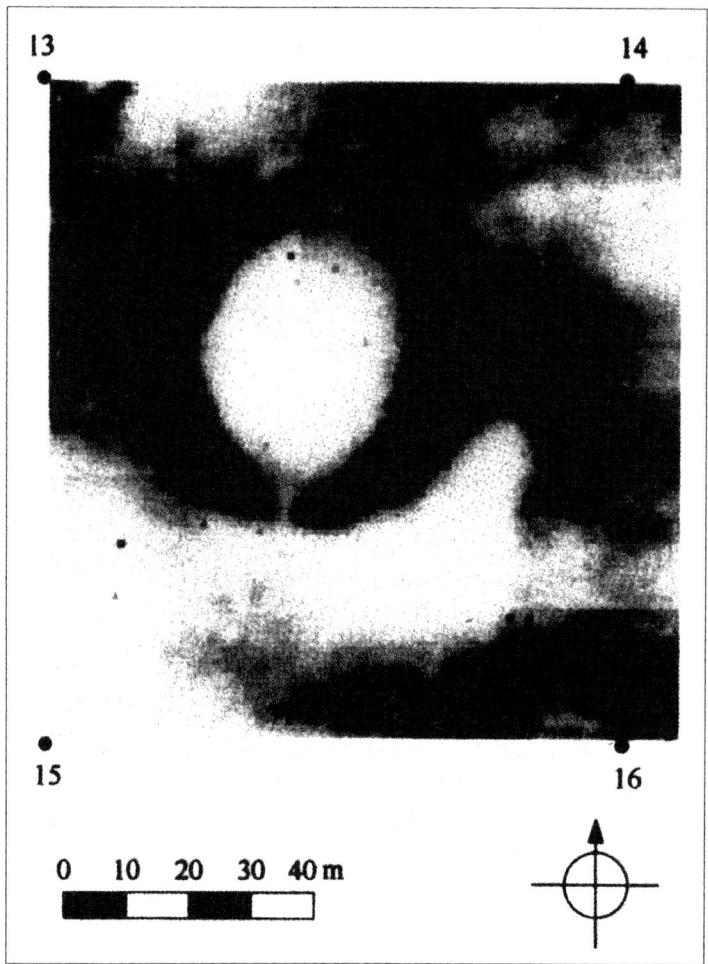

65 Geophysical survey of the amphitheatre at Caistor St Edmund. *John Wiley and Sons*

Caerwent (Venta Silurum)

The supposed amphitheatre at Caerwent (*66*) was discovered during excavations within the Roman town in the early years of the twentieth century.[54] It was a late construction, superimposed during the third century upon a north–south road and the demolished buildings that had been ranged on each side of it. The main part of the structure consisted of a simple wall, 610mm thick enclosing an approximate oval, 43.5 x 36.3m. The only entrance to the arena was on the east side and was 2.6m wide, with a pivot stone surviving on its south side. The feature that helped to confirm the identification of this as an amphitheatre was a small portion of a concentric outer wall lying 7.62m out from the arena wall. This wall appears from the published plan to have a return at its eastern end, which turns towards the

THE SITES: THE SOUTH AND EAST

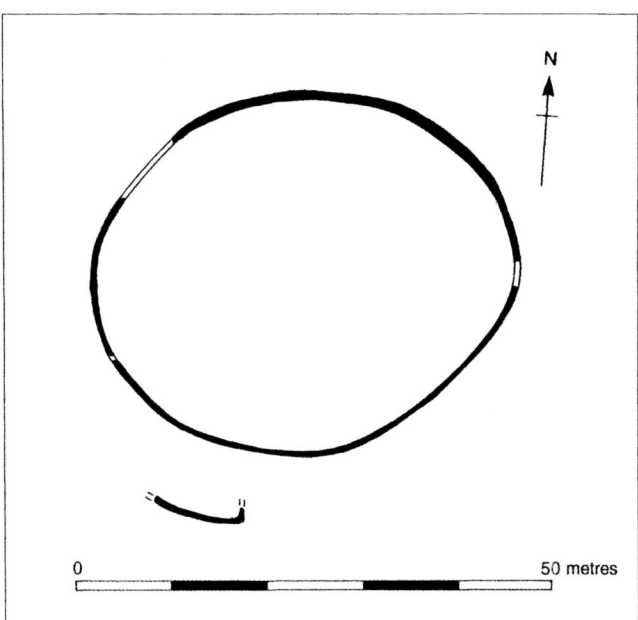

66 Plan of the Caerwent amphitheatre. *Chris Evans, after Ashby et al. 1905*

arena. It is just possible that this was the side wall of an entrance, though if so the entrance did not extend as far as the arena and must simply have served the *cavea*. The excavators interpreted the structure as possibly unfinished. The arena dimensions are close to those at Cirencester, though the form is unusual without, apparently, a hollowed-out arena. Furthermore, if this is an amphitheatre, it is the only one in Britain to have been built within the walls of a town, though this may simply have been because, unlike other urban amphitheatres, this is a late structure, which would have been built chronologically after the city walls. The interpretation of the building as an amphitheatre is not proven, and an alternative idea that it was a livestock market place has been suggested.[55]

Richborough (Rutupiae)

The amphitheatre at Richborough was first noticed by Stukeley,[56] who wrote that,

> upon an eminence is the carcas of a castrensian amphitheatre made of turf; I suppose for the exercise and diversion of the garrison

referring to the garrison of the nearby Saxon Shore fort. Stukeley illustrated the amphitheatre as he saw it (*9*) and also the location with relation to the

67 William Stukeley's engraving of the relationship between the Saxon Shore fort and the amphitheatre at Richborough *(Stukeley 1723)*

fort (*67*), where the vertical scale is greatly exaggerated. The problem of the date and context of the Richborough amphitheatre has been mentioned above (p. 55). Recent geophysical survey has revealed that Richborough was an extensive town following the Roman conquest of Britain. It always had the status of a principal entry point to the province and this was marked by the existence of a huge triumphal arch marking the gateway to Britain[57] (the foundation of this monument is the cruciform feature on Stukeley's engraving). In the late third and early fourth century, however, this monument was first fortified and then demolished for the construction of a new military fort of the Saxon Shore series, constructed to defend the coast against the threat of seaborne raiders.[58] This site was the first British amphitheatre to be examined by excavation, in 1849, and in 2001 it was the subject of a major geophysical survey (*68*).[59]

The resistivity survey of the site shows an amphitheatre with an oval arena measuring approximately 62 x 50m and a broad entrance at each end of the long axis. It is possible that there is a stone outer wall, it is also possible that the structure was of two phases. On each side of the short axes are large, almost circular anomalies some 15m in diameter. These are difficult to explain. They might be extraordinarily well-preserved vaulted entrances, or the rubble from collapsed entrances, perhaps including the tribunals. In a radar survey, these showed as more deeply founded than the *cavea* walls and were, therefore, major structures. It is very atypical that this amphitheatre is built on a hill (or at least

THE SITES: THE SOUTH AND EAST

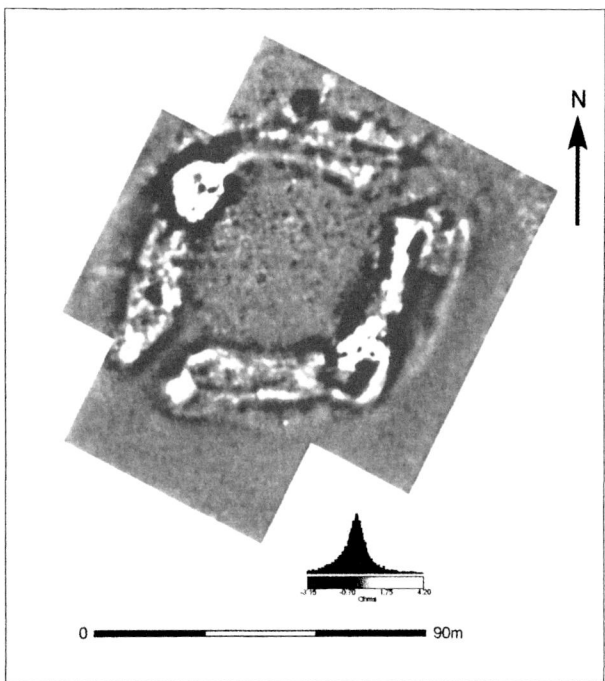

68 Geophysical survey of the amphitheatre at Richborough. *English Heritage*

the highest point in the area) and the excavators make a point of the views from this commanding position to:

> the sister fortress Regulbium [Reculver], the whole of the south side of the isle of Thanet, the ocean, and even the white cliffs of Gaul between Calais and Boulogne, together with the estuary extending several miles in the direction of Durovernum [Canterbury].

The amphitheatre does not, as would be more usual, appear to take advantage of the flank of the hill, and this suggests that it was meant to be visible from a distance. If built at the same time as the Saxon Shore fort it might have been intended to replace the great monumental arch as a visible sea-mark and aid to navigation.

The excavation results seem to have been misinterpreted with the arena wall thought to be the limit of the building. The published plan (*10*) differs greatly in dimension and orientation from the geophysical plot, however the observations are still valuable. The stone walls were 1.3m thick, composed of flint rubble faced with chalk blocks, with levelling courses of tile and stone. The excavators comment that the masonry is exactly like that in the walls of the Saxon Shore fort, suggesting that the two might have been contemporary. The arena was clearly hollowed out to a depth of around a metre and the excavated material forms the *cavea* banks. The distribution of entrances is the point where the report begins to be difficult to understand. Entrances are claimed on the west, south and north sides, in other words on one end of the long axis and both ends of the short. The geophysics clearly shows entrances on each end of the long axis, and it seems likely that whatever the two circular masses are, they at least include entrances. The three recorded entrances follow a descent down a ramp into the arena. Survival is good, with walls standing to almost 2m in places, with signs of the provision of arches. Door-stops were also recorded.[60] The early excavations and geophysics demonstrate that Richborough has a high potential for future research.

THEATRE-AMPHITHEATRES

Verulamium
The Verulamium theatre was discovered and first excavated in 1847 when a farmer notified the antiquary R. Grove-Lowe of the presence of curvilinear walls in his field. Though well conducted for its time, the excavation did not establish a chronological sequence for the building.[61] Virtually total excavation was carried out in 1933-4 by Kathleen Kenyon[62] after which the site was consolidated as a publicly accessible monument. An unusual book by Anthony Lowther[63] attempted to interpret the theatre through imaginary vignettes of episodes in its history.

The first phase of the building more closely resembles an amphitheatre than a theatre (*69, 70, 71*), whereas later phases emphasise the theatre plan. To reflect this I will use amphitheatre terminology for the first phase and theatre terminology for the second. The structure was built no later than *c*.AD 140 on a site within the city walls close to the *forum*, which may have been reserved since the foundation of the city *c*.AD 50 for a public building.[64] It lay in the same *insula* (Insula XVI) as a Romano-Celtic temple placed within a rectangular *temenos* which was enclosed with a stone wall. It is highly likely that the theatre formed part of a religious complex and functioned in association with the temple. Mortar pads found to the north-east of the rear of the stage, along the Watling Street frontage, may have formed an arcaded screen separating the theatre precinct from the street.[65]

The first phase structure was very simple (*69*). The arena was circular, 24.34m in diameter, and like most amphitheatres was hollowed into the existing ground surface, the gravel excavated from the arena being deployed around it as the basis of the *cavea*. As at Chester (p. 137), the earliest element of the structure was a free-standing, stone-built outer wall. This wall was 1.14m wide at the foundations, narrowing to 910mm above a brick-capped offset course, which was at ground level on the west side, but well above this level on the downhill, eastern side. Once this wall was raised, the arena was excavated and the gravel

THE SITES: THE SOUTH AND EAST

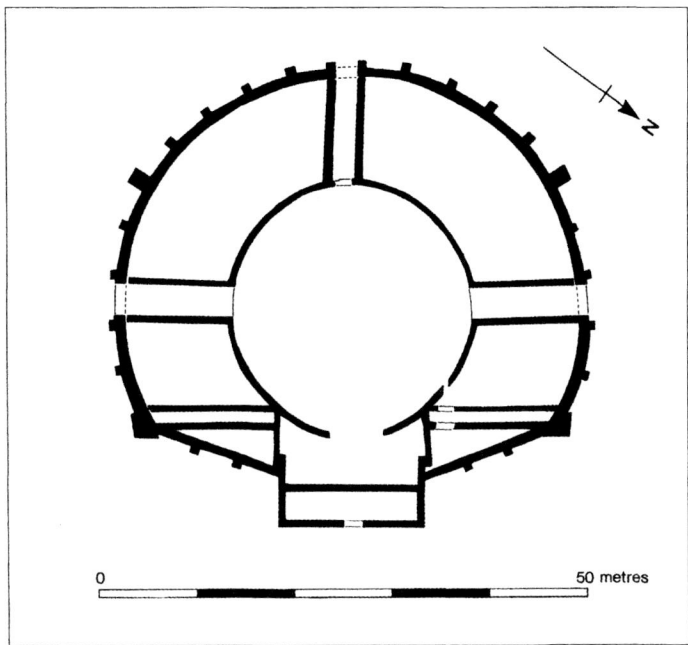

69 Plan of the first phase of the Verulamium theatre. *Chris Evans, after Kenyon 1935*

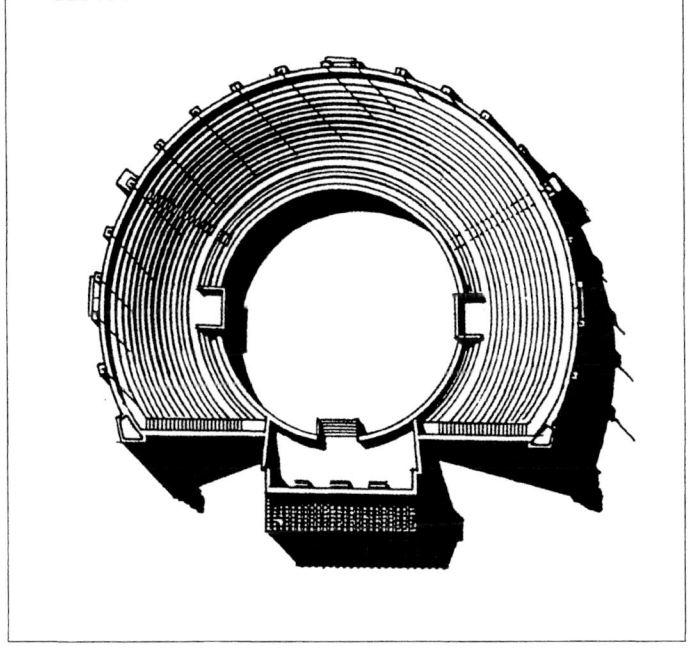

70 Verulamium. The theatre in the first phase as reconstructed by Anthony Lowther

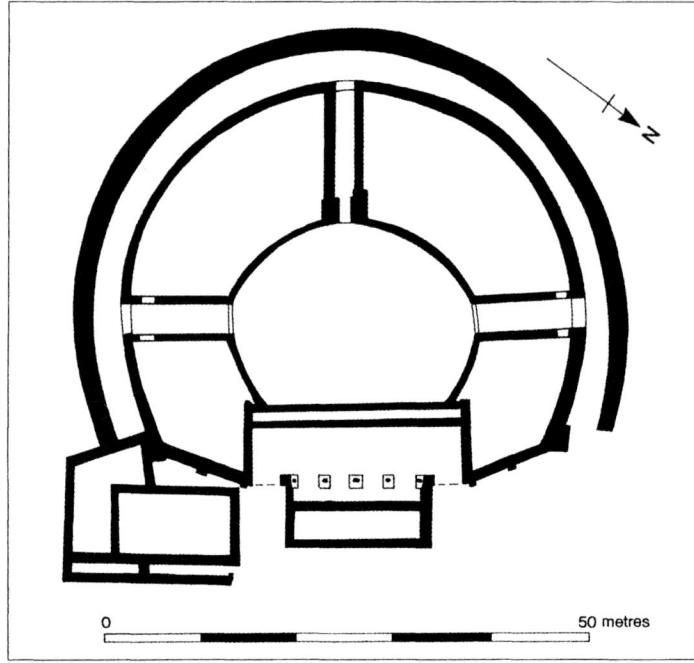

71 Plan of the fourth-century phase of the Verulamium theatre. *Chris Evans, after Kenyon 1935*

from the excavation was piled against it. The excavated arena and piled spoil was then retained with an arena wall, which stood at least 1.22m high.

The outer wall was supported with shallow buttresses 910mm wide, set at regular 4m intervals. On the two western quadrants of the building, symmetrically placed, were two larger buttresses, 1.75m wide, projecting 1.67m from the face of the wall. These are interpreted as the supports for wooden external stairways, which were the only means by which the seating could be reached. Three entrances led into the arena, on the west, north, and south sides. The east side was occupied by the stage. The three entrances gave level access into the arena. The north and south entrances were wider (2.91m) than that to the west (2.28m). In the south entrance the side walls near the arena survived to a height of 1.98m, but no springer for a vault was visible. This might indicate that the inner portion of the entrance passage was open, while the outer part was vaulted, however it seems more likely that the whole passage was vaulted with seating carried over it, as in the reconstruction by Lowther (*70*). The eastern ends of the outer wall, where the circuit was interrupted for the stage, were terminated with piers. These helped support end walls to the *cavea*, which converged on the stage. The stage structure was very simple. The curve of the arena wall was carried round the front of the stage, probably interrupted by a flight of steps linking it with the arena. The stage was 14.78m wide at the front, and behind it was a small rectangular room. Post-holes suggest that the stage was floored in wood.

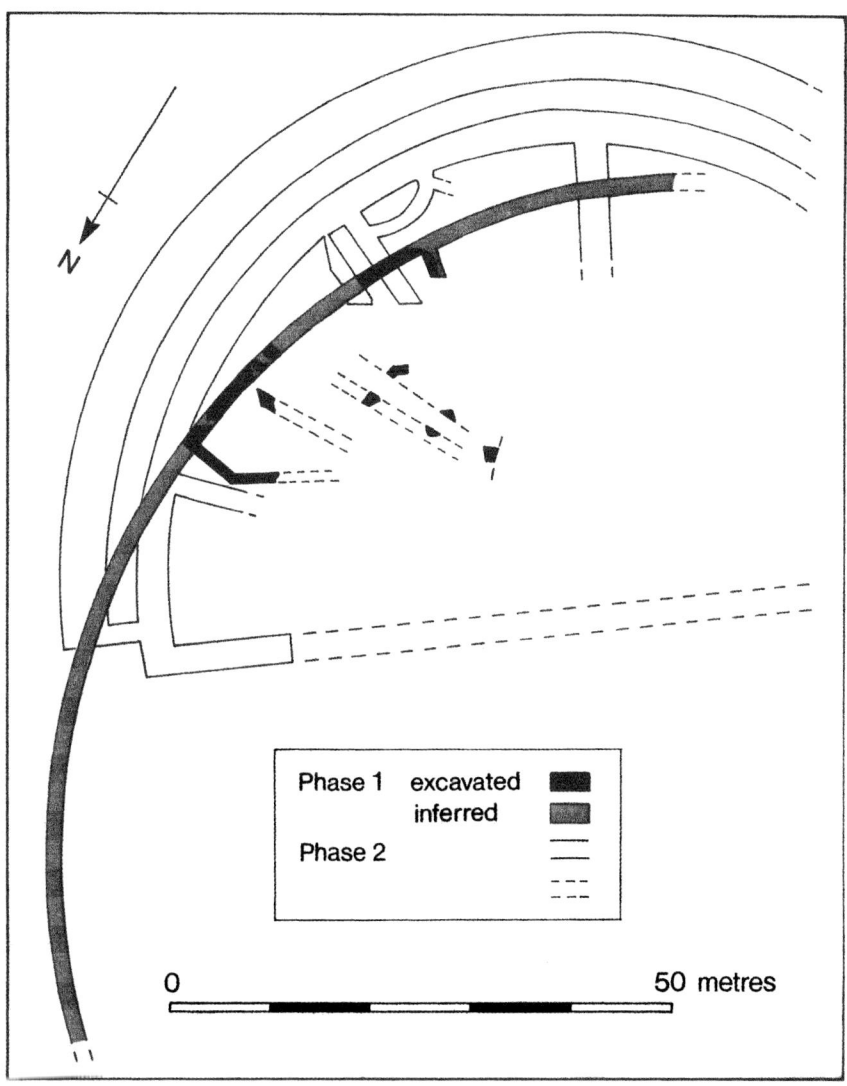

72 Plan of Canterbury theatre showing later classical-type theatre in outline, and the curve of the wall of the primary theatre-amphitheatre. *Chris Evans, after Frere 1970*

The layout of the theatre was such that the concentration of spectators would have been on the arena, not the stage. Those seated in the north-eastern half of the building would have had either no view, or at best an impeded view of the stage. The focus of attention on the arena is confirmed by traces of arena furnishing. This takes the form of a cross-shaped slot with arms 4.05m long and 457mm wide. In the centre was a deeper section. This seems to be provision for a cruciform timber base-plate with a central upright. There was evidence that the base-plate was pegged down. The excavator suggested that this could have been 'a maypole, a gibbet, or post to which baited beasts could be chained'.[66] Though the arena was small, it may be compared in size to the amphitheatres of auxiliary forts, such as Tomen-y-Mur, and may have been used for the animal baiting, small wild beast hunts and wrestling which were vividly imagined by Anthony Lowther.[67]

During Period 2, beginning c.AD 150-60, the emphasis was placed upon the stage and the arena ceased to exist. The western half of the former arena, behind the lateral entrances, was covered with timber-framed seating, while the stage was thrust forward by constructing a wall between the ends of its side walls, which was a chord of the former arena. The space between the front of the wooden seating and the stage now became an orchestra in the true sense of a classical theatre and was floored with a new mortar surface. In addition, 1.60m inside the back wall of the stage, three piers, 1.45m square, were built, flanked by two pilasters. These supported columns, probably 5.79m high, surmounted by Corinthian capitals, one of which was recovered in the excavation (*colour plate 14*). This was a version of the classic architectural backdrop or *scaenae frons*. The stage was still of wood and beneath it lay a drainage soakaway pit. The access pattern was changed in the lateral entrances. The side walls of the passage were breached immediately inside the entrances and lateral stairs were made leading up to the seats on either side. This plan remained the same until Period 3, when the stage was rebuilt, thrust further forward and improved in the early third century.

It has been suggested[68] that the changes at this time may have been due to the erection of an amphitheatre proper. The account of the martyrdom of St Alban mentions an amphitheatre, locating it outside the city walls and across the river to the east of the town. If an amphitheatre existed here, however, no trace has been found to date.

In the early fourth century a virtually total rebuild took place (*71*). A new outer wall was built, concentric with the first. The levels within the lateral entrances and the entrance opposite the stage were raised, and it is possible that the vaults were removed. This conclusion would, however, be inconsistent with the idea that the space between the two outer walls became a barrel-vaulted corridor. There are problems with this interpretation. Though the three entrances opened into the space between the walls, which would suggest a corridor, the presence of buttresses against the primary outer wall would block such a passage. The stage front retreated to its Period 2 line and the seats in the former arena were removed. The portion of the *cavea* facing the stage was moved forward by the erection of a new wall, which gave the curve of the front of the seating a flatter appearance. There is no doubt that the building was maintained as a theatre as, despite the removal of the wooden seating, the orchestra was too small to have reverted to its mid-second-century function.

Canterbury

Post-war excavation in St Margaret's Street, Canterbury in 1950 revealed the remains of a Roman theatre. The building was of two phases. The second was the best understood. It consisted of a Classical style, semi-circular theatre dating to the early third century, with a diameter of 70.71m. Its predecessor was larger, with an outer wall diameter estimated at 100.28m, projected from a short stretch of wall. The remodelling of the theatre amounts to a total rebuild, off the line of the primary building (*72*). The excavator suggests that the wide curve is more reminiscent of the oval of an amphitheatre, and that this large diameter suggests that the building was a Romano-Celtic type of theatre like that at Verulamium. The outer wall was 1.2m wide, stone built on deep foundations and retained a substantial gravel bank; the core of the *cavea*.[69] Despite a paucity of dating evidence, a Flavian date has been suggested for the first theatre.

RURAL AMPHITHEATRES

Charterhouse on Mendip

The earthwork which has been claimed as an amphitheatre is high in the Mendip hills, on a hill-slope above a Roman fortlet and lead mining site. The small fortlet was certainly a Claudian foundation, showing that the exploitation of Mendip lead began early during the Roman period.[70]

The identification was first suggested by the Rev. H.M. Scarth in 1858:

> at Charterhouse are very interesting remains of a Roman station and a perfect amphitheatre. … The farmer pointed out the site of another amphitheatre about half a mile distant to the south.[71]

As we have seen (p. 32) Scarth's idea that this was an amphitheatre was scorned by Hadrian Allcroft,[72] whose suspicions were justifiably aroused by Scarth's claim that there were two amphitheatres. Recent ideas on the auxiliary amphitheatres of the German *limes* have suggested that sites with two small earthwork amphitheatres, like that at Zugmantel, might have been erected at particular times for special events, and this may be the context of the apparent pair of amphitheatres at Charterhouse. The second earthwork was partially back-filled when Scarth visited a second time and has now vanished from sight. It was about the same size as the amphitheatre,

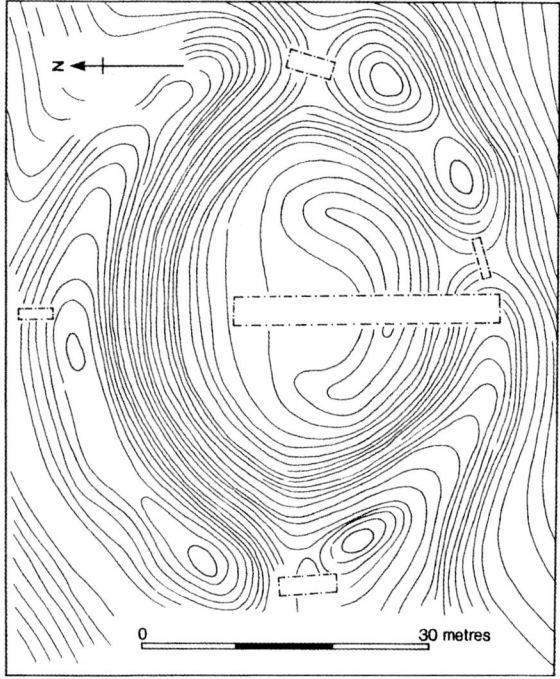

73 Plan of the amphitheatre at Charterhouse on Mendip showing excavation trenches. *Chris Evans, after Gray 1909*

but showed no signs of any entrances. The Charterhouse amphitheatre was surveyed and partially excavated by H. St George Gray in 1909.[73] The excavation took place over two wet fortnights in June and July 1909, and even the excavator found the results thoroughly unsatisfactory. A total of six trenches were excavated, three of which formed a partial north–south transect of the earthwork.

The earthwork (*73, colour plate 15*) is of elliptical plan, and has entrances at each narrow end, to west and east. The arena is 32m long (east–west) and 24.38m wide (north–south). The overall measurements over the banks are 71.62 x 61m, with the banks averaging some 20m wide. It is of very similar dimensions to the auxiliary amphitheatre at Tomen-y-Mur (p. 153). The banks slope generally slightly shallower on the inner faces than they do on the outer. The two axial entrances are some 3.05m wide. Gray adds the caveat that the whole monument had been ploughed over within living memory and therefore the height of the banks could not be recovered.

It is important to note that the natural fall of land from north-west to south-east is pronounced, and the northern side of the earthwork is a natural hillside. It is possible today to see that the earthwork is, like many other British amphitheatres, built into a natural depression, in this case the head of a natural valley. The arena was cut into the hillside and the redeposited sand, which comprised the south bank, was apparently won from the excavation of the

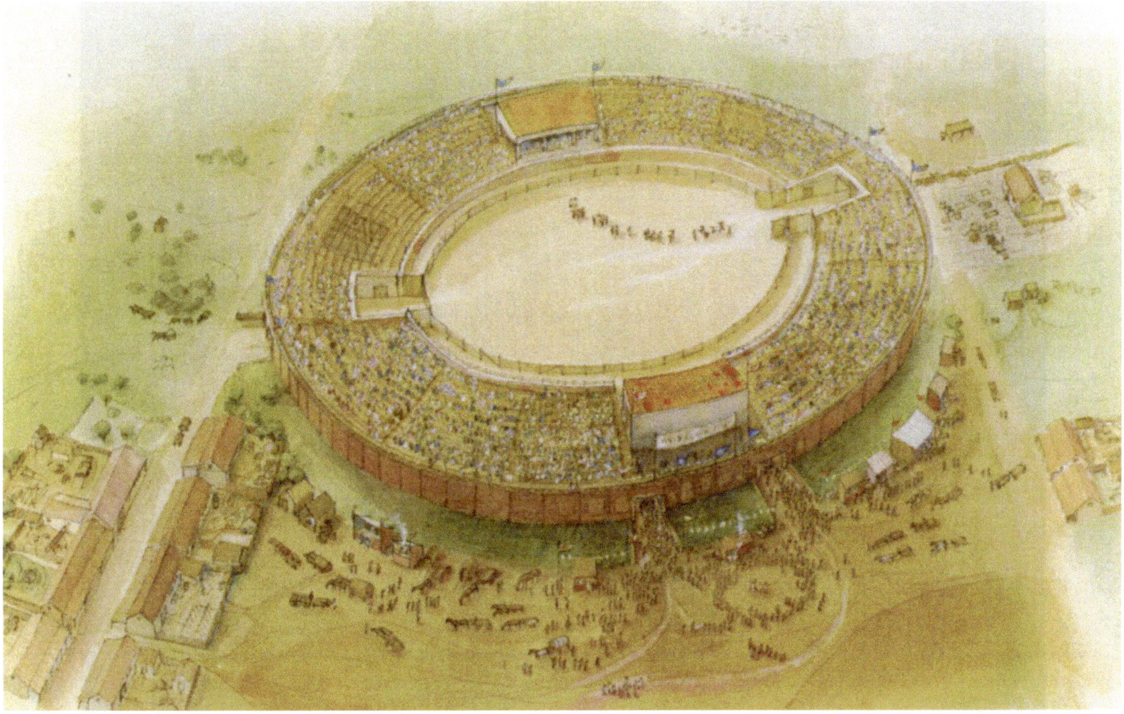

1 Reconstruction painting by Judith Dobie of the London amphitheatre c.AD 120.
Museum of London Archaeology Service

2 Computer reconstruction of the first Chester amphitheatre. *Julian Baum*

3 Excavations of the Chester amphitheatre in 2005. The walls overlain in blue are of the first amphitheatre, those in red of the second amphitheatre. *Cheryl Quinn, Chester City Council / English Heritage*

4 Artist's reconstruction of the amphitheatre at Caerleon. *CADW*

5 Chester amphitheatre excavation in 2005, clearly showing the radiating slots provided for the base-plates. *Chester City Council/English Heritage*

6 Base-plate, diagonal brace and uprights of timber seating framework for the Chester amphitheatre in Phase 1a. *Chester City Council/English Heritage*

7 Computer reconstruction of the second Chester amphitheatre. *Julian Baum*

8 East entrance to the London amphitheatre, showing *carceres* flanking entrance of the second, stone amphitheatre, and post-holes for the entrance passage to the timber predecessor. *Museum of London Archaeology Service*

9 Timber-lined axial drain in the arena of the London amphitheatre. *Museum of London Archaeology Service*

10 The Silchester amphitheatre from the south

11 The Dorchester amphitheatre from the north entrance, the same viewpoint as Stukeley's in 1723 (see *59*)

12 The Cirencester amphitheatre from the north-west

13 The Carmarthen amphitheatre from the north

14 Arena and stage of the Verulamium theatre

15 The amphitheatre at Charterhouse-on-Mendip

Opposite 16 Aerial photograph of the amphitheatre at Caerleon. *Crown Copyright: Royal Commission on the Ancient and Historical Monuments of Wales*

17 Semicircular niche built into the eastern entrance at Caerleon in the third century

18 Aerial photograph of the forts at Newstead. *Crown Copyright: Royal Commission on the Ancient and Historical Monuments of Scotland*

19 Aerial photograph of the fort of Tomen-y-Mur. The amphitheatre site is indicated.
Crown Copyright: Royal Commission on the Ancient and Historical Monuments of Wales

20 Reconstruction on site of the *gyrus* at the Lunt

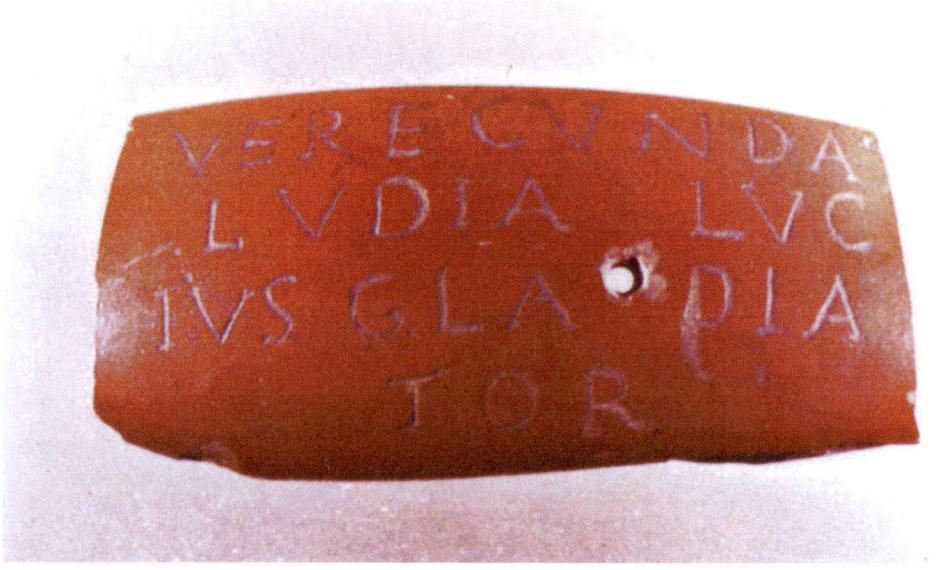

21 Graffito on a potsherd from Leicester commemorating Verecunda the actress and the gladiator Lucius. *Leicester City Museums*

22 Bignor villa mosaic; detail of gladiator frieze showing block and ring to be compared with that found at Chester. *By kind permission of the Tupper family*

23 The Rudston Venus mosaic. *D.S. Neal and English Heritage*

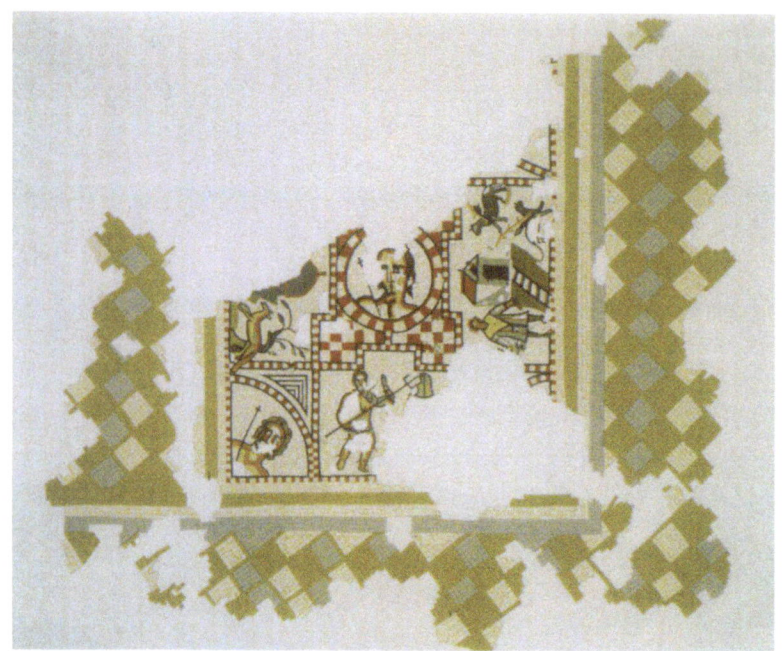

24 The Brading hunt and gladiator mosaic. *L.J. Thompson*

25 Wall painting depicting a surrendering gladiator from Colchester *(Colchester Museums)*

26 Bignor villa mosaic, showing bust, possibly of Diana-Nemesis, and frieze of cupids as gladiators. *By kind permission of the Tupper family*

27 Miniature samian ware bowl depicting gladiatorial scenes from Chester. *Chester City Council/English Heritage*

28 Painted glass bowl depicting combat between a *secutor* and a *retiarius* presided over by a *summa rudis*. From the Roman part of Vindolanda, Northumberland. *Vindolanda Trust*

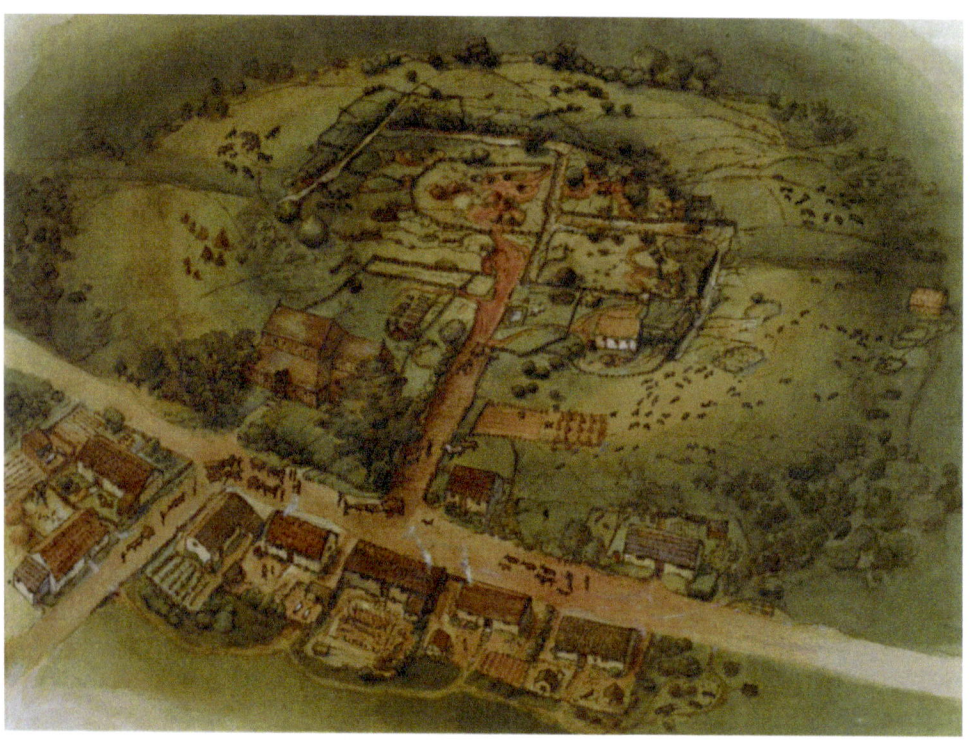

29 Reconstruction of the area of the London amphitheatre during the eleventh century. *Museum of London Archaeology Service*

THE SITES: THE SOUTH AND EAST

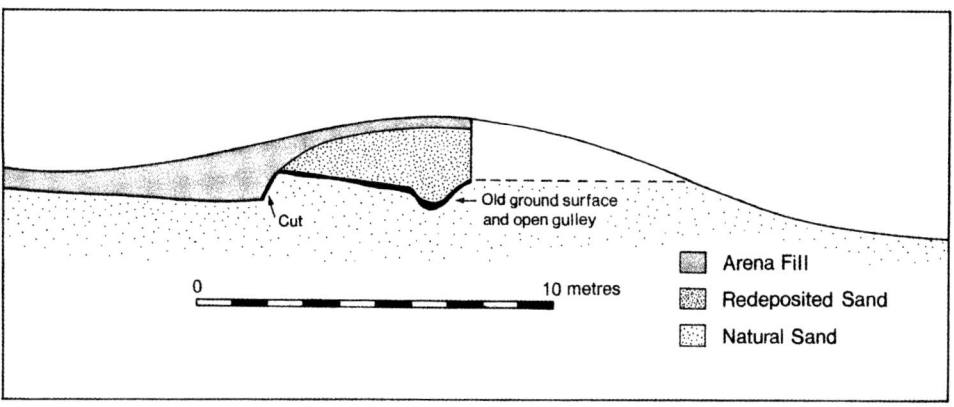

74 Simplified interpretive section through the bank of the amphitheatre at Charterhouse on Mendip. Chris Evans, after Gray 1909

arena. The hill had seen previous occupation, and the excavation cut into and revealed in section earlier features, notably a large ditch on the uphill side, and a disturbed land surface into which was cut a gully on the southern side. This surface and gully were covered with a spread of clay and lead-mine waste.[74] The land surface was cut by the excavation of the arena, and was sealed, and the gully filled, with the upcast sand, which formed the south bank. In Figure 74 I have tried to interpret the excavator's section in the light of this interpretation.[75] While the ditch contained no finds, the sand beneath the land surface contained a number of flint implements. Unsurprisingly more prehistoric flintwork was redeposited with the sand which formed the south bank.[76] It is probable that we should interpret the face of the cut of the arena and the redeposited sand bank as the construction of the 'amphitheatre'. Debris, including clay and lead-mine waste dumped against the face of this bank look like dumping following the disuse of the amphitheatre rather than part of its construction. In the arena, natural, undisturbed sand overlay bedrock, but there was no sign of a deliberately smoothed floor. Though disappointing to the excavator, such floors have proved elusive in most excavated amphitheatres. Excavation in the two entrances showed that they were original. In both, a similar, earlier ground surface was seen beneath the redeposited sand of the banks, including on the east side two distinct phases of pre-amphitheatre post-holes. The two entrances had become silted-up since the amphitheatre went out of use.

The dating evidence for the earthwork is poor. As the excavator observed, the best evidence was the presence of a few fragments of Roman pottery, including one of samian ware, in the buried land surface beneath the earthwork in the east entrance. Roman pottery was also found in the upper levels of the redeposited sand of the south bank and on the surface of the natural sand in the arena. Despite the paucity of finds material there can be little doubt that the earthwork is of Roman date, though it is impossible to be more specific.

The Charterhouse amphitheatre in its outward appearance is as convincing as that at Tomen-y-mur (p. 156). The excavation showed a number of features common to amphitheatres, the most persuasive being its position in a natural depression and the fact that the arena was dug out to provide the spoil to form the banks. The recovery of many prehistoric finds is not surprising, as the landscape around has many prehistoric monuments, such as barrows, and recent excavations on the site of the fortlet and Roman mining site have similarly produced prehistoric material. It seems reasonable to conclude that this was in fact a small amphitheatre, built on the lines of the auxiliary amphitheatres to provide entertainment for the mining community, probably including miners and the military, who appear to have supervised production; a hard audience indeed.

Frilford

At the time of writing the site of Frilford is under excavation and its interpretation is mutable. Frilford is situated in the Vale of the White Horse in the Thames Valley. It has long been known that there is a Romano-British temple in the environs of the Noah's Ark pub.[77] Survey and excavation around this temple site over recent years have revealed a number of Romano-British structures close to the temple building, as well as the *temenos* wall around the religious compound. Outside this enclosure to the north-east is a large circular structure, which was discovered in 1976 by aerial photography and first interpreted as an amphitheatre by Richard Hingley[78] following small-scale excavation (75). Between 2001 and 2006 excavations by Oxford University have sought to explore this structure and to clarify its use.[79] The structure is circular and consists of a walled enclosure or arena 40m in diameter. The wall, built of mortared chalk blocks, measures 1.75m in height – its original height – and has a plastered surface on which are traces of painted decoration. Behind the wall is a low mound, but the profile ('whale-backed') and dimensions of this bank do not allow for seating, terracing, or even a substantial area of grassed surface, which might accommodate an audience. There are also as yet no traces of timber supports for any timber-framed seating structure. There were deliberate deposits of Romano-British objects at the rear of the bank on the south side, which are not immediately suggestive of amphitheatrical activity. Though originally interpreted as an amphitheatre, the excavators became unsure of this interpretation in 2002, proposing the alternative idea that it might have been a ritual pool, formalising the outlet to a spring, which was venerated within the temple complex. Interpretation is still developing as excavation

THE SITES: THE SOUTH AND EAST

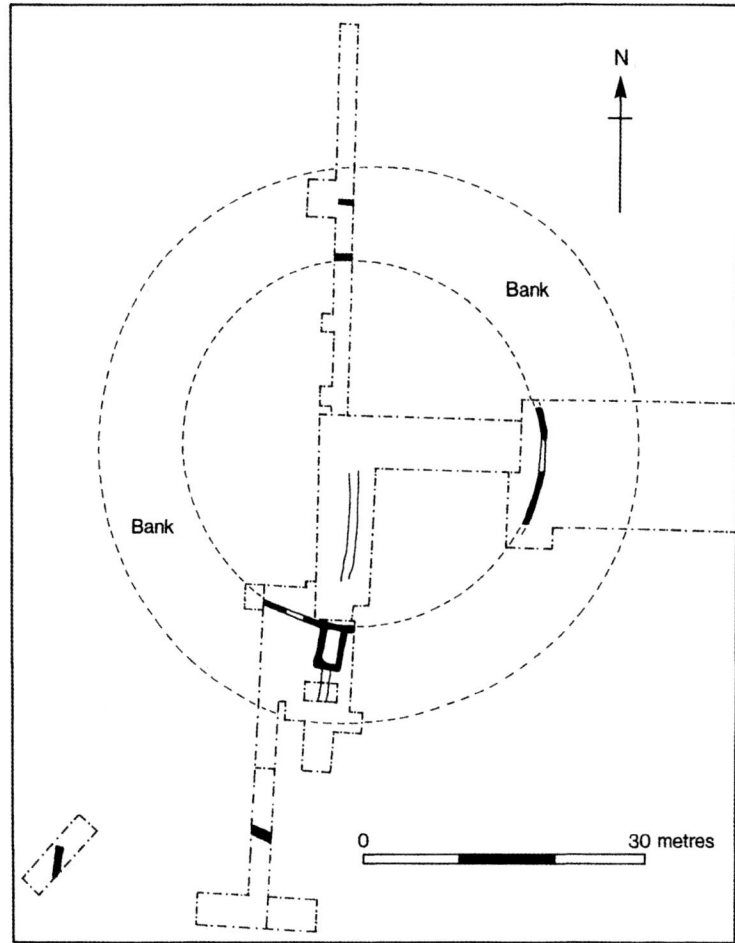

75 Plan of the amphitheatre (?) at Frilford showing excavation trenches. *Chris Evans, after Gosden and Lock 2005*

continues, but the validity of an interpretation of the structure as an amphitheatre, at least in the conventional sense, may increasingly be doubted.

The structure was cut into a natural circular hollow, possibly originally a pool. The initial bank was raised and the wall was cut into the face of the bank. Geophysical survey showed traces of structures on the cardinal points around the 'arena', which were originally interpreted as entrances or recesses. The original interpretation of the feature on the eastern side of the 'arena' as an entrance proved unsafe, as there was no sign of a slope or steps down into the 'arena', or any point of access to the bank. This feature has tentatively been identified as access to a platform or viewpoint overlooking the 'arena', perhaps a tribunal. On the north side, surfaces and post-pads suggested a number of interpretations. These might have been the foundations of a timber colonnade. The excavators preferred to interpret this as a fomal display area situated outside the 'arena' in which pillars or statues were displayed. On the south side of the 'arena', a stone chamber was one of the features discovered during early excavations and was tentatively interpreted as a *carcer*. In fact this was clearly a later addition to the whole complex and may have served a function related to the main drain, which ran beneath it. The laying of drains required the partial demolition of the wall and its reconstruction, the southern chamber was built as part of this operation, and finally the 'arena' was surfaced with gravely clay.

Currently the structure is seen as the enclosure of an existing natural feature, within the context of a structural formalisation of existing religious practices. Deposition around the outside of the bank has a strong votive feel, as does a possible focus for the erection of statues, even personal dedications. Perhaps the 'arena' was used as a venue for formal events, ceremonies and observances of various kinds (which could, given the religious origin of such events, of course include *munera*). Whatever the final interpretation, this fascinating site is clearly not a conventional amphitheatre. The excavators have suggested that the enclosure of a previously venerated natural pool or piece of wetland draws on native religious traditions, but that the banked enclosure was also a structural form maintaining links with prehistoric antiquity. In this context they also invoke the fact that Maumbury Rings was a prehistoric henge monument and that part of the reason for its reuse might have been a reverential link with the past, given a new identity within the novel Roman *milieu*.[80]

REJECTED SITES

Winterslow, Wiltshire
The Winterslow earthwork had been regarded as a long barrow before its identification as a possible amphitheatre following excavation in 1959.[81] It is located on the southern edge of Salisbury Plain. The Roman road between Old Sarum and Winchester runs some 300m to the north. The surviving part comprises a roughly crescentic earthwork, facing uphill, around 36.57m wide. The uphill half of what appears to have been a circular earthwork is discernible in the ploughland to the north-east. The entire structure would have measured 110m in diameter, and there was an appearance of a single entrance. Excavation showed that the earthwork was constructed in three stages. Firstly a low platform of soil in an irregular semi-circle was formed. Flints were found scattered on the surface of this. Secondly, the central part of the circle was quarried out to the level of natural chalk, entailing the removal of the original surface and the flinty clay subsoil, and the material won from the hollow was piled to form the 'secondary core'. Lastly a final bank was constructed using grey clay, the origin of

which being undetermined. The form of the bank had a steep face on the inner side, with the slope falling gradually away to the outside. The hollow was filled with rain-washed soil from the bank.

At the base of the final bank was a layer of iron-pan which sat above the earlier bank phases. This immediately raises doubt as to whether the entire structure was of one build, as such a deposit would tend to accumulate beneath an earthwork raised on an older, solid surface. The report states that 'many sherds' of Roman pottery were found embedded in the bank. In fact the accompanying pottery report[82] shows that there were only six Roman sherds and only in the final bank. This can be compared with the quantity of evidence for prehistoric occupation on the site, comprising 303 sherds of prehistoric pottery. 'During construction' of the final bank a Roman well was sunk through the chalk. This timber-lined well, 18m deep, contained Roman pottery. All of the Roman pottery from the site dated to the late third and fourth centuries. The excavator recorded that cracks had developed in the 'secondary core',[83] and that the surface of the bank was prone to cracking in hot weather. This raises the possibility that some, or even all, the Roman pottery within the bank might have been intrusive, having worked its way down through cracks in the bank.

The site is clearly overdue for re-assessment, but it seems unlikely that the identification as an amphitheatre can stand. The iron-pan layer suggests that the final bank is a later modification of an existing earthwork, but the date of the modification is uncertain. The well is the only thing certainly Roman on the site and it is unclear why the excavators thought this was created during the construction of the earthwork. An additional problem is the fact that, apart from the road, there is little known Roman occupation in the immediate area. The Winterslow earthwork would have been a very large amphitheatre, comparable to or larger than the urban amphitheatres at Cirencester and Silchester, for example, and it is impossible to see where the audience would come from. The Roman pottery from the site comes from a period when amphitheatres were not being constructed (save the possible exception at Richborough (p. 55). The presence of prehistoric material, its circular form and single entrance suggest a henge monument, though there are problems with this interpretation as well. At present it seems reasonable to think of the monument as prehistoric, with an element of later Roman occupation.

Woodcutts, Dorset

Woodcutts is a small Romano-British village settlement situated on Cranborne Chase in Dorset. The village was occupied at least from the first to the fourth century. It was excavated by General Pitt Rivers and was thoroughly reported in the first of the General's celebrated and pioneering excavation reports.[84] The earthwork which he called the 'amphitheatre known as "Church Barrow"' sits astride the road leading southwards from the village, which he called the 'southern fosseway'. This road was not metalled and was defined by the fact that it lay between two ditches. The overall dimensions of the earthwork were some 40m x 30m, with a central 'arena' measuring 21m x 15m. The banks were some 12m wide. The bank on the western side was curvilinear, resembling the shape of one side of an amphitheatre *cavea*, however the eastern side was somewhat more straight, giving a D-shaped plan to the whole. The centre of the 'arena' was lower than the surrounding ground level. The published account provides grounds for the belief that the two banks are not contemporary. The roadside ditch on the west side seems to have been diverted in order to run around the outer curve of the bank, before butt-ending, and seems to have respected a pre-existing earthwork. On the east side, however, Pitt Rivers records that the roadside ditch ran continuously beneath the bank, although he did describe a slight curve, which may have been related to the shape of the west bank. There is no reason to suspect that the roadside ditches did not function together and were not contemporary, therefore the two banks of the 'amphitheatre' could not be contemporary. Roman pottery was found in the eastern roadside ditch beneath the bank, but only in the butt-end of the western ditch against the west bank. The sequence seems to be that the curving west bank was built first at an unknown time and for an unknown purpose. The road ditches were subsequently laid out to define a route, possibly during the Iron Age or early Roman period. The lack of surfacing suggests that this was not a road, but possibly a droveway. If the ditches were provided to stop cattle straying from a predetermined route, this would explain why the ditch was interrupted where the west mound stood – the mound would serve this function as well as the ditch did. Finally, during the Roman period, the east mound was added. It seems likely that the area between the mounds was reduced in height to provide material for the east mound.

In its final form the use of the earthwork is difficult to determine. If it was reused for the purposes of entertainment, then it was at best a very makeshift 'amphitheatre'.

7

THE SITES: THE NORTH AND WEST

> I imagine the terrace at top in our work was designed for the men of arms: for they are by no means to be excluded, seeing one of the primary intents of these diversions was to inure them, as well as the people, to blood and murder. Hence, before they went upon any great expedition, or foreign war, these feasts and butcheries were publicly celebrated.[1]

As we have seen, the sites of the north and west are primarily related to military installations, and the three classes of structure catalogued here are the legionary and auxiliary sites together with the *gyrus/vivarium* at the Lunt and possible related structures. Finally, three sites where amphitheatres have been claimed are noted, together with the grounds for rejecting the interpretation. The urban amphitheatres of South Wales, at Carmarthen and Caerwent, have been examined in the previous chapter.

LEGIONARY AMPHITHEATRES

Chester (Deva)

The legionary fortress at Chester appears to have been established *c.*AD 74-5. It is possible that this was the culmination of earlier military activity, and that earlier camps or forts remain to be found on the site. The amphitheatre site produced a small assemblage of material which might have derived from such occupation. Once the fortress was established, a civilian settlement, or *canabae*, began to develop. By the end of the first century AD this settlement extended eastwards of the fortress for some 300m beyond the defences. The early garrison of the fortress was Legion II *Adiutrix*, but for most of the history of the site it was occupied by Legion XX *Valeria Victrix*.

76 The first photograph of the Chester amphitheatre, published by W. Williams in 1929. *Chester City Council/English Heritage*

The Chester Amphitheatre lies on high ground on the banks of the River Dee, just outside the south-east corner of the legionary fortress of *Deva*. It was built in a commanding position, visible to anyone approaching from the south and west and from the river. The amphitheatre was discovered by W.J. Williams in 1929 during the installation of heating to the Dee House convent school (*76*). Before this, the only evidence for such a structure was the discovery in nearby Fleshmongers Lane of a slate relief depicting a gladiator (a *retiarius* armed with trident and net) in 1737[2] (p. 166; *94*). Williams' identification of the scant remains as an amphitheatre was an interpretative *tour de force*[3] and was confirmed in the following years by excavations carried out by R.N. Newstead and J.P. Droop.[4] Between 1960 and 1969, extensive excavations of the northern half of the amphitheatre by F.H. Thompson culminated in the consolidation of this part of the site and its opening as a public monument in 1972.

Thompson's excavation report was forthcoming about the flaws in his methodology.[5] In particular he acknowledged that his wholesale clearance of the arena by machine down to what were believed to be Roman levels had destroyed evidence for the post-Roman periods on the site. Thompson's conclusions have been widely accepted and influential in the interpretation of amphitheatre excavations in Britain. The discovery beneath the seating bank of timber slots running concentrically and radially to the arena wall led to the conclusion that the first amphitheatre was entirely of timber construction. Thompson's second amphitheatre was stone built and he believed that all of the stone elements were contemporary. These were the arena wall, the main outer wall, the stone-built gates and entrances, and a wall 1.8m inside the outer wall which Thompson termed the 'concentric wall'. Archaeological dating evidence for the timber phase was not forthcoming, so this phase was dated theoretically to the mid-AD 70s, as it was assumed that the amphitheatre was contemporary with the earliest timber phase of the legionary fortress. The stone phase was dated by archaeological means to *c*.AD 100; a date derived from finds from the construction of the arena wall. In the centre of the arena itself a complex of post-holes was interpreted as the foundation for a platform associated with arena activities such as military parades.

In 2004-6, new excavations took place, funded and implemented jointly by English Heritage and Chester City Council, and directed by Tony Wilmott and Dan Garner. So far only interim statements on the findings have been published and at the time of writing, analysis is continuing. Despite this, it is clear that most of Thompson's conclusions can be overturned. The following account is based on the interim reports and current understanding,[6] though the analytical phase of the work will generate new interpretations. The phases in construction superimposed on the excavation, are shown in colour plate 3.

The probable survey method is described in an earlier chapter (p. 83). The earliest amphitheatre structure (Phase 1) was an oval or elliptical stone building, and Thompson's 'concentric wall' may now be understood as its outer wall. It measured 88 x 76.5m overall. The outer wall was built first and the arena was then excavated, though to what depth we do not know. The arena measured 57.9 x 48.7m. The spoil from the arena was dumped against the outer wall to form a seating bank. The date of this construction has not yet been determined, but the presence of dumps of rubbish incorporating Roman finds in the primary bank suggests that settlement was well established before its construction. An estimate of *c*.AD 80-90 is reasonable at present. An arena wall would also have been necessary, and it is probable that in this incarnation the amphitheatre comprised a stone-built outer wall and arena wall, with an earthen seating bank, possibly supporting timber seats. Metalled surfaces developed outside the outer wall. Access to the seating was probably via one of four entrances, the positions of which dictated the location of entrances in succeeding phases.

It was probably not long before the amphitheatre was radically altered (Phase 1b, 77). Though the outer wall remained, the seating bank was cut away, forming a

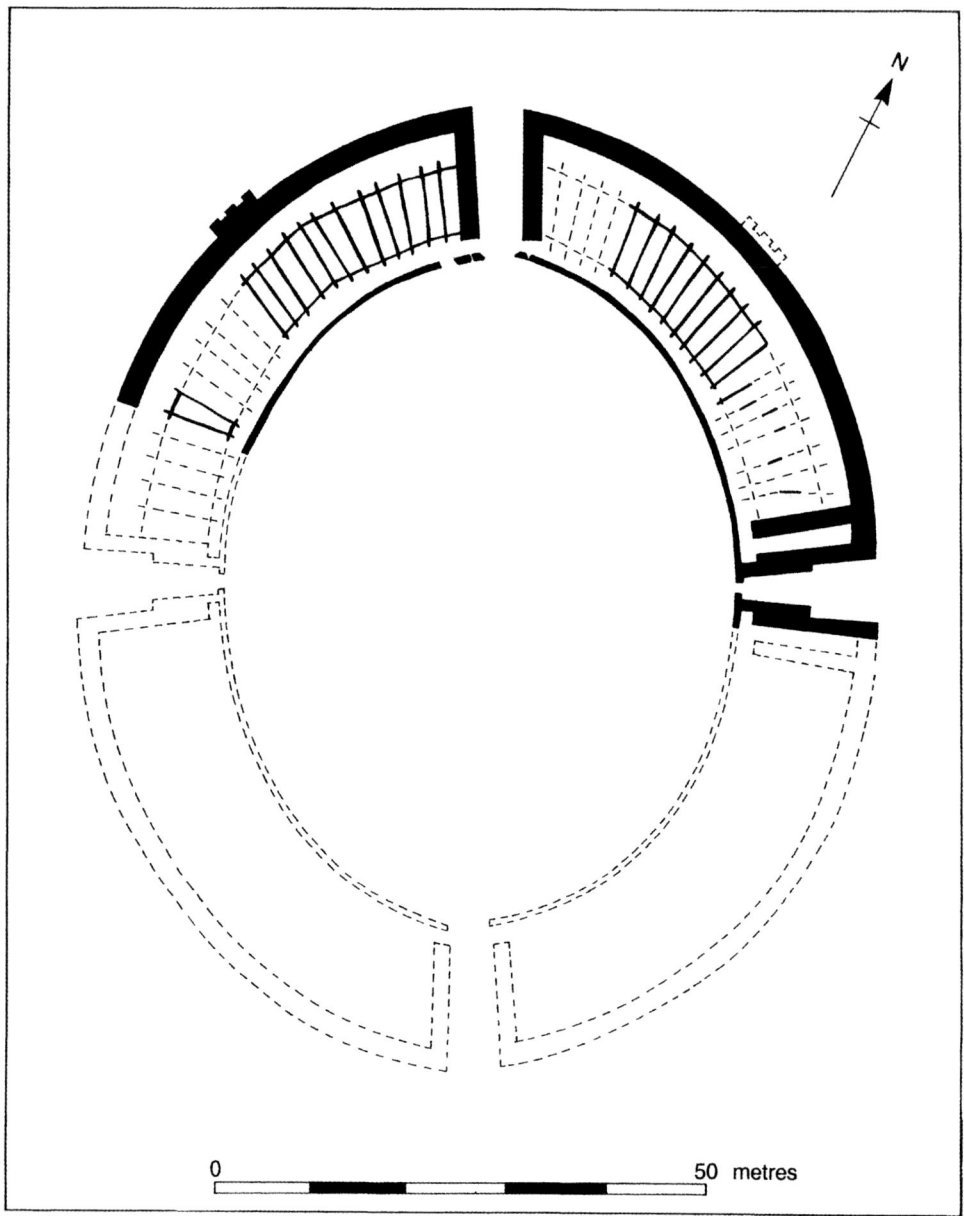

77 Plan of the first amphitheatre at Chester (Phase 1b). *Chris Evans*

flat terrace. On this terrace was built a system of timber-framed seating. Slots were cut into the terrace, radiating from the arena wall, and these were linked by a pair of concentric beam-slots which were also concentric to the line of the outer wall and the arena wall (*colour plate 5*). Thompson had interpreted this beam-slot pattern as the footings for a wholly timber amphitheatre. The data recovered has the

78 Robbing trench of the buttressed exterior stair of the Chester Phase 1b amphitheatre. *Chester City Council/English Heritage*

potential to tell us a great deal about the way in which this was constructed. The timbers survived in semi-mineralised form and it will be possible to recover their dimensions. Ground-fast beams and upright and diagonal members were recorded (*colour plate 6*). The various members were not jointed, but simply nailed. Some of the nails retained the imprint of wood grain, from which it is possible to say that the timber used was not oak and may have been beech. The position of the nails with relation to the timbers and the ground shows that the timber frames were prefabricated and were installed working in an anti-clockwise direction. Once the timber framework to support the seating was erected, the arena was deepened, and it was probably at this stage that it was excavated to bedrock. This would necessitate a new arena wall. Upcast from the excavation of the arena was again deposited in the *cavea*, this time to hold in position the base-plates of the timber framework. On the south side of the *cavea* limited excavation suggested that there were no timbers and that the seating bank deposits were 'topped-up' with a mixture of domestic rubbish, sand and clay. The date of these changes was well established, as a coin dating to AD 96 was found in the foundation slot of one of the radial timbers.

At the same time as the new timber seating was installed, new access arrangements were provided to the upper seats in the form of a stairway engaged against the outer wall (*78*). The foundation for this stair cut the metalled surface of Phase 1. The dimensions of the stair and a preliminary calculation of practicable gradients suggest that the outer wall stood to a height of some 4m. This stair is virtually identical in dimensions to that at the amphitheatre of Paestum in Italy (*45*). At about the same time as the external staircase was erected, the service road running around the circumference of the amphitheatre was moved away from the outer wall creating a concentric zone about 1.7m wide, and its new edge was defined by a formal kerb. This may have been done to prevent the new staircase from causing an obstruction to the regular flow of traffic outside the amphitheatre (*colour plate 2*).

THE ROMAN AMPHITHEATRE IN BRITAIN

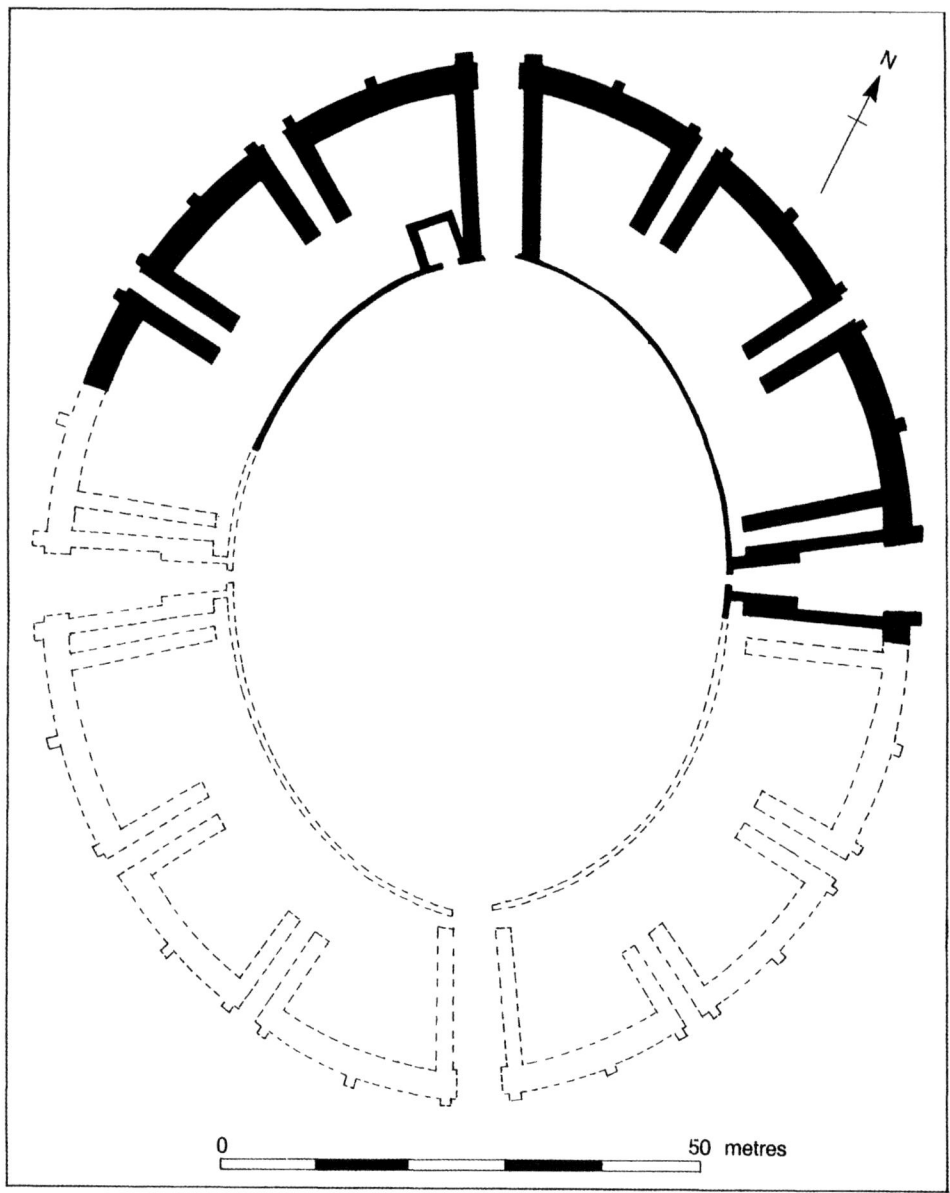

79 Plan of the second amphitheatre at Chester. *Chris Evans*

The deposits which built up around the outside of the amphitheatre during Phase 1a are a unique survival, protected as they have been by being enclosed within the shell of the second amphitheatre. These deposits give unrivalled evidence for the activities that took place outside amphitheatres during their use (p. 178).

THE SITES: THE NORTH AND WEST

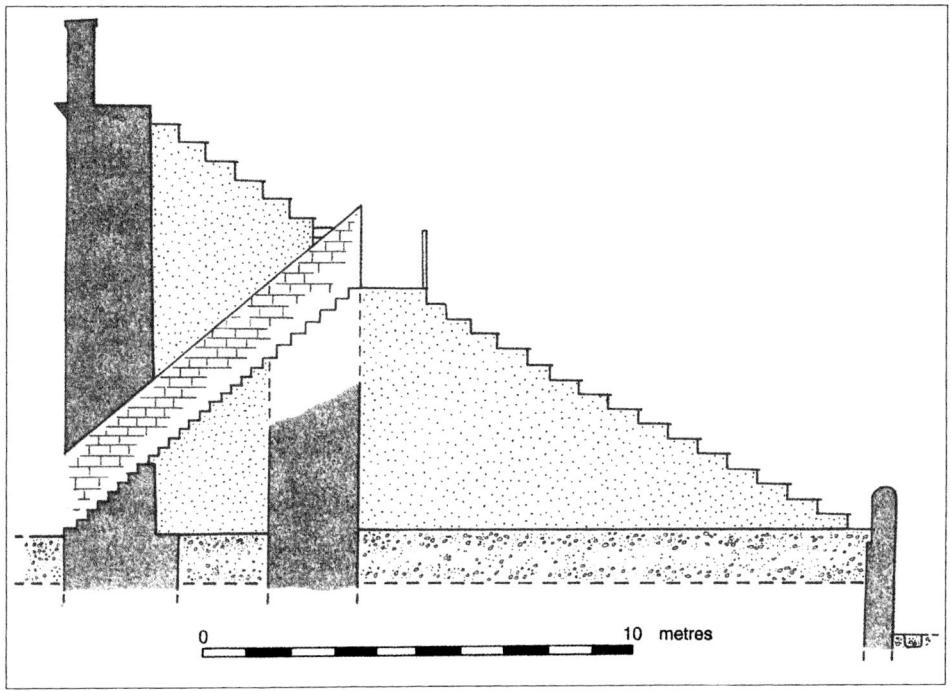

80 Section through one of the *vomitoria* of the second Chester amphitheatre showing staircase rising to *cavea* across the robbed stub of the wall of amphitheatre 1. *Chris Evans*

At some time, probably in the late second century, though the dating evidence is yet to be analysed, the amphitheatre was extended and enlarged (Phase 2 (*79*)). A new outer wall, almost 2m thick, was constructed 1.8m outside the outer wall of the first structure. This wall had foundations over a metre deep, and was founded on bedrock. A small part of the superstructure survived; the bottom two courses of the inner face of the wall were bonded in lime mortar and more carefully dressed and laid than the masonry of the outer wall of the first amphitheatre.[7] Although the original four entrances into the arena were retained, the upper part of the auditorium was now accessed by *vomitoria*, vaulted stairways within the structure of the building which led directly into the face of the *cavea* (*80*). This suggests that the outer wall was now very much higher than before, and that it was no longer possible to use external stairways. Two *vomitoria* were provided in each quadrant of the amphitheatre. Marking-out lines for the bottom step found in the one threshold excavated demonstrate that the stairs opened direct from the street. The arrangement was almost certainly intended to cater for an increased audience capacity as the new system of *vomitoria* represented a much higher level of crowd management. Both the major and minor entrances were

81 Stone block with iron fitting secured with lead, in the centre of the arena of the second Chester amphitheatre. *Chester City Council/ English Heritage*

flanked by a pair of piers and between each entrance and each *vomitorium* was a single pier. Thompson interpreted these as buttresses, however they were only one stone thick and did not penetrate to the base of the foundations. In two cases semi-circular mortar pads on the upper face of these blocks betray their true identity; these were foundation stones for substantial engaged pilasters, possibly half-columns (*49*). This suggests an exterior decorative treatment extraordinary for the northern provinces (*colour plate 7*) and seldom found north of the Alps. If there was one storey of such pilasters, laws of proportion would demand that there should be another storey above, with an entablature in between. The most obvious and grandest parallels to this form of ornament are the Colosseum itself and the amphitheatre of El Djem, Tunisia. It is hoped that analysis of the architectural scheme according to Classical proportions, and the angle and rise of the *vomitorium* stairs, will enable us to reconstruct the height and grandeur of the second amphitheatre.

The east entrance seems to have comprised three entrance passages to the arena separated by walls, and it is possible that these were used to control the entry of animals into the arena, or to separate animals from human participants. Thompson's original suggestion that a tribunal sat above the east entrance seems to be strengthened by the presence of these walls. Keith Matthews' re-examination of the upstanding masonry in the eastern entrance in 2001-3 revealed a complex sequence of modifications to the central passage, and it is possible that the two narrow outer passages were blocked at a relatively early stage. Later, in a complex sequence of developments, the arena end of the entrance was narrowed on at least two occasions; two rows of decorative columns were added to the narrowed entrance. Part of a series of steps on the southern side of the entrance leading to an upper level were heavily worn through use. Perhaps in the early post-Roman period the outer end of the entrance was completely sealed by a blocking wall.

THE SITES: THE NORTH AND WEST

Excavation in the centre of the arena revealed a large stone block placed virtually in the geometrical centre of the amphitheatre. This had an iron fitting fastened into its upper surface with lead, and was certainly a piece of arena furniture (*81*). A very similar block is depicted twice on the gladiator mosaic from the villa at Bignor, West Sussex, where a pair of gladiators fight across a block with an iron ring in the top (*colour plate 22*). It can only be interpreted as a point to which arena victims, probably animals, could be chained during spectacles (p. 162).

Chester is one of the very few sites where there is now fairly substantial evidence for the post-Roman fate of the amphitheatre and this is discussed in a later chapter (p. 183).

Caerleon (Isca)

The legionary fortress of Caerleon was founded in *c*.AD 70-74 during the governorship of the Flavian governor, Julius Frontinus, by Legion II *Augusta*, which remained its garrison throughout the following centuries. It is situated in modern south-east Wales, on a tongue of land overlooking the River Usk and commanding the road crossing over the river. The fortress appears to have been maintained continuously until around AD 290.[8]

The Caerleon amphitheatre, excavated in 1926, remains the most accessible, most complete and one of the two most completely excavated amphitheatres in Britain.[9] Until its excavation in 1926, the site was known as King Arthur's Round Table.[10] Its recorded history goes back to the twelfth-century writings of Giraldus Cambrensis (p. 21). As late as 1908, Hadrian Allcroft listed the Caerleon site as only a 'probable' amphitheatre,[11] but in 1909 the Liverpool Committee for Excavation and Research in Wales and the Marches carried out the first formal excavations and discovered that the remains were well preserved. In 1926, funds were made available by the *Daily Mail* newspaper and the Loyal Knights of the Round Table of America for a project to totally excavate the whole site, and to open it up to public view. The work was overseen by Mortimer Wheeler, with V.E. Nash Williams supervising the first six weeks of the excavation, J.N.L. Myers the following four months and Mrs T.V. Wheeler the remaining eight months. The site was then handed over to the Office of Works for preservation as a national monument.[12]

The amphitheatre (*colour plate 16*) was built, probably *c*.AD 80, on a site possibly previously occupied by the builders of the fortress.[13] Deposits pre-dating the amphitheatre contained a great deal of Flavian pottery of *c*.AD 60-80.[14] It lay on a site very close to the fortress between its south-west gate and south-west corner. The site was limited, and in order to squeeze the amphitheatre in it was necessary to partially fill the fortress ditch and to modify the rear of the existing bath-house. This shows clearly that the amphitheatre was provided after the fortress was well established.

The chosen site was shelved to the south, and the arena was excavated and levelled to the level of a sandy subsoil stratum, the spoil being used mainly to build up the seating bank in the southern quadrant. The arena seems to have been designed to measure 140 x 190 Roman feet. This is approximated by the actual measurement of 41.6 x 56.08m. The survey technique described in a previous chapter (p. 83) produced a good oval shape, though the effect is somewhat marred by the fact that the side walls of the entrances at the ends of the oval were planned to lie parallel with the long axis of the arena, rather than splaying radially with the end curves. This means that the curve has been replaced with a straight line at these points. The arena was clearly laid out first and accurately, as the outer wall is not regular in width, and the outer curves are irregular and not parallel with those of the arena. The overall dimensions of the building to the outer wall were 81.38 x 67.67m. The inner ends of the eight entrances were laid out at the same time as the arena wall (*82*). This is shown by Entrance C, which is regular at the arena wall, but twisted to fit the irregular position of the outer end.

The arena floor was of sand, though was later made up of other materials (p. 183). The main drain beneath the arena ran from the main north entrance to the main south entrance, meeting with the main drain from the adjacent bath-house and discharging into the River Usk. The arena wall was treated with a thick mortar rendering and no traces of painting were observed.[15]

The outer wall of the building was faced internally and externally. This does not necessarily mean that it was built as a freestanding wall, but that the weight of the seating banks within would require a substantial and well-built wall to support them. Around most of the building the outer wall is 1.4m thick, rising to 1.8m on the south-eastern, down-slope, portion. This is presumably in order to retain a greater weight of piled loose material within the bank. In this quadrant the outer wall was provided with both interior and exterior buttresses. The equally spaced external buttresses (2.94m apart) were continued as narrower pilasters around the entire circuit of the wall. This was probably intended as a decorative external architectural treatment, conceivably even featuring a series of blank arcades, though no arch stones have been found to confirm this.

The seating in the *cavea* was supported upon a bank of earth and gravel 12.3-13.6m wide. The maximum surviving height of 5.8m for these banks is probably the full original height.[16] Wheeler stated that the seating must have been timber-built, a statement which was confirmed in 1962, when metre-square pits for timbers 300mm square in section, two of which were linked by a beam slot, were discovered in the bank in the north-east quadrant, between Entrances D and E.

THE SITES: THE NORTH AND WEST

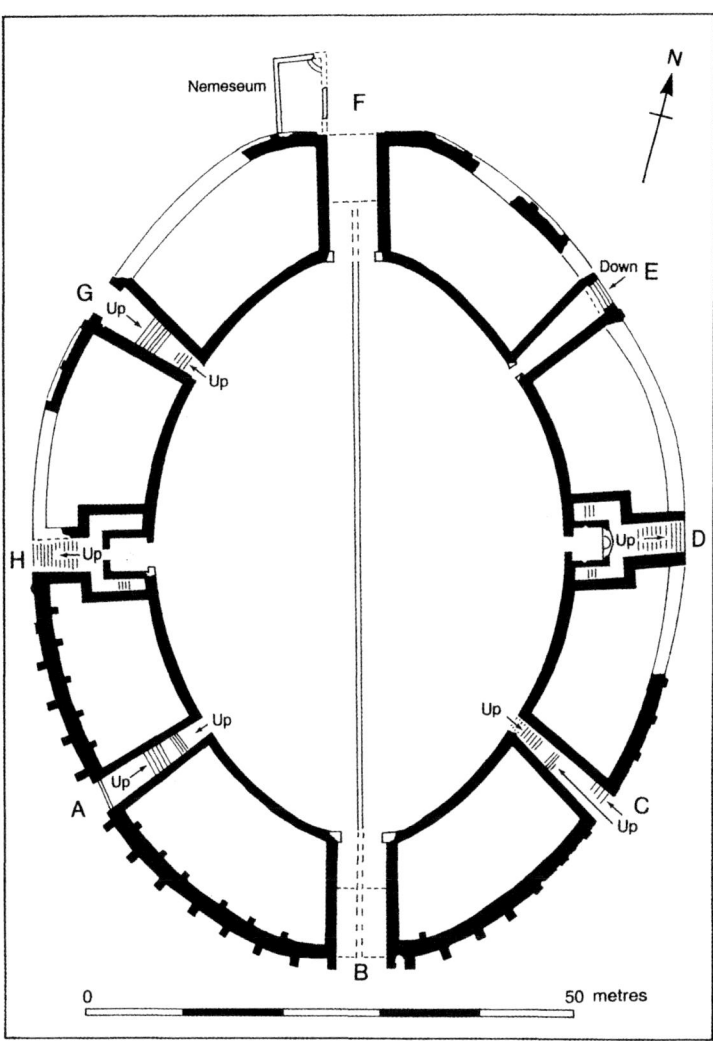

82 Plan of the Caerleon amphitheatre. Chris Evans, after Wheeler and Wheeler 1928

These are almost certainly part of an open-framed timber stand like that which is presumed for the first phase in Chester. The outer supports of the stand were probably embedded within the fabric of the outer wall and the appearance of the building was probably similar to that shown on Trajan's Column, where the amphitheatre Dacia is depicted with a stone outer wall, vaulted entrances and a timber-framed stand (*48*).

The entrances provided a complex pattern of access to the amphitheatre. The entrances situated on the ends of the long axis, sloped downwards from the outside to the level of the arena, which they served with no evidence of access to the seating. Gate piers at the outer end of the gate passage and piers half-way down, show that the outer half of the entrance passages were roofed with barrel

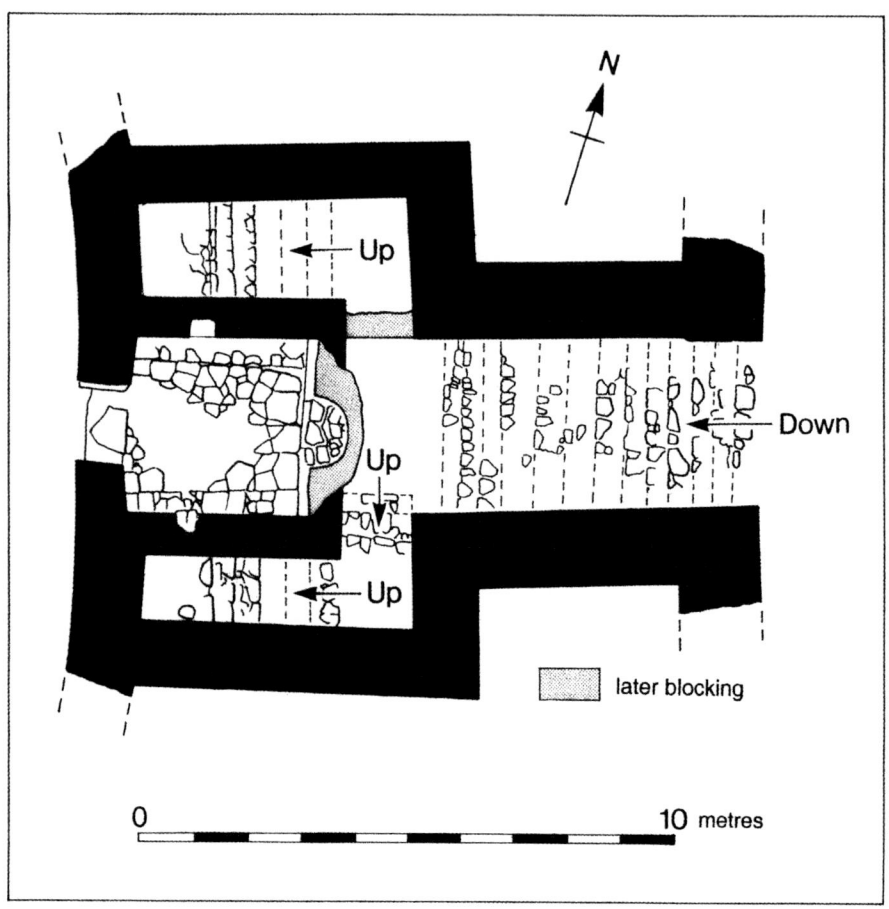

83 Plan of entrance on the short axis at Caerleon. Chris Evans after Wheeler and Wheeler 1928

vaults, as shown by the existence of external jambs and inner piers and arch (*46*). Arch imposts survived on the outer arches, showing that the crown of the arch was at a level 7.5m above that of the arena (4m above exterior ground level).[17] Though originally it was thought that the seating was directly on the bank and directly above the barrel vault, the discovery of the post-holes in the bank shows that a timber-framed structure was built above, as shown in the reconstruction (*colour plate 4*). The inner half of the barrel vault must have remained unroofed, as any continuation of the vault beyond the mid-point of the passage would have made the roof ridiculously low.

The entrances on the short axis were more complicated. Here the outer part of the entrance was again formed by a ramp, sloping steeply from the outside, and possibly furnished with steps. This was roofed with a barrel vault. From the

THE SITES: THE NORTH AND WEST

84 View of entrance on the short axis at Caerleon

base of the ramp, above the level of the arena, opened three brick arches. The one in the centre gave access to the arena via a square, brick-faced, barrel-vaulted chamber, probably a *carcer*, or beast pen, in which animals (and possibly humans) were kept before their turn in the arena. The other two arches led to stairs, which broke at right angles around the chamber (*47, 83, 84*). In both entrances the northern stair was wider than that to the south, and it has been suggested[18] that the wider stairs led to boxes over the chambers, while the narrower stairs led to the general seating.

The remaining four entrances were situated one in each of the quadrants of the *cavea* between those on the long and short axes. These provided access to seating for the majority of the audience. Again, the outer parts of the entrances were barrel vaulted, as shown by a surviving arch springer for the inner end of a vault. The ramps led downwards following the gradient of the barrel vaults to meet flights of steps up to the auditorium (*85*). At first sight, this seems similar to the situation in the short-axis entrances, however there is a problem. On the arena side of the stair to the auditorium is a further stair down to the arena. The steps up to the auditorium perhaps emerged onto a wooden landing, from

147

THE ROMAN AMPHITHEATRE IN BRITAIN

Left 85 Stair up to the podium and down to the arena in a subsidiary entrance at Caerleon

Opposite 86 Plan and section of subsidiary entrance at Caerleon. Chris Evans, after Wheeler and Wheeler 1928

which the arena steps could be accessed by means of trap-doors (*86*).[19] No other explanation seems feasible, as the steps are not high enough to have shared a broad mutual landing.

The exterior appearance and decoration of the amphitheatre is hinted at by some surviving detail. The barrel vaults of the entrances were built of tufa, banded with tile and stone. There are traces that the walls were rendered and picked out with false ashlar joints highlighted in red paint.[20] A number of coping stones for the parapets of the arena wall and the top walls of the open entrance sides were found, some with holes in the quarter round moulding for railings. These were made, like the piers of the entrances, in fine oolitic limestone, while the rest of the squared rubble of the walls was in local sandstone. The walls are of standard legionary work,[21] and the role of the legion in its construction is demonstrated by the presence of many centurial stones recording the work of individual centuries (*43*).

Over the following couple of centuries the building was changed on a number of occasions. The evidence for these changes could be seen mainly at the entrances. Around AD 90 part of the timber seating seems to have been destroyed by a fire, which affected the extra-mural area of the fortress, and may have produced the burning on the seating banks observed by Wheeler.[22] Perhaps the seating was replaced or repaired on the original lines at this time, but significant alteration took place in Period 2, possibly shortly after AD 140.[23] The work involved the removal of all barrel vaults except for those over the main entrances on the long axis. This may have been due to a rise in floor levels required to counter flooding. Large buttresses, 1.2 x 1.8m in size were built on

THE SITES: THE NORTH AND WEST

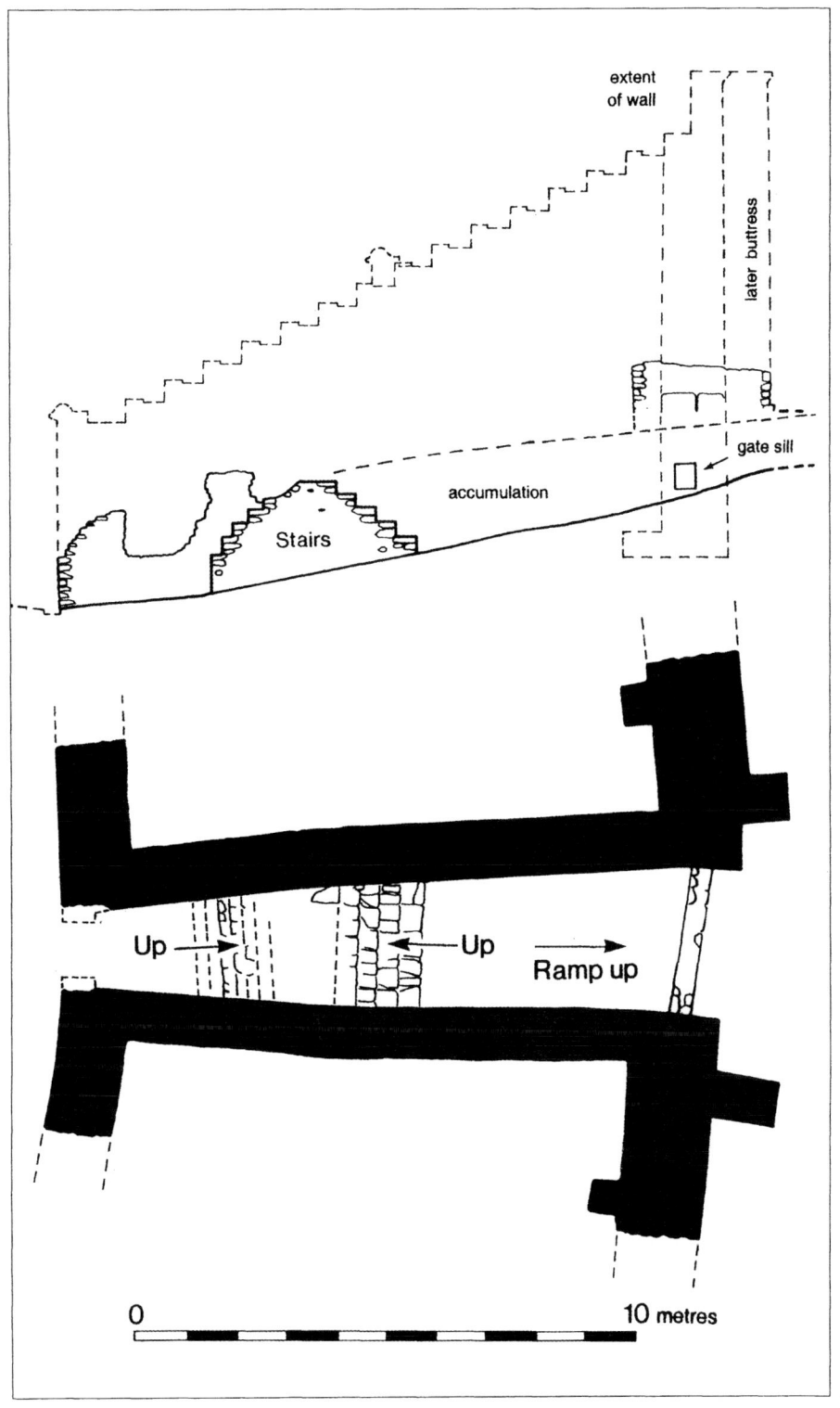

the north-west quadrant to replace original shallow pilasters. This may have been to counter strains exerted by the timber-framed seating where it was keyed into the wall, 'augmented by the vibrations caused by an excited audience'.[24] Levels in all entrances were raised, resulting in re-flooring and the replacement of steps. It is odd that in both short-axis entrances the broad, northern stairs were filled in and walled-up, as this suggests that the probable boxes went out of use. This seems to be confirmed by the fact that the barrel vaults of the chambers beneath the boxes were demolished and replaced by flat wooden ceilings, the side walls being heightened with reused brick voussoirs. One of the strangest interpretations made by Wheeler at Caerleon was of a large stone – a reused voussoir – placed by the angle of the southern stair in the west entrance. He thought this was 'probably a stand for a policeman, ticket-collector or other official'.[25] This is still there. In the east entrance the access from the main ramp to the arena was blocked by the insertion of a cupboard into the doorway of the chamber.

The final period of reconstruction (Period 3) is dated to *c*.AD 213-222 by the use of tiles stamped LEG II AVG ANTO – the last being the title *Antoniniana* awarded by Caracalla (AD 211-17) to many units. The stamp ceased to be used following the *damnatio memoriae* of Elagabalus in 222, so the date is quite tight.[26] Entrances A, D, E, G and H were filled to the level of the exterior ground surface, allowing a horizontal approach for spectators. A new stone stair was inserted in the north half of Entrance C, and admission to the block of seats to the east of Entrance B was provided by the addition of an exterior semi-circular flight of steps. Outside entrance F rising levels were held back by an L-shaped retaining wall. New buttresses were again constructed and the work was distinguished by the lavish use of hard white mortar.

In the east entrance on the short axis (D) the rear wall of the chamber leading off the arena was furnished with a semi-circular niche built of the *Antoniniana* tiles. This perhaps hints at the use of this chamber as a shrine (*colour plate 17*). However, a further addition to the plan was a small oblong room constructed on the east side of Entrance F. This had a stone bench on the west side and a square platform in one corner. It was built in an analogous position to the building at Carnuntum, Austria, which is known to have been a *Nemeseum*.

The amphitheatre appears to have been deserted in the later third century. Indeed this seems to have been the fate of Caerleon as a whole. It has been suggested that the garrison moved on, partly to Cardiff, and in part to man the new Saxon Shore fort at Richborough, where Legion II *Augusta* is mentioned in the fourth-century *Notitia Dignitatum*. It is just possible, as already noted (p. 55), that the Richborough amphitheatre was built at the same time as the Saxon Shore fort garrisoned by Legion II and therefore that the Richborough amphitheatre was the direct descendant of that at Caerleon.

THE SITES: THE NORTH AND WEST

AUXILIARY AMPHITHEATRES

The interpretation of elliptical or oval embanked features at auxiliary forts as amphitheatres has been doubted over the years. The discovery of the very definite auxiliary amphitheatre of Kűnzing in Bavaria (p. 60), however, allows us to be more certain of these identifications. This group must be regarded cautiously however. While the sites at Newstead and Tomen-y-Mur are very good candidates, that at Inveresk is very odd; the Forden Gaer site is a possible candidate for consideration, but the proposed amphitheatre at Walton may be rejected, and the antiquarian notion of an amphitheatre at Housesteads on Hadrian's Wall has long been dismissed (p. 31).

Newstead, Roxburghshire (Trimontium)

The Roman fort of *Trimontium* near Newstead lies on the strategic crossing of the main Roman penetration route into western Scotland, Dere Street, over the River Tweed. The surrounding region is one of the most fertile arable farming areas in this part of Scotland, and is dominated by one of the two largest hillforts in southern Scotland, Eildon Hill North. *Trimontium* was clearly regarded by the Romans as one of the most strategically important centres in the Scottish Lowlands. There are eight marching camps in the vicinity, as well as two permanent forts which were built during the two main advances into Scotland. These took place during the Flavian governorship of Agricola and the period of advance into Scotland under the Emperor Antoninus Pius, which resulted in the occupation of the Antonine Wall. During the first of these periods, Newstead was occupied for about 20 years after *c.*AD 80, and in the second for about 40 years after *c.*AD 140. It was an unusually large fort, probably a base for up to 2000 legionary and auxiliary troops, but appears also to have been the main supply and reinforcement centre for the Roman army throughout Scotland.

A hollow close to the north-east corner of the fort on the hillslope of Leaderfoot Brae has long been recognised as an artificial feature (*colour plate 18*), and Sir Ian Richmond suggested that it was a clay pit from which material was quarried for the construction of the late Flavian fort.[27] The surface appearance of the feature is an oval depression 70 x 60m, lying 100m to the east of the north-east corner of the fort. During the early 1990s the suggestion was made that it might be a small amphitheatre,[28] prompting Bradford University to undertake contour and geophysical surveys. Geophysics confirmed the existence of an arena and encircling bank, but it was the contour survey that showed that the centre of the hollow was at least 250mm lower than the lowest point of the bank – a pattern that would not have been likely to result from any natural process.

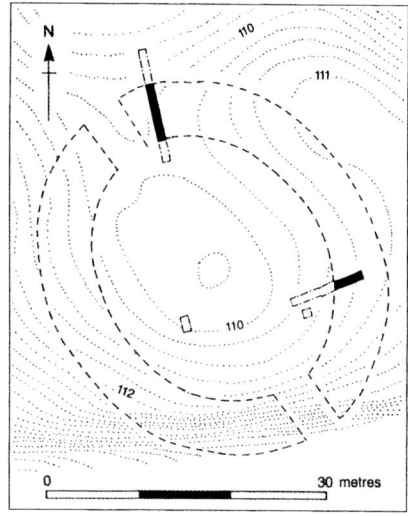

87 Plan of the Newstead amphitheatre. Chris Evans, after Clarke et al. 1996

Following the survey, Bradford University carried out limited excavation in order to confirm the identity of the site and this summary is compiled from their interim reports[29] (*87*). Two trenches in the centre of the arena showed that it had originally been 1m deeper, and the silting was devoid of modern finds. The arena surface was simply beaten earth, though the free-draining gravel subsoil would have prevented it from flooding. Trenches through the bank showed that the material quarried from the arena had been piled to form the banks around it. The bank survived to a height of 500mm and had been eroded by silting into the arena and subsequent ploughing. The surviving inner edge of the bank was almost vertical, and had been retained by a timber arena wall. A 200mm wide timber slot for this revetment was identified on the north side of the arena.

Despite the small scale of the work, it was possible to assess the probable size and shape of the amphitheatre. The arena appears to have been elliptical, measuring $c.37 \times 30$m (an area of $c.870$m^2), which is remarkably similar to the size of the arena of the excavated auxiliary amphitheatre at Künzing (36.5 x 30m).[30] The bank width was examined only on the north side, probably close to the north entrance, which is indicated by the slight appearances of a gap in the bank. On this downhill side, where most effort was required to create the bank, the surviving width was 7m, which has been estimated as sufficient for a seating capacity of 1000-2000.

Finds from the excavation were sparse and much poorer than the assemblages from other areas of the site. This is unsurprising, as amphitheatres are not the kind of location where rubbish would be deposited. It might be expected that the area would be clear of finds other than casually lost personal objects such as dress fittings and coins. This was borne out by the very few finds recovered.

THE SITES: THE NORTH AND WEST

Tomen y Mur, Merionethshire

The auxiliary fort of Tomen-y-Mur lies at the centre of an extraordinary and complex archaeological landscape, which has largely been revealed through aerial photography (*colour plate 19*). It includes the second largest concentration of Roman 'practice camps' in Wales (at least 14 in number),[31] the auxiliary fort and its civilian settlement, a partly excavated bath-house, a parade ground and the amphitheatre.[32] The fort was reused as the bailey of a substantial Norman motte, which is celebrated in Welsh myth.[33] The phasing and dating of the various Roman features is not well understood, as little excavation has taken place here.

The fort is sited in the heart of Snowdonia. It occupies a small promontory on the east side of the Ffestiniog Vale, about half way down the slopes of Myndd Maentwrog. A small stream runs down the south-eastern side of the defences, flowing eventually into Llyn Trawsfynydd, the lake which is overlooked by the fort. Excavation within the fort in 1962 provided a basic sequence.[34] The first fort was of Flavian date, probably *c*.AD 78 and was built of turf and timber. Its area was 1.75ha. Its smaller, stone-built successor (only 1.34ha in area) was early Hadrianic in date (*c*.AD 110-20) and seems to have been abandoned *c*.AD 140.[35] No garrison unit has been identified. To the north-east of the fort is an artificially levelled area, 123 x 98m, which is interpreted as a parade ground, and beyond this lies the amphitheatre.

Thomas Pennant wrote the first description of the amphitheatre in 1784:

> ... close by the roadside on the common at a small distance from the camp is an oval inclosure about 36 yards long and 27 wide in the middle surrounded by a high mound of earth, but without a foss. There were two entrances, one opposite the other.[36]

A fuller description was published by Allen in 1888, who described a circular enclosure, 81ft in diameter inside, encircled by a mound 21ft wide and 10-12ft high[37] (*12*). Allen was in no doubt as to its function, writing that:

> ... it was probably used for the gladiatorial exhibitions to which the Romans were so much addicted.

In 1938, Gresham recorded the damage that had befallen the monument.[38] The entrances recorded by Pennant were at the ends of the long axis of the structure (which runs north–south), and the line of a slate works tramway, which was driven through the earthwork, created two further gaps, on the east and west sides of the amphitheatre. In addition, Gresham pointed out that a sheep-dip, pens and a field wall had cut the south side of the structure, and that the banks had been much 'mutilated' over time. Though the tramway is long gone, the additional east and west gaps are visible in the encircling mounds, and the field wall over the south-west quarter of the monument is still there.

The amphitheatre consists of an oval, earthen bank enclosing an arena some 32 x 26m, with its long axis running from north to south (*88*). Gresham estimated the original bank height and width at 3.05m and 9.10m, and despite the growth of marsh grasses both in the arena and around the banks, this seems accurate. It is clear that the centre of the arena was hollowed out to form the surrounding banks – a signature of all earthwork amphitheatres in Britain. The original northern and southern entrances are much clearer than the additional gaps to east and west, and are some 2.5m broad. The banks are built of stony soil and the internal face is relatively vertical suggesting the presence of some form of arena wall. Wilding has suggested that this might have been created using vertical slate slabs of the kind used nearby in field boundary walls.[39] This is an attractive idea, but could not be proved without excavation. The arena size is somewhat smaller than that of the auxiliary amphitheatres at Künzing and Newstead,[40] but it feels very small when one stands in the middle. At the most there would perhaps be room for two pairs of gladiators to fight simultaneously. The arena walls would have had to have been low given the height and circumference of the banks, and

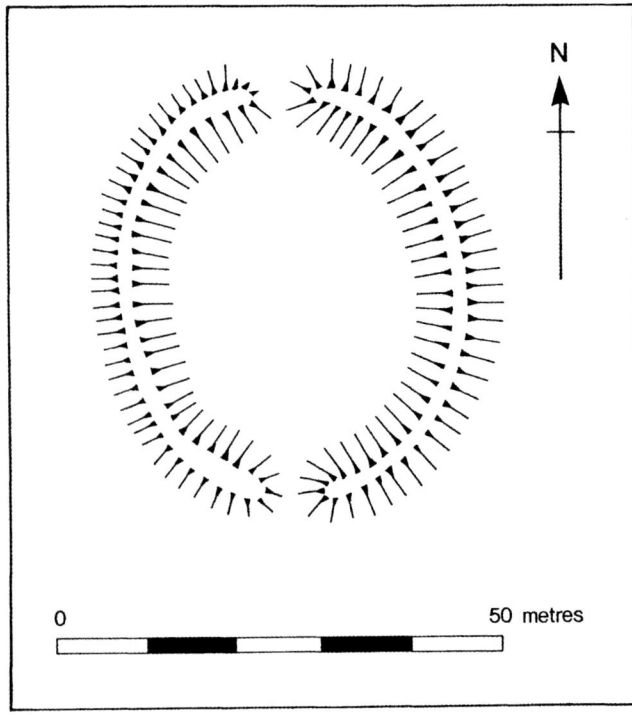

88 Plan of the earthwork amphitheatre at Tomen-y-Mur. *Chris Evans*

THE SITES: THE NORTH AND WEST

one cannot imagine that wild beast spectacles could have been safely performed unless the animals were tethered; perhaps the most one could visualise would be a tethered bear, baited by dogs.

AMPHITHEATRE-LIKE STRUCTURES

The Lunt, Baginton

Excavation at the 'Lunt', an auxiliary fort of the Neronian period near Baginton, Coventry, in 1970 showed that the fort plan was different to any found before (or since) in the Roman Empire. The eastern defences followed a sinuous, curving course in order to enclose a circular structure of a type unique within any Roman fort. This took the form of a circular arena surrounded by a wooden palisade (*89*). The arena measured 34m in diameter. Its floor was cut into the gravel subsoil to a depth of 800mm in order to provide a completely level surface on what was otherwise a sloping site. Around the perimeter of this flat area, against the face of the cut, a series of some 50 half-round posts 220mm in diameter had been placed. These supported a framework to which vertical planks were fixed to create a continuous smooth internal face (*colour plate 20*). The imprints of vertical timbers were clearly seen in the fill of a 300mm wide palisade trench around the circumference, the fill of which helped to retain the timber structures. On the western side of the circumference the palisade was broken for an entrance 3.04m wide, which was probably equipped with a single gate. From this entrance a timber-lined passage constructed like the ring, extended for a distance of at

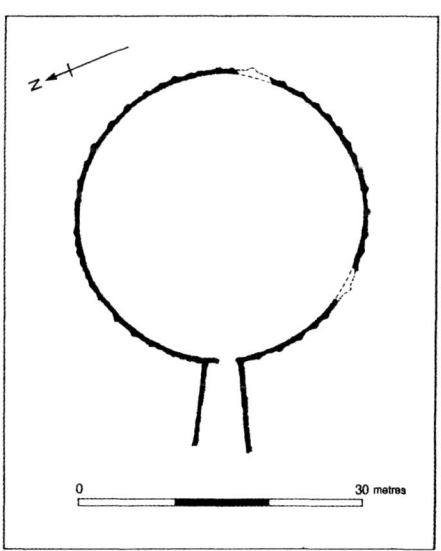

89 Plan of the Lunt *gyrus*. *Chris Evans, after Hobley 1973*

least 6m. In the north-east quarter of the structure, six clay pads may have been the foundation for a timber structure.[41]

Inveresk, Midlothian

The Roman fort of Inveresk, one of the most important in Scotland, is located 8km east of Edinburgh on the south side of the Firth of Forth at the head of two Roman roads, one coming from Newstead, the other from Elginhaugh. It is sited on the high eastern terrace of the River Esk, at a point where this forms a narrow spur overlooking the river and harbour. It was one of the forts built in the mid-second century, as part of the advance into Scotland under Antoninus Pius in AD 139-40, and the consolidation of Roman control over the Scottish lowlands following the construction of the Antonine Wall. It is the site in Roman Scotland for which most is known about activity outside the fort.

The supposed amphitheatre lies on the Park Lane site, situated some 500m east of the fort – an unusually long distance from the fort for an amphitheatre. The structure was hailed as an amphitheatre in 1997,[42] an interim report appeared in 2002 and a full report in 2007.[43] The structure consisted of a curved fence of timber uprights set in post-holes (*90*). A 25m length of this curved fence was revealed in the excavation. Adjacent to the fence was a rectangular arrangement of post-holes measuring about 8.5 x 7m overall. The grid of posts was slightly splayed, to respect the curve of the fence, and there is no doubt that they worked together as part of one structure. The interpretation of the structure as an amphitheatre postulates a fenced arena with a small segment of seating on its side, large enough for less than 200 spectators (*91*). The floor of the fenced area was of natural sand. No sign of the curving fence was found in a southern trench, so the whole structure would need

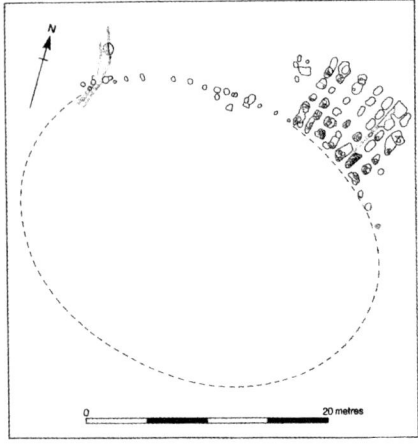

90 Plan of the Inveresk *gyrus* (?). *Chris Evans after Neighbour 2002*

THE SITES: THE NORTH AND WEST

91 Reconstruction of the seating area at Inveresk. *Drawn by Alan Braby, CFA Archaeology*

to be contained within the area north of this trench. This would allow space for an oval arena measuring some 31 x 22m. Though somewhat elongated, this dimension is not impossible or unprecedented. What is unprecedented for an amphitheatre is the tiny *cavea*. Alternative interpretations are that the Inveresk 'amphitheate' was either a *gyrus* or a *vivarium* for the capture of animals for use in amphitheatres, interpretations that have also been discussed for the structure at the Lunt fort.

Forden Gaer, Montgomeryshire (Lavobrinta)

This auxiliary fort of 3.25ha lies on the road connecting Caesws and Wroxeter. It was long-lived, being founded in the mid-Flavian period and undergoing a series of alterations and refurbishments, the last of which occurred in the mid-fourth century.[44] The feature in question lies some 110m north of the north-west corner the fort. A thorough survey of the area of the site by Peter Crew[45] revealed a large concentration of features, most of which seem to be Roman, and which echoes the group of features around the Tomen-y-Mur fort. The feature comprises part of a shallow open bowl of figure-of-eight shape measuring 76 x 50m within which water stands for long periods in winter. The flat base of the circular areas is very hard compacted gravel in distinct contrast to the ground around. The clear evidence of surrounding ditches and the long sinuous approach suggest that it is more than a mere pond. Its setting in an apparently natural bowl and the hard footing of the circles suggested to Crew and others some form of exercise area, possibly a *gyrus* like that at the Lunt.

157

THE ROMAN AMPHITHEATRE IN BRITAIN

Chesters, Northumberland (Cilurnum)

Chesters is one of the forts on Hadrian's Wall and stands at the crossing point of the wall and the North Tyne River.[46] Geophysical survey in 2003 revealed, 40m from the south-east corner of the fort, within the extra-mural area, a circular structure some 50m in diameter.[47] The fact that Chesters is known to have been a cavalry fort strengthens the interpretation of this feature as a *gyrus*.

REJECTED SITES

As the following three sites appear in the literature of amphitheatre studies,[48] it is worth describing them and explaining why their identification has now to be rejected. At two of the three, Catterick and Walton, the 'amphitheatres' are now interpreted as Neolithic henge monuments. It is interesting to note that the auxiliary fort at Newton Kyme, North Yorkshire (SE 457 454) is situated immediately to the north-west of a henge monument of some 215m in diameter. The ribbon development *vicus*, or civilian settlement, associated with the fort extends from the south gate of the fort and passes the henge to the west, and Paul Bidwell has suggested that the henge might have been used as, or converted into, an amphitheatre.[49] This raises the interesting idea that henges may in some cases have been used as impromptu arenas. This may have been the case at Catterick, though the relationship of the monument with a main Roman road perhaps makes this unlikely. As we have seen, at least one amphitheatre, Maumbury Rings, Dorchester, was created by altering an existing henge monument. It would be an interesting study to examine the incidence of Roman settlements placed next to henge monuments.

Aldborough, North Yorkshire (Isurium Brigantium)

Aldborough, the *civitas* capital of the Brigantes, was a moderately sized walled town. Surprisingly little research has taken place on the site and the best understood part of the Roman town is its defences.[50] Recently the extramural area has been surveyed.[51] A plan of an amphitheatre, without further comment, appears in R.G. Collingwood's *The Archaeology of Roman Britain*, published in 1930.[52] The site thought to be an amphitheatre was the earthwork known as Studforth Hill, which lies immediately south-east of the walled area[53] and the name of which has been fancifully derived from the word 'stadium'.[54] Collingwood's is the only reference to an amphitheatre here, later works on the town have not mentioned it,[55] and it is not now thought to be the correct

THE SITES: THE NORTH AND WEST

interpretation.[56] A letter to the *Gentleman's Magazine* of 1811,[57] refers to:

> ... a curious site of ground, which evidently marked out the site of an amphitheatre, for the celebration of the *ludi Romani* has been only very lately demolished.

Where this was, and whether it really was an amphitheatre, of course, can no longer be determined.

Catterick, North Yorkshire (Cataractonium)

Excavations during 1995 at the racecourse at Catterick in North Yorkshire were at first hailed as having revealed an unknown amphitheatre – indeed the predecessor of the racecourse itself as a place of entertainment.[58] The site in question lay some 700m to the south of the Roman small town and limited evidence for Roman period occupation was identified there. The initial aim of the excavation was to examine a small Iron Age settlement. Mechanical sectioning revealed that adjacent to the settlement there was a substantial bank, which incorporated the remains of a large cairn. This was initially thought to be the seating bank of an amphitheatre.

Subsequent analysis of aerial photography has demonstrated that this was the wrong conclusion.[59] Though the boundary ditches of the Iron Age settlement (which was dated by pottery from inside one of the round houses) formed a basically rectangular enclosure, its western boundary was curved, mirroring the line both of the early cairn and the banked feature. This suggests that the cairn and bank were earlier than the settlement, and that the settlement took its shape from the existing bank. The cairn, which produced early Bronze Age pottery, was a round platform of densely packed river cobbles, and the bank was constructed of gravel and cobbles. The bank had become so flattened and spread over time that it had gone unnoticed by the many antiquarians and archaeologists who had worked in this area over three centuries, though sources suggest that the bank was visible as a broken series of tumuli in around 1800. Crucially the excavation discovered that both the cairn and the primary deposits of the banked feature sealed the same old soil level, suggesting that they were close together in date.

The diameter of the monument is hard to judge accurately, but the internal diameter lies in the range 90-100m, the external at 135-45m. The bank would have been 35-45m wide. No British amphitheatre reached this size and the settlement at Catterick was not large or important enough to justify one of the largest amphitheatres in the Roman Empire! The site is, furthermore, too distant from the town itself. Perhaps the most important factor is that Roman Dere Street, the major road to the north, and the *raison d'être* for the siting of

Catterick, which lies on the crossing of the road over the River Swale, appears to cut across the feature, suggesting that they could never have been contemporary. The conclusion from all this is that the feature was actually a prehistoric henge monument, an interpretation which was confirmed by a thorough examination of historic aerial photography. The examination also enabled the complete reconstruction of the monument, one third of which had been destroyed by quarrying by the late 1980s.

Walton, Radnorshire

Three Roman marching camps have been identified through aerial photography at Walton.[60] The marching camps lie side-by-side and appear to be contemporary with each other. They may also be contemporary with the marching camp at nearby Hindwell Farm, and would seem to indicate an element of an early military push into Wales during the conquest phases of AD 48-78.[61] A feature close to the marching camps is identified in the regional Sites and Monuments Record as a possible *gyrus*, like that at the Lunt, or an amphitheatre.[62] The feature seems to consist of a ring-ditch with a single entrance facing south-east. This raises two problems immediately, as an amphitheatre is likely to be embanked with a hollowed out arena in the centre and would not appear as a ring ditch, furthermore such a building would tend to have more than one entrance. The fact that marching camps are by nature short-lived and temporary structures would make it most unlikely that a *gyrus* or amphitheatre would be provided, and there is no other Roman settlement in the area with which it could be associated. The key is that the aerial photograph seems to show that the circular feature is cut by one of the Roman ditches. The landscape around Walton is replete with prehistoric archaeology including two possible cursus monuments, standing stones and pit alignments. This last feature probably associates the monument with a far earlier ritual landscape. The ring-ditch and single entrance instantly recalls Neolithic henge monuments, and it seems likely that this is the correct identification for the Walton feature.[63]

8

THE ARENA SPECTACLE

Saying anything of the games here practised, [I] suppose them much the same in all points with those used at Rome, and other places, and with suitable grandeur and magnificence; whether in relation to hunting or fighting of wild beasts, of the same or different kinds, with one another, or with men; of the gladiators, wrestlings, of the pageants …[1]

In 1851 during excavations in Bath Lane, Leicester 'for public purposes'[2] (actually for the installation of mains drainage), a red pot sherd was found upon which an inscription had been scratched (*colour plate 21*). It read:

VERECVNDA LVDIA : LVCIVS GLADIATOR

or 'Verecunda the actress, Lucius the gladiator'. This is one of the most evocative personal objects from Roman Britain and obviously 'records a romantic contract between these two forgotten professionals'.[3] It is also the only direct evidence for the presence of a named gladiator ever found in Britain. The inscription was scratched on a sherd after the bowl from which it came was broken, and it was pierced, possibly to hang around the neck as a love token.[4] For many years this was thought to be a sherd of samian ware, common in Britain.[5] It is not. In 1971 the late Brian Hartley recognised the sherd as a type of red ware not generally found outside Italy.[6] The circumstances and date of the discovery of the piece suggest that the sherd was an ancient import, rather than something brought in as an eighteenth- or nineteenth-century travel souvenir. In other words Verecunda and/or Lucius had come to *Ratae Corieltavorum* (Leicester) from Italy in Roman times and lost this object then. The possibilities are as limitless as the mind of a romantic novelist could invent: were they visiting performers,[7] perhaps part of a professional entertainment troupe? If so we have evidence for an Italian professional gladiator in Britain. Were they ever *both* in Britain? Perhaps Lucius had been killed in combat in Italy and Verecunda had continued to carry the sherd in his memory? If so we lose our only named gladiator from the province. It is all very tantalising.

Despite the paucity of direct evidence from Britain for the individual participants in arena spectacles, the very existence of amphitheatres in Britain shows that such spectacles took place (though their frequency can be debated). In this chapter we will look at evidence from a variety of sources in an attempt to identify the nature of the spectacles that took place in the British arenas, the response of the spectators and what the amphitheatre may have meant to the different communities in Britain. There is a certain amount of evidence for *venationes* and for gladiatorial *munera* derived from a number of sources, all of which reflect an enthusiasm for the arena. These we will examine first, afterwards moving on to look at the limited evidence for what went on around the amphitheatres. We will then examine evidence for cult in the British amphitheatres.

VENATIONES

Much of the British evidence relates to *venationes*. These might have involved beasts paired in different ways, hunts of beasts by men, or the spectacle of the condemned being thrown to animals in the form of execution known as *damnatio ad bestias*. Several of the British buildings include *carceres*, or beast pens. These are particularly apparent on the arena ends of the entrance passages on the long axes of the amphitheatres of London, Cirencester and Chester. In all of these, two entrances were provided, one from the entrance passage and one from the arena. This would allow animals to be put into the pens, having either been driven, led or carried in transport crates, and when the time came, to be released into the arena by way of the second door. It is probable that they would need to be encouraged into the arena, perhaps by slaves with lit torches entering the pens from the entrance passage side. At Cirencester the arena entrance was a metal grille, at London it was a sliding door.

In 2005, excavations in the centre of the arena at Chester revealed a large stone block with a lead plug in its top surface, which secured into position an iron staple or ring. There is little doubt that this was a tethering block, used to secure animals in the centre of the arena (*81*). In the iconography of the arena, I am aware of only one picture showing a similar feature and that is the gladiatorial frieze of the mosaic from the villa of Bignor in Sussex. Here, two gladiators are

THE ARENA SPECTACLE

92 Scene of bull and bear from the paintings on the arena wall of the Pompeii amphitheatre

seen fighting across such a block (*colour plate 22*). This has led to the conclusion that unwilling apprentices were tied to the stone.[8] The most important aspect of this depiction is probably that nothing is, in fact, secured to the stone. It is a piece of arena furniture that is present, but not explained. It might even be intended to be a shorthand reference, within a mosaic depicting gladiators, to animal spectacles. The block would have ensured that anything chained to it would remain in the centre of the arena and would therefore remain visible to all spectators. This would counter the natural tendency of a threatened animal to seek greater shelter and security by going to bay against the arena wall, where a substantial portion of the audience would not see what was going on.[9] The tethering block might be used in the context of an animal pairing which appears both in the painting on the arena wall in Pompeii (*92*) and on the mosaic from Zliten in North Africa, showing a bull and a bear chained together.[10] Perhaps two victims were chained to the block? Perhaps the chain was passed through the ring on the block and was free to be pulled either way? The provision for an upright timber post in the centre of the arena of the Verulamium theatre-amphitheatre in its first phase may have served a similar function to the Chester block.

There is little direct evidence for *venationes*. The only substantial evidence is from London, where the distal humerus of a brown bear was found behind the arena wall, and the skull of a large bovoid, possibly a bull, in one of the perimeter drains.[11]

Across the Roman Empire, arena spectacles were commemorated in the decorations of private villa dwellings. In Britain this is rare, and there are only two mosaics that can be assumed to feature arena *venationes*, though there are others where hunts in the wild are probably shown. The first of the two is at Rudston in North Yorkshire (*colour plate 23*).[12] The mosaics from Rudston also include one depicting a charioteer, and the owner was probably a fan of all types of spectator sport and spectacle. The lively, if crudely executed, Venus

93 Compartment from the Rudston Venus mosaic depicting the bull 'TAVRVS OMICIDA', and showing the crescent-headed staff of the *Telegenii*. D.S. Neal

pavement features a figure of Venus in a central circle; there are quarter-circle compartments in each corner containing figures of birds. Four semicircular compartments occupy the sides of the pavement and there are four concave-sided spaces between the circular panels. Each of the semicircular panels contains an animal – a lion, a stag, a leopard and a bull. In the concave-sided spaces are human figures, clearly meant to represent hunters. One of these is missing. One hunter holds a spear, another is empty-handed, and a third is caught in the act of casting a large net. The main interest of the pavement is in the animal panels. The stag runs through a wooded landscape and a circular object, possibly a shield discarded by a hunter, accompanies the leopard. The lion has been pierced through the body by a spear and the wound drips blood. It is accompanied by an inscription, long restored as (LEO) F(R)AMMEFER – the spear-bearing lion, though it has been convincingly argued recently that we should interpret it as (LEO) F(L)AMMEFER – the fiery lion.[13] The bull is also named TAURUS OMICIDA – the man-killing (homicidal) bull. The bull's compartment also contains a strange item resembling a curious pole-arm – a staff with a crescent-shaped object at the end (*93*). It is possible that the empty-handed hunter is meant to have thrown this. This item, and the names given to the animals reveal this mosaic as relating to arena *venationes* rather than generally to hunting. Though the naming of animals on this mosaic is unique in Britain, it is a common practice in the arena hunt mosaics of North Africa[14] and occurs also in frescoes in the Hunting Baths of Lepcis Magna (Tunisia).[15] The name OMICIDA is applied to a bear on a mosaic from Thuburbo Majus (Tunisia).[16] These names are presumably stage names used in the arena. The crescent-on-a-stick is the most persuasive evidence for North African influence at Rudston. Like the millet stalks at Brading (below), it is the emblem of a well-attested, much-travelled and professional troupe of beast hunters (*venatores*) known as the *Telegenii*. They are depicted, with their emblem of a crescent-headed staff, on the famous Magerius mosaic from Smirat (Tunisia),[17] where a lengthy text records the payments made to the *Telegenii* in a form of contract, and where the four leopards shown being killed are also named. A mosaic from El Djem (Tunisia) shows members of five of these troupes drinking at a semicircular table around five sleeping bulls. The representative of the *Telegenii* is again depicted with the crescent-headed staff.

The Rudston mosaic is not the only one in Britain to show a *venatio*, or to be influenced by North African iconographic styles. The other instance is at Brading on the Isle of Wight (*colour plate 24*). The central panel features a bust of Bacchus and the only corner panel to survive also depicts a Bacchic bust.[18] A partial rectangular panel shows what appears to be a fox running past a tree towards a small domed structure, a hut or hillock. The animal may be intended as a dog and would then be balanced by a quarry animal in the other corner. The only complete rectangular panel has excited a great deal of comment since its discovery in the nineteenth century.[19] A small gabled building approached by a ladder or stair stands on a knoll and may be a small temple. On one side is a figure with a human body and a cock's head wearing a striped tunic, and on the other side is a pair of griffins accompanied by an odd branch-like object. For many years the cock-headed figure has been interpreted as a Gnostic deity, Abraxus,[20] but recent studies have reinterpreted the mosaic as showing arena scenes.[21] It seems that the mosaic is based upon themes common in the hunting mosaics of the Mediterranean, particularly in North Africa. The domed structure and the building with steps may represent architectural elements in a landscape. The tunic worn by the cock-headed man is paralleled in hunting mosaics across the Empire, and it has been suggested that the cock head may be a pun on the name of a *venator*.[22] The griffins are not out of place in hunting scenes, in that they appear in the great hunt mosaic at Piazza Armerina (Sicily)[23] and on the silver hunting casket from the Walbrook Mithraeum (London),[24] both of which depict the hunting, capture and transport of animals in the wild for the arena. In Britain the only other griffin not in an Orpheus mosaic is on a hunting mosaic from Dewlish in Dorset,[25] though there is no evidence that either this or other British hunting mosaics are amphitheatre related. The Dewlish pavement features a leopard leaping onto the back of a Dorcas gazelle – a distinctive North African species. The branch-like motifs accompanying the Brading griffins have been interpreted by Pat Witts as millet stalks. These were widely used in the context of hunting and amphitheatre mosaics in North Africa, in particular they are the emblem of several of the professional guilds of wild beast hunters who operated in North Africa.[26] Millet stalks are used as symbols on mosaics such as the already-mentioned Magerius mosaic from Tunisia.

The named animals and the emblem of the *Telegenii* at Rudston, the millet stalks and griffins at Brading, and the gazelle at Dewlish are all evidence of North African influence on the style and content of these mosaics, however there is no reason to suppose the mosaics consciously depict North Africa. These influences have been seen as part of an empire-wide repertory and would have come to Britain indirectly to be used by mosaicists who were unaware of the original sources, and might misinterpret their source material.[27] The crescent-headed stick at Rudston is an excellent example; it must have been derived from a pictorial source, but its meaning had been lost. It seems to have been interpreted as a pole-arm, dropped or thrown by one of the hunters. There is, therefore, no reason to think that the mosaics at Rudston and Brading do not show enthusiasm for arena *venationes* held in Britain, merely because the idiom of the depictions ultimately derives from Africa. The fact that they took place is attested in the architecture of the amphitheatres.

GLADIATORIAL *MUNERA*

We have seen how uncertain the interpretation of the Leicester graffito of the gladiator Lucius is as evidence for gladiators in Britain. It is just possible that another named gladiator, Victor, might be attested by the inscription on a bone slip found in a Roman cemetery at York in 1873, on the breast of an inhumed individual. It reads DOMINE VICTOR VINCAS FELIX – 'Lord Victor may you have a lucky win' – though this is a formula used for both gladiators and charioteers.[28] Also from York a stone capital, probably from a tomb, depicts a crudely carved *retiarius*.[29]

From the amphitheatres themselves, the best evidence comes from the legionary sites. At Chester (*94*) a relief depicting a gladiator of the class known as a *retiarius* was discovered in 1738 by workmen digging in the foundations of a house in Fleshmongers Lane, within the walls of the legionary fortress and close to its east gate. By 1742 it was owned by the collector Dr Richard Mead and in 1836 it was in the collection of the Saffron Walden Museum, where (despite the fact that it had become misidentified as a marble piece from Pompeii) it was re-identified as the Chester find by Ralph Jackson in 1983.[30] The stone is north Welsh slate, and the scene is contained in a border on all three sides but the left, where it has been broken. It shows a *retiarius* facing to the left, holding his two main weapons, a trident (*tridens*) in his right hand and a net (*rete*) in

THE ARENA SPECTACLE

94 Relief of left-handed retiarius *from Chester. Saffron Walden Museum*

the left. He wears a belted loincloth (*subligaculum*), his right arm is protected by a padded sleeve (*manica*) secured by leather straps and on the right shoulder he carries a metal shoulder guard protecting the neck and face (*galerus*). His opponent has been broken from the panel, but a discarded curved rectangular shield and a dropped *gladius* suggests that he was a *secutor* and that the relief depicts the moment of his surrender, perhaps kneeling in submission. The relief may be part of a frieze. It has been suggested that it might have been from a tomb, perhaps of the *editor* of *munera* in Chester. This is unlikely, as the *canabae legionis*, or civilian settlement, spread over 200m beyond the east gate, and the nearest burials known on this side of the fortress are 2km away at Boughton. The find spot is very close to the site of the amphitheatre, and it is most likely that this frieze originally adorned the building. The Chester *retiarius* is unique in one crucial respect – unlike all other representations of the *retiarius*, he holds the trident in the right hand and the net in the left. More to the point, the *manica* and *galerus* are worn on the right arm rather than the left as is the case in every other *retiarius* portrayal in sculpture, painting, mosaic and on small objects throughout the Empire. Juvenal, in his *Satires* is clear on the technique of these gladiators when he says:

> ... see how ... with poised *right* hand he has cast the trailing net in vain ...[31]

Though ineptitude or artistic licence have been suggested to explain the Chester portrayal,[32] a more intriguing possibility is that the panel depicts a specific gladiator, well known to the Chester audience, who happens to have been left-handed.

At the other legionary amphitheatre, Caerleon, gladiatorial combat is reflected in two poorly executed carvings on building stones. One has the central motif of

95 Graffito from Caerleon showing a trident between two shoulder guards of *retiarii* (*galerus*), and palm fronds denoting victory. *National Museum of Wales*

a trident flanked by two oddly shaped objects, interpreted as the shoulder guards (*galerus*) worn by *retiarii* (*95*). There are also two crude palm fronds, the symbol of victory. The second piece has a central rosette flanked by another *galerus* and a ladder-like object, which may represent the laminated metal arm-guard worn on the sword arm of the *secutor*, the traditional adversary of the *retiarius*.[33]

Only one item of probable gladiatorial equipment has been found in Britain. This is the Hawkedon helmet (*96*), found in Essex and interpreted as a piece of loot taken from Colchester during the Boudiccan revolt. As the centre of the Imperial cult, this was a likely place to have seen *munera* during the early years of occupation. There is no amphitheatre at Colchester, so such events would have taken place in other venues. The object is a bronze helmet with a wide neck-guard and bronze binding. Rivet holes over the eyebrows suggest a lifting, hinged visor. The helmet was tinned, so that it would shine like silver, but the most remarkable fact is that it was more than twice the weight of a contemporary legionary helmet.[34]

Across the Empire it is common to find sculpture and mosaic representations of named gladiators, where memorable *munera* are commemorated. Examples are numerous, including a third-century mosaic from Kos,[35] a mosaic in the House of the Gladiators at Kourion, Cyprus,[36] the famous fourth-century gladiator mosaic at the Villa Borghese in Rome[37] and the extraordinary mosaic depicting the fight between Astanax and Kalendio, now in the Madrid museum.[38] In Britain there is only one such example, the famous Colchester vase (*97*).[39] This

THE ARENA SPECTACLE

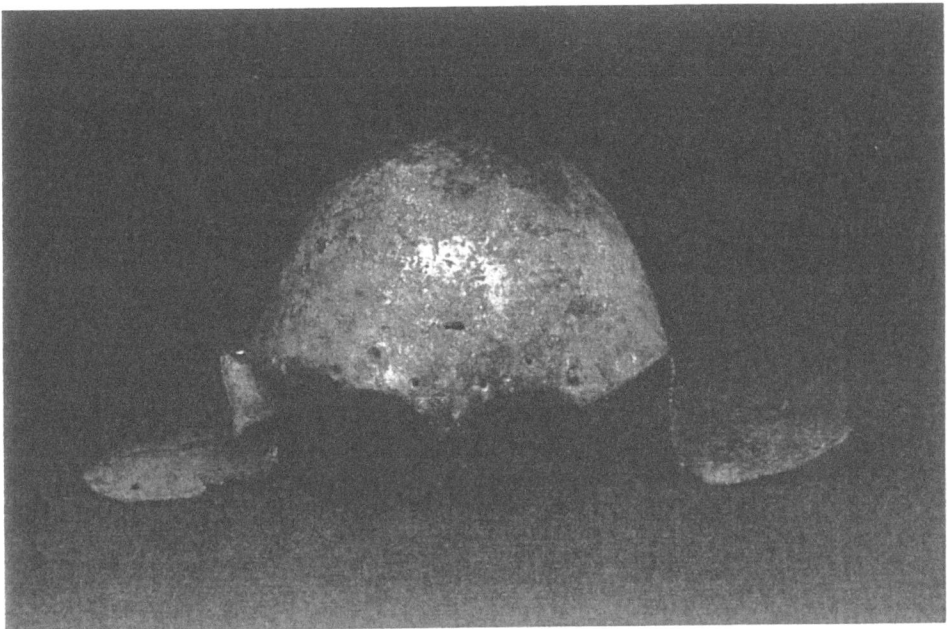

96 Gladiator's helmet from Hawkedon, Essex. *Trustees of the British Museum*

is a colour-coated vessel in red fabric, with gladiatorial decoration in barbotine, and is accepted as a product of the Colchester kilns. It was found in a grave at West Lodge in 1848. It shows both principal aspects of arena events. On one side are two *venatores*, one wielding a whip over the head of an animal, probably intended to represent a bear. The names SECVNDVS and MARIO are inscribed above the head of the man with the whip. On the other side is a famous scene of a *retiarius*, his trident dropped to the ground and his index finger raised in the gesture of surrender before the attack of a *secutor*, who is advancing, shield forward and sword upraised. Interestingly, the *secutor* is shown as a left-handed swordsman. The gladiators are identified in inscriptions which, like those over the *venatores*, were cut onto the vessel after firing:

MEMNON SAC VIIII VALENTINV LEGIONIS XXX

This seems to mean 'Memnon, the *secutor*, nine victories; Valentinus of the thirtieth legion'. The inscription over the figure of Memnon is typical of inscriptions over figures of gladiators seen, for example, in graffiti from Pompeii.[40] The identification of Valentinus with the thirtieth Legion (Leg XXX *Ulpia Victrix*) is more unusual, not least because this legion was stationed far from Britain at Xanten in the province of Lower Germany. It has been suggested that the

97 The Colchester vase.
Colchester Museums

gladiators were part of a troupe attached to the legion, either far famed in the western provinces,[41] or a troupe which went 'on tour'. This is the only certain example of such a military 'stable' to be found,[42] and other references to gladiators and spectacles in a military context are literary; thus Suetonius describes Tiberius attending garrison games at Circeii, during which he threw javelins from the president's box at a wild boar in the arena,[43] and Tacitus' account of the accession of Tiberius in AD 14 mentions that Q Junius Blaesus, commanding Legions VIII, IX and XV in Pannonia, had gladiators as slaves in his household.[44] The fact that the inscription was cut after the vase was fired might lead to the suspicion that the vessel was in origin a generic piece, with the names of particular arena performers scratched on later, perhaps after the owner had witnessed a combat the result of which neatly matched the subject shown. The fact that the *secutor* is left-handed, however, suggests that a left-handed *secutor* named Memnon existed and was deliberately depicted with an actual opponent. In this case the post-firing inscription would have been added as part of the manufacturing process.

Gladiators are also depicted in wall paintings and on mosaics, though infrequently. Again at Colchester, excavations during the long hot summer of 1976 in the remains of a late first-century timber-framed building outside the Balkerne Gate, revealed a collapsed panel of painted wall plaster including the only painted arena scenes yet found in Britain. The decorative scheme includes rectangular panels containing pairs of duelling gladiators on a green background. The most complete of these (*colour plate 25*) is the lower right portion of a panel in which a defeated gladiator shown in three-quarter view moves to the right, raising his hand to petition for mercy. He has dropped his semi-cylindrical shield, but still holds his blood-dripping sword. He wears an arm-guard (*manica*), greaves and a belted loincloth (*subligaculum*), while his heavy, crested, bronze helmet marks him out as the class of heavily armed gladiator known as a *hoplomachus*. Parts of at least one other gladiator have survived – the back of the head, shoulder and torso of a gladiator with sword and shield raised ready for an attack. He too faces right, so could not be the opponent of the defeated gladiator. This indicates that there were at least two pairs on separate panels. A shield, also held in readiness, and moving right suggests a third figure. The standard of workmanship is very high, and the artist was probably continental, using a figure type – the pleading gladiator – from an established repertoire of conventional figure types.[45] He appears, for example, on stucco at Pompeii, on the mosaic from Zliten (Libya), on a terracotta relief in Brussels, and is a standard figure type used on Central Gaulish samian ware.[46] The archaeological context of the painting shows that it was executed in the last quarter of the first century. This is contemporary with the construction of the earliest British amphitheatres, and the householder who showed his interest in the arena by commissioning this painting may have become familiar with such entertainments elsewhere. Possibly he was a trader or a legionary veteran. We might certainly speculate that he was someone who would welcome the building of the new amphitheatres in the province, which would enable him to pursue his interest.

Only three known mosaics from Roman Britain feature scenes of gladiatorial combat, all of which have been found in rural villas in the south-east of England, at Eccles (Kent), Bignor (West Sussex) and Brading (Isle of Wight). At Eccles (*98*) the central square panel of a mosaic has been painstakingly reconstructed from many fragments.[47] Though the surviving part of the panel is small, it seems to depict a pair of gladiators. Among the diagnostic fragments are their legs, and a fragment showing a wrist and hand bound with leather thronging and a red sword pommel. The initial dating for this mosaic was *c*.AD 65, but subsequent work has suggested a date closer to AD 120.[48] Like the Colchester wall painting, the early date would have indicated that the pavement was commissioned by someone who had witnessed games abroad; the later date makes it possible that he had attended the amphitheatre in Britain as this is contemporary with, or slightly later than, the main period of amphitheatre building in Britain.

98 Gladiator mosaic from Eccles, Kent. *D.S. Neal*

At the palatial fourth-century villa of Bignor, winged cupids take the role of gladiators on a frieze (*colour plates 22, 26*) forming a division between a main pavement showing Bacchic scenes and an apse containing a female bust. This is usually interpreted as representing Venus,[49] though L. Foucher[50] has suggested that the head is that of Diana-Nemesis. There are four distinct groups of figures in the Bignor frieze. Reading from right to left, the first shows a classic pairing of *secutor* and *retiarius* watched by the *summa rudis* or umpire who carries a wand (*rudus*). The gladiators fight across a stone block into which an iron ring is fastened, and which we have already discussed. In the second scene the *secutor* has disarmed a *retiarius*, but the *summa rudis* intervenes in the fight, brandishing his wand. Next, the *secutor*, bareheaded and leaning on his shield, receives his helmet from an attendant or slave as the *summa rudis* leads an apparently unwilling *retiarius* into the fray. Finally, the *retiarius* lies downed and helpless as the *secutor* prepares to deliver the *coup de grâce*. In the background of this scene the stone and ring is repeated. Costume and equipment are well depicted. The *summa rudis* wears a belted tunic, the gladiators wear loincloths and broad belts. The *retiarius* wears a padded left arm-guard and carries a net and trident. The *secutor* has padded or armoured right arm and left leg and is equipped with a heavy helmet and a large curved rectangular shield. The frieze format of the Bignor mosaic recalls a frieze from Zliten (Libya), which shows a range of arena scenes including *damnatio ad bestias*, wild beast hunt, musicians and gladiatorial combat, including the intervention of a *summa rudis*.[51] The combat of *secutor* and *retiarius* in the presence of a referee is a popular theme in Roman arena art, appearing (for example) on mosaics now in museums at Verona (Italy) and Madrid (Spain) and at the villa of Nennig (Germany), as well as on a spectacular painted glass jug from Ismant el-Kharab (Egypt)[52] and an equally spectacular painted glass bowl from Vindolanda on Hadrian's Wall (*colour plate 28*). It is noticeable that many of the gladiatorial representations in Britain, as elsewhere, portray the moment of truth – the point at which a gladiator's life hangs in the balance. This was a popular and potent image.[53]

The gladiators at Brading (*colour plate 24*) are part of the complex pavement that includes the scenes identified as *venationes*. Indeed it is the presence of gladiators on this pavement that identifies it as an artefact of the arena. The gladiator scene is a single panel showing the classic pairing of a *retiarius* dressed in a tunic and armed with a dagger[54] and a trident, and a heavily armed opponent, presumably a *secutor*, whose armoured head and shoulder only survive.

PUBLIC ATTITUDES

A great many small objects from Britain, as elsewhere, depict arena scenes. These were purchased by people with an interest in the arena, or in its symbolism, and the spread and variety of these objects is a clear indication of how ubiquitous such interests were. Gladiators are often represented and these clearly refer to *munera*. When animals are shown, however, there is doubt as to whether these are meant to depict nature, hunting in the wild, or arena *venationes*.

Arena scenes often appear on pottery and ceramic objects. The familiar and common red gloss samian ware often shows arena scenes. In London, a statistically significant proportion of samian ware from the amphitheatre site was decorated with scenes appropriate to the arena. Though statistical analysis has not been

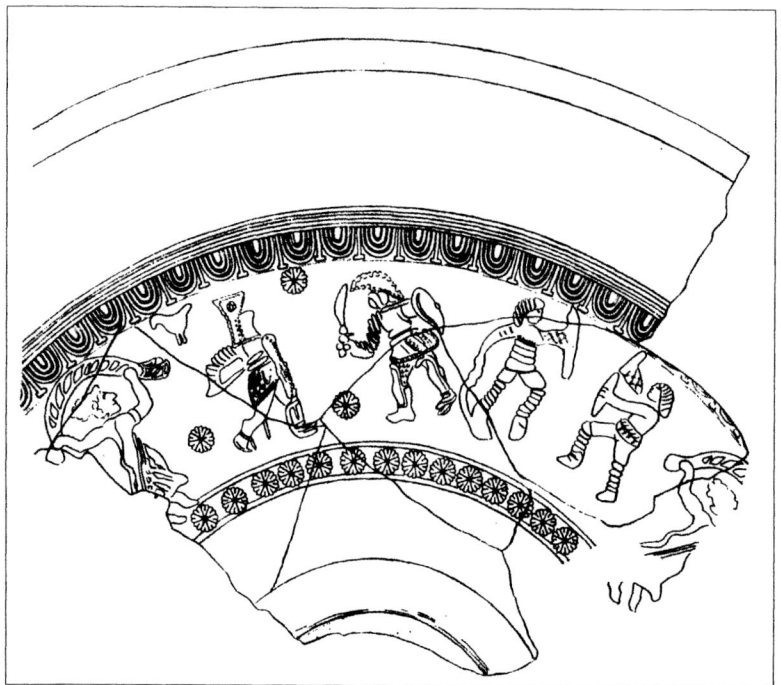

99 Mould design for imitation samian pottery from Colchester depicting gladiatorial combat. *Hull 1963*

performed on the samian ware from Chester, this may also be true here, and these vessels were probably purchased as souvenirs. At Chester, archaeological deposits around the outside of the amphitheatre produced a miniature samian bowl decorated with gladiators (*colour plate 27*). In London, decoration included representations of bullfights, figures of *damnati ad bestias*, and a panel showing Bacchus, who is associated with the games in other contexts, and Silenus. At Chester, there are a large number of vessels showing lions, and a smaller number portraying gladiators. These vessels are, of course, Gallic imports, but the ubiquity of this kind of decoration must indicate that these images were popular. In Britain, the Colchester potters who made imitation samian ware used a variety of figure types in moulds used to create figured bowls. Most of the moulds found in excavation included one or more of the gladiator pairs (*99*) and/or a bound captive attacked by beasts (*100*),[55] and a second captive figure and a *venator* with a spear also appears in the repertoire. A further object from the kilns was a mould for the manufacture of a gladiator figure in relief.[56] Also from Colchester, a ceramic plaque, now lost, but found in the nineteenth century at Union House, shows a *secutor* apparently fleeing, together with another gladiator, from a ferocious looking dolphin (*101*). This may be an oblique reference to the

THE ARENA SPECTACLE

100 Mould design for imitation samian pottery from Colchester depicting prisoners condemned to the beasts (*damnati ad bestias*). Hull 1963

retiarius, whose net and trident were derived from the kit of a Mediterranean fisherman.[57]

As well as pottery, glasswares were frequently decorated with arena scenes. Some of these were cups blown into a mould, producing the same design. These have been found showing circus scenes as well as gladiators. One type of ovoid vessel shows both an upper register of charioteers, and a lower showing the gladiators Petraites and Hermes.[58] The cylindrical mould-blown cups have a single register of gladiators, the most common design showing named gladiators in various poses, surrendering with finger raised, downed, fighting and holding a victory palm branch (*102*). The find spots of these cups are spread all over Britain, from Devon to Kent and from London and Colchester to Leicester and Wroxeter. A gladiator is engraved on a fragmentary glass vessel from Whitehill Farm, Northamptonshire (*103*), and from Vindolanda, near Hadrian's Wall, come fragments of a truly exceptional glass vessel with painted scenes of a *summa rudis* refereeing a combat between a *secutor* and a *retiarius* (*colour plate 28*). None of these objects would have been made in Britain, but all were acquired because of an enthusiasm for the subject matter.

A popular expression of this enthusiasm throughout the Roman Empire (for example at Budapest (*Aquincum*), Hungary[59], Cologne, Germany,[60] and Avenches (*Aventicum*), Switzerland[61]Church) was the carrying of clasp knives decorated

THE ROMAN AMPHITHEATRE IN BRITAIN

101 Ceramic plaque from Colchester depicting a *secutor* pursued by a dolphin, possibly intended to represent a *retiarius*. Hull 1958

102 Design from a series of mould-blown glass vessels. *Drawn by P. Compton*

with figures of gladiators, and such knives have been found in many provinces. The iron blades pivoted and folded into the handles exactly like a modern folding penknife, and the handles are often small three-dimensional figures of gladiators. Several handles have been found in Britain, made in copper alloy, ivory and bone. It is likely that price varied according to quality and it is probable that similar, cheaper items were also made in wood. A beautifully modelled and complete knife was found during excavations at Piddington (Northamptonshire) in 2000, in an archaeological deposit dated to AD 200-250.[62] Despite being only 70mm long, it is one of the most detailed and vibrant gladiator images from Britain (*104*). The *secutor* stands in the *en-garde* position, sword levelled at waist-height, and a curved rectangular shield held guarding his left side. His helmet is closed, with only two small eye-holes, a dorsal crest and an all-round flanged neck-guard. The slight turn of the head gives an impression of watchfulness, while the stance, both legs flexed, the forward left leg slightly advanced, shows a readiness which any modern fencer would immediately recognise. Apart from the helmet he wears a loincloth (*subligaculum*) with a broad belt (*balteus*) and quilted padding

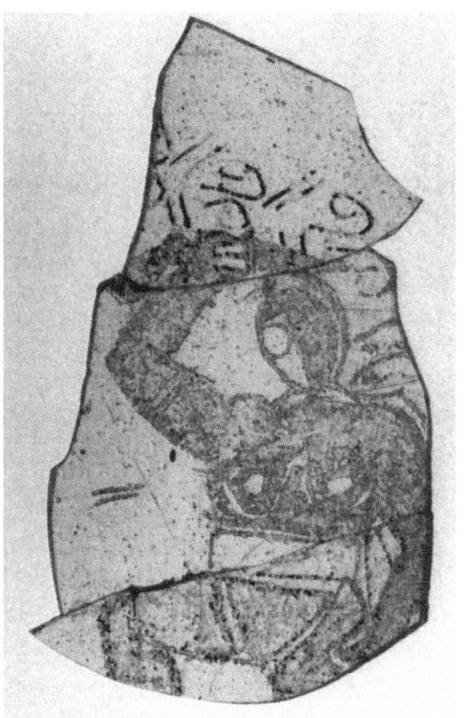 

Left 103 Glass vessel with decoration from Whitehill Farm, Northamaptonshire. *Jeremy Cooper and the Whitehill Farm Roman Villa Project*

Right 104 Clasp knife depicting a gladiator from Piddington, Northamptonshire. *Photograph courtesy of Simon Tutty, Roy Friendship Taylor and the Trustees of the British Museum*

on the left leg and right arm (*manica*). An ivory handle from South Shields (Tyne and Wear) again shows a *secutor*. He is bare headed, dressed like the Piddington gladiator, except for the fact that he is bare-headed and wears a short shin-guard on his sandaled right leg, and a short greave (*ocrea*) as well as padding on his left. He stands defensively behind a large curved rectangular shield decorated with a pattern of diamonds in a raised border, possibly representing quilted leather. His right hand holds a *gladius* across the top of the shield. He dates to the late second or early third century.[63]

Also from the Hadrian's Wall area, at Corbridge (Northumberland), comes a copper alloy handle which also shows a *secutor* standing behind a curved rectangular shield, this time with a central boss and incised decoration. He is dressed like the South Shields and Piddington figures, and the helmet is crested and closed, with small eye holes. The left hand is clenched to hold a *gladius* upright against the face of the shield.[64] A knife handle, albeit not for a clasp knife, from Carmarthen, though crudely carved, clearly represented a helmet. It seems likely that this was intended to be a gladiatorial helmet rather than a military parade-helmet, despite the fact that it seems to have no crest and a high peak.[65]

AROUND THE AMPHITHEATRE

We know very little about the activities that took place around the amphitheatres. This is mostly because of the concentration in excavations upon the arenas and entrance structures. It is likely that the spectacles would require different kinds of service buildings, religious structures might have existed in the vicinity of amphitheatres and it is thought that trading stalls were erected during festivals. Actual evidence for these activities is very sparse. Stratified deposits relating to the use of amphitheatres from the area beyond the walls are exceptionally rare throughout the Roman Empire and in Britain have only been excavated at Chester. Post-holes and surfaces suggest the existence of short-lived timber buildings, possibly temporary stalls erected for the duration of a festival. These existed within a pattern of deposition leading to the accumulation of almost a metre depth of material. The predominant element of these deposits was fine yellow sand, quite different to the coarse red sand native to the site and clearly imported, probably from the area of Boughton 2km upstream on the River Dee. It seems likely that this represented sand imported to the amphitheatre for use in the arena. A number of factors, not least the presence in this material of a human tooth, suggest that this was deposited during the clearing of the arena after spectacles had taken place. Close to the north entrance of the amphitheatre was a small, three-sided, stone-built structure with a plastered and painted interior. This was probably a small shrine. Other finds from these external deposits included animal bones and fragments of portable ceramic ovens or *clibani*, possibly relating to the sale and consumption of snack food, and a miniature samian ware bowl depicting gladiatorial combat, which was conceivably sold to a spectator as a souvenir of an event (*colour plate 27*). The London excavation produced eight vessels decorated with arena scenes outside the east entrance of the amphitheatre and these too were interpreted as possibly having been used by food sellers at the games or sold as souvenirs.[66] A glass cup with moulded scenes of chariot racing found in the road make-up of an entrance at Caerleon may similarly have been a souvenir accidentally dropped and broken.[67] Again at Chester, two large cess-pits situated outside the north-west quadrant of the first amphitheatre may well have been public latrines.

RITUAL AND CULT IN THE AMPHITHEATRE

We have already seen that the amphitheatre was allied to and an expression of the Imperial cult. The Imperial cult sanctuary at Lyons (*Lugdunum*) in Gaul incorporated an altar to the cult and an amphitheatre. At Colchester, the precinct of the temple of the Divine Claudius, the centre of the Imperial cult in Britain, included only a theatre, however it is possible that *munera* related to the cult were held in this theatre, given the large amount of gladiatorial imagery which, as we have seen above, has been found in the city, and the probable provenance of the Hawkedon helmet.

The cult most closely associated with the amphitheatre as far as the British evidence is concerned is that of Nemesis. Nemesis' association with the arena seems to spring from the spread of arena spectacles to the areas where she was worshipped in the east. The cult of Nemesis was associated with the emperors and the Roman state, and a temple to her existed on the Capitoline by AD 77. Iconography on coins linked Nemesis to the emperor, victory and peace delivered through victory, particularly noted in the victory of the Flavian dynasty under Vespasian. Part of the reason she was worshipped in the arena was because this place confirmed the primacy of the order established by the Roman state through the symbolism of the execution of criminals, insolent slaves and wild beasts, and through the *munera*, where barbarians and enemies were represented by different types of gladiator. Nemesis was equated to Fortuna, and was depicted with Fortuna's attributes of the wheel and the rudder. She was sometimes equated specifically in inscriptions to Fortuna. She could reward as well as punish, as could the emperor and the state. This aspect is reflected by the fact that most dedications to Nemesis were made by members of the army, the administration and the priesthood. Her presence in the amphitheatre is wholly understandable. She was amoral, a distributor of good and bad fortune, of success or failure, of life and death. She could, through ritual and offering, intercede with the workings of destiny.[68] These aspects meant that her favour would have been important to the *editor* of games, wishing for success and the favour of the crowd, as well as to a gladiator.

Shrines to Nemesis (*Nemesea*) are found in amphitheatres throughout the Empire. These were not uniformly placed. Often they were placed on one end of the short axis, with connection to the presidential box above, sometimes on the long axis, and sometimes outside the building against the outer wall, close to a main entrance. Examples are numerous. In Spain, at Italica, dedications to Nemesis from a main entrance were made by members of a range of social groups, including women and a town priest, while at Merida a plaque, also from a main entrance, invokes *Dea Invicta Caelestis Nemesis*.[69] *Nemesea* have been suggested

105 Altar to Nemesis from the Chester amphitheatre. *Chester City Council/English Heritage*

in several British amphitheatres, including as identifications for the recesses on the short axes at Dorchester and Silchester, and the late tile-lined recess in the short axis east entrance at Caerleon.[70] Also at Caerleon, a building outside the amphitheatre, against the north wall, was suggested as a *Nemeseum* by analogy with the shrine in this position in the amphitheatre of Carnuntum, Austria.[71] Nemesis was often identified with Diana, and dedications to Diana-Nemesis have been found in the vicinity of the civilian amphitheatre at Carnuntum. Diana-Nemesis was an important patroness of the amphitheatre, and as Diana was the goddess of the hunt, this personification was of particular relevance to *venationes*.[72] The idea that the female bust in the apsidal panel of the gladiator mosaic at Bignor (*colour plate 26*) is Diana-Nemesis has been mentioned. At Cologne Diana-Nemesis was invoked in a dedication made by a gladiator of the Thracian class named Avitus.[73]

Both Diana and Nemesis appear in association with British amphitheatres. At Chester a small stone altar (*105*) was found in the chamber at the arena end of the main north entrance, which seems to have started as a *carcer* and later converted to use as a *Nemeseum*. This reads:

DEAE NEMESI SEXT MARCIANVS > EX VISU

To the Goddess Nemesis, Sextius Marcianus, the centurion, set this up after a vision.[74]

THE ARENA SPECTACLE

106 Small painted shrine outside the north entrance of the first amphitheatre at Chester. *Chester City Council/ English Heritage*

It may well have begun life in the small painted shrine located close to the north entrance of the first amphitheatre (*106*). On the amphitheatre sites at Caerleon and London lead curse tablets begging for divine retribution on petty thieves have been found dedicated respectively to Nemesis and Diana. The Caerleon example reads:

> Lady Nemesis, I give thee a cloak and a pair of boots; let him who took them not redeem them (unless) with his own blood.[75]

The curse from London also concerns the theft of clothing:

> I give Diana my headgear and scarf less one third. If anyone has done this, I give him, and through me let him be unable to live.[76]

The speculation that these curses reflect the sneak-thieving of clothing laid aside in a crowded amphitheatre is irresistible.

In Caerleon a temple of Diana appears to have been situated in the vicinity of the amphitheatre. An inscription on a metal tablet found near the amphitheatre site records the restoration of the temple in the mid-third century by the legionary legate T Flavius Postumius Varus.[77] Dedications to Nemesis and Diana in British amphitheatres are limited to three locations: Caerleon, Chester and London. This must be significant, as these three places housed large concentrations of the very classes from which the majority of Nemesis dedications come, Empire-wide, the legions and the administration.

A further deity of the amphitheatre was Mercury who in the guise of Hermes Psychopompus would conduct the souls of the dead to the underworld. Tertullian describes masked attendants in the amphitheatre, dressed as Dis Pater, and as Mercury, wearing a winged cap and with his wand, or *cadeuceus*, heated in order to establish whether the fallen were actually dead.[78] This seems to have taken pace during the midday executions in the arena rather than after gladiatorial fights. It seems likely that the discovery of a tinned bronze statuette of Mercury, albeit unstratified, at the amphitheatre of Caerleon is connected with this kind of imagery.[79]

9

AFTER THE ROMANS

Whenever refurbishments continued in the amphitheatres one can be confident that arena events took place. In general, however, there is evidence that the amphitheatres had fallen out of use by the mid-fourth century. The period between their disuse and their rediscovery is relatively obscure both because of the lack of excavation and because in the past excavation tended to be oriented towards the discovery of the Roman history of the structures, the post Roman being disregarded. The most obvious example of this tendency was at Chester, where F.H. Thompson, during his excavations in the 1960s, removed the fill of the arena by machine without any recording taking place until he reached the level he interpreted as that of the Roman arena floor.

In London the amphitheatre was abandoned in the mid-fourth century and seems to have been used for a time as the town dump. Subsequently, and at any event later than AD 367, the stone elements of the amphitheatre were robbed, possibly in order to refurbish the walls of the city. After abandonment and robbing, the site was covered over in a thick layer of grey earth[1] and forgotten. The theatre at Verulamium was also used as a late Roman municipal dump. It is possible that this development was the result of increasing Christianisation during the fourth century, with amphitheatres, theatres and temples falling out of favour. Their association with pagan religion, and the system of Imperial cult and pagan festival, began to end with the adoption of Christianity by the Emperor Constantine. Towns lost their places of entertainment, but organised rubbish disposal implied that administrative authority continued.[2] The same pattern may have occurred at Chichester, where the fill of the arena was 650mm deep below the level at which the earliest medieval sherds were found.[3]

At only two of the excavated sites has information come to light about any immediate post-Roman use of the amphitheatres, Cirencester and Chester. At

Chester, recent excavations have helped in the interpretation of features found in the 1960s. Within the arena, overlying an accumulation of loam, which contained a number of third-century coins, were patches of stone paving. It seems very unlikely that such paving was laid when the arena was in use, as this would have provided a hard surface inconsistent with arena performances. In the centre of the arena were four apparent rows of post-holes forming a rectangular structure. Thompson interpreted this as a platform used in the Roman period, possibly for military presentations, when the legionary commander would stand on a raised central platform.[4] Such a structure would be unparalleled elsewhere. Over the central drain in the arena was a kerbed and metalled path, which ran from the north entrance to the timber structure. Excavations in 2005 on a part of the arena not previously explored showed how much had been lost by the earlier clearance. Although the area excavated was only small, it showed that following the end of the use of the arena it was used for occupation. No fewer than seven phases of activity were recorded, with the evidence consisting of intercutting pits and post-holes. Only the final phase could be clearly understood, when a small timber building was constructed. There can be no doubt that the post-holes recorded by Thompson were part of the same phenomenon. Despite sieving all of the archaeological deposits associated with these phases, no dating evidence was found. All we know is that this occupation took place between the end of the Roman use of the arena and the eleventh to twelfth century, when the walls of the amphitheatre were robbed to extend the town walls and to build the cathedral church of St John. Work continues on the analysis of the evidence at the time of writing, though the lack of finds might indicate that the occupation is earlier rather than later within this period. There was some evidence that the east entrance was walled up in the late period. One of the *vomitoria* was certainly treated in this way. This is of great interest, as the essence of an amphitheatre is to get people in and out – walling up entrances would be highly counter-productive. This process implies that the amphitheatre was no longer being used as such and instead that people were being kept out. It is possible that the amphitheatre was used in the period from the fifth century as a fortified settlement for occupation or as a refuge. If so, the north entrance may have been the only one retained, as indicated by the metalled path leading from this entrance to what we might now interpret as timber buildings in the centre of the arena. To fortify the enclosure would have been a simple process, as all that was needed was the closing of most entrances. This use of amphitheatres as early post-Roman fortifications is seen elsewhere in Europe, particularly clearly at Trier in Germany.[5] Clearly this settlement lasted some time and it may have been of high status, perhaps becoming the base of a local warlord or petty king, and thus a seat of local power. It is possible that the siting of the church of St John immediately outside the east entrance to the amphitheatre by the Mercian King Æthelred in the seventh century was the result of the existence of such a settlement, though it could also have been because of an association of the amphitheatre with Christian martyrdom, or, of course, both.[6] It is possible that the east entrance of the amphitheatre was actually reused as the crypt of the seventh-century church. The sixth-century monk Gildas mentions the martyrdom of two Christians, Aaron and Julius at a place called *Legionum Urbs*, or the city of the legions. Though traditionally this has been thought to refer to Caerleon, the name might also apply to Chester with its old Welsh name *Cair Legion*, which, like Caerleon, is a direct translation of *Legionem Urbs*.[7]

The various patches of stone flagging and other types of surfacing in the arena at Chester are reminiscent of the excavators' description of the arena at Caerleon. Here the arena, which was floored primarily with natural sand, 'had been made up at various indeterminate times with trodden earth, broken brick, stones and occasional patches of slabbing'.[8] It is possible that these surfaces in both amphitheatres were the remnants of sub-Roman buildings. At both the Roman town of Wroxeter and the Hadrian's Wall fort of Birdoswald[9] it has been found that buildings at the very end of Roman Britain tend to be timber structures, built on the surface and thus leaving no post-holes, but with solid floors. Indeed, at Wroxeter the different floor surfaces were all that betrayed the existence of buildings to the archaeologists.[10] It is conceivable that such buildings were erected in both legionary arenas. The location of these two sites, on the western side of Roman Britain, where *Romanitas* seems to have survived longer, is also an interesting indicator.

The other site to have provided evidence for the sub-Roman period is also in the west, at Cirencester. Here, the amphitheatre had certainly fallen out of use by AD 350-60, when the north-eastern entrance passage was demolished and the stone removed.[11] The demolition appears to have been undertaken to allow a wider metalled access into the arena and one which could be used by wheeled traffic, as attested by wheel ruts worn into the cobbled surfaces which ran through the entrance. When the masonry walls were demolished, the seating banks were cut back on both sides of the entrance to provide a road 8m wide at the outer end, funnelling in to enter the original arena entrance. The sides of the seating bank were revetted by timber shuttering retained by large posts which required replacement from time to time, possibly as slumping took place. Both in the arena and in the passage, various metalled surfaces were laid successively, the latest containing a coin dated to AD 388-402, demonstrating that the new function of the amphitheatre continued into the fifth century. John Wacher[12] has suggested that the new use was as an out-of-town marketplace. At some date probably well into the fifth century, the entrance to the arena was narrowed into a pedestrian access only 1.6m wide and, probably at the same time, a fence or palisade was used to block the entrance further along. Wacher[13] has suggested the use of the amphitheatre as a sub-Roman fortified retreat, though these blockings do not appear very defensive. Following this the gate was abandoned. Four sherds of grass-tempered pottery were found in a turf line above the abandonment layer. This ware, dating to the fifth to eighth centuries, has not been found on any site within the walls of Cirencester and the nearest find spot is associated with sixth-century burials cut through the ruins of the Roman building at the Barton, 1km away. The latest surfaces in the arena were cut by five large post-holes, which represent part of a substantial timber building. The author of the report associated the building with the period of the grass-tempered pottery, and sees the single twelfth-century sherd found in one of the post-holes as intrusive, given the total lack of any other evidence for this period.[14]

In other amphitheatres the immediate post-Roman evidence is for dilapidation and desertion. At Silchester it is thought that the stone amphitheatre was built in the mid-third century and that intermittent use continued until the mid-fourth century, this interpretation being based on archaeological finds of coins of this date in the latest arena deposits.[15] After this, the west wall of the north entrance passage began to lean, ultimately collapsing, and it is possible that this collapse occurred before the end of the fourth century.[16] Following this the arena began to receive silt, and the stone walls were robbed for building material. Though this robbing could have begun immediately after the Roman period, in practice there was no use for the stone until a few centuries later. The robbing is more likely to have taken place in the eleventh to twelfth century, 7-800 years after the amphitheatre had ceased to be used.

The two amphitheatres overlain by medieval town development are London and Chester. In London the site, already robbed of its stone, was a boggy hollow by the eleventh century, when there was a phase of large-scale dumping and levelling. Efforts were made to drain the site, while it was used largely for livestock and animal husbandry. In the south-west corner was a burial ground, probably associated with a timber precursor to the later church of St Lawrence Jewry, which was built on the higher, drier, south *cavea*. The thoroughfare later known as Lawrence Lane ran virtually through the south entrance of the former amphitheatre, across the arena, conceivably to the site of a timber hall built upon the north *cavea*, which would have been a forerunner to the medieval Guildhall[17] (*colour plate 29*). Houses lay along the line of the lane. The early streets of the City shown on the earliest maps have pronounced curves as they run around the amphitheatre site. This is also true in Chester, where the earliest map we have, that of John Stow, shows a street curving around the northern side of the robbed and obscured amphitheatre (*107*). This curving street, with hindsight, is an

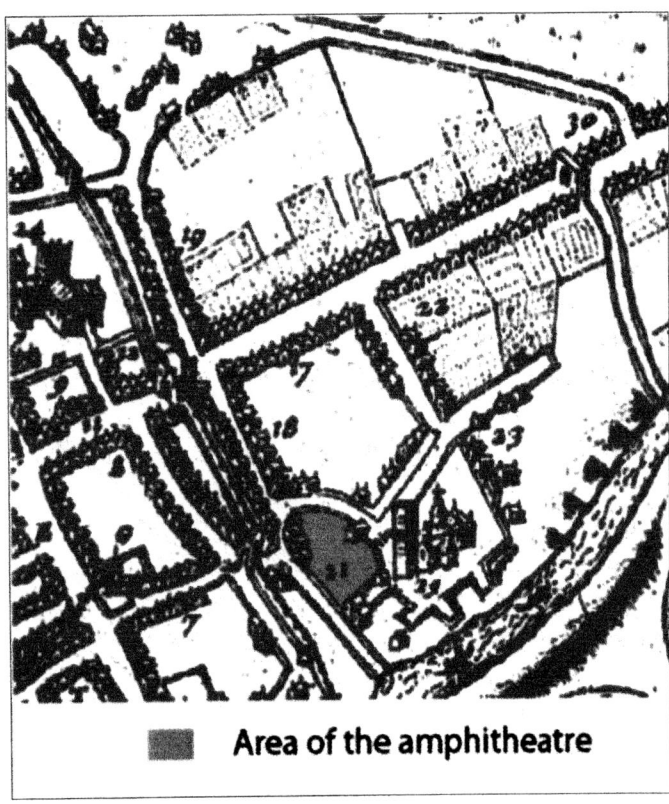

107 Extract from John Stow's 1610 map of Chester showing the area of the amphitheatre. *Chester City Council/English Heritage*

obvious indication of the existence of the amphitheatre, given its relationship to the site of the corner of the old legionary fortress and the fact that most of the other streets in Chester are straight and laid out at right-angles. It is clear that in Chester and London the shapes of the amphitheatres were still very visible long after they disappeared from view. In York there is a suggestion in early mapping that early streets were laid out around a large oval structure, and therefore that an amphitheatre may have lain between St Andrewgate and St Saviourgate, to the immediate east of the legionary fortress.[18]

The presence of churches on the *cavea* in London and just outside the east gate at Chester might suggest that at both sites there was an appreciation of the nature of the sites. Also, the common knowledge in the medieval church of the role of amphitheatres in Christian martyrdom, derived from the writings of early church fathers,[19] might have lent the sites an element of sanctity. Such sanctity would not have required the knowledge of specific martyrdoms, only the knowledge or understanding that these structures were, in fact, amphitheatres. The lane leading across the arena in London to a possible predecessor to the Guildhall, in the tenth century, is at least reminiscent of the path from the north gate at

Chester to a timber building in the centre of the arena. In both cases associations seem to exist, albeit at different times between the fifth and eleventh centuries, between amphitheatres, churches and probable high-status secular buildings. The robbing of the outer wall at Chester was apparently undertaken in earnest in the eleventh and twelfth centuries. London, of course, never had a stone outer wall. In London, a stone Guildhall building was constructed by the later thirteenth century, but the twelfth century saw a reawakening of interest in the Classical past, which may have aided recognition of the amphitheatre site. At any event, Guildhall Yard, an open space on the site of the arena, was certainly in existence by the mid-thirteenth century and continued as such down to the present.[20] It seems unlikely that this is simply coincidence. In Chester the northern curve of the amphitheatre may have survived in part as a boundary, a portion of the bounds of the Bishops Borough, a distinct precinct around the church of St John, which is mentioned in Domesday Book.[21] Although there is evidence for building on the *cavea* of the amphitheatre, the arena seems never to have been completely built up, remaining a garden area for the best part of a millennium.

Those amphitheatres that remained in the countryside seem, as far as is currently known, simply to have merged into the landscape. At Caerleon enough survived for Gerald of Wales to comment on in the eleventh century, however obliquely, and the site was certainly robbed from the fourteenth century onwards, but for most of the other sites there is simply no evidence before their rediscovery.

Reuse of amphitheatres as fortifications in later times is attested at two sites. At Silchester, the western side of the arena was occupied by a post-built, single-aisled building, which was clearly utilising the amphitheatre earthwork as an enclosure. At the same time the southern entrance was revetted with timber again, and there are traces of a palisade around the crest of the bank. The dampness of the site did not encourage permanent occupation and it seems most likely that the defensive capability of the earthwork was being exploited. There are good reasons, given the twelfth-century date for this development, to believe it to have been used as a short-lived defensive ring-work during the Anarchy; the civil wars of the reign of King Stephen (1135-54).

Another, very much later civil war, resulted in the last known reuse of a British amphitheatre. Maumbury Rings, Dorchester was remodelled in 1642 by the Parliamentarian defenders of the town to form an outwork of the town defences commanding the Weymouth road. A survey of 1649 refers to the site as 'the fort called Mambry'.[22] Despite the arrival of artillery, and the completion of earthwork defences, the town surrendered to the Royalist Lord Carnarvon in August 1643 without resistance.[23] The amphitheatre was remodelled by the insertion of ramps and parapets to adapt it to its new function. The southern ramp is very visible today, running from the centre of the arena to a platform constructed over the filled-in south entrance. This would have been a perfect gun platform from which to sight down the Weymouth road. To east and west are a pair of ramps, both of which ran across the face of the *cavea* rising to a platform at the centre of the arc of the *cavea*, and then sloping back to arena level. The platforms were possibly surfaced with flint nodules. These ramps would allow men or artillery to reach the crest of the earthwork, where parapets were raised for protection. A ditch discovered close to the south entrance appears to have served as a covered way, that is to say a ditch, flat bottomed and flanked by a pair of banks, allowing the defenders of the outwork to get back into the town under cover. A flat-bottomed ditch with the same function was recently excavated between Pontefract castle and a church used as an outwork during the siege of the castle in 1642.[24] Finally, a perimeter ditch appears to have been cut around the outside of the amphitheatre. This latter feature, together with a pair of human burials within a single grave, appeared beneath a turf line, which ante-dated the southern and western ramp. These features, though post-medieval in date, need not therefore have belonged to the Civil War re-fortification. A well excavated in the arena was probably allowing water to be supplied to a garrison in case they were cut off from the town by the severing of the covered way. The Dorchester amphitheatre was thus used in the way assumed in Leland's description of its counterpart at Richborough (p. 22).[25] It is apparent from Stukeley's account that that the Dorchester amphitheatre was used to house the town gallows after the Civil War, indeed after the first notice of the site by Sir Christopher Wren. This final, and rather appropriate use of Maumbury Rings ended in 1767.[26]

10

CONCLUSIONS: AMPHITHEATRES AND SPECTACLES IN BRITAIN

The architectural, archaeological and artefactual evidence for the Roman amphitheatre in Britain now add up to a good body of data. Although research on this aspect of Roman Britain is a relatively late-flowering field, as we saw in Chapter 3, the mass of new information that has been gathered during the second half of the twentieth century and the beginning of the twenty-first about our small group of relatively unimpressive amphitheatres begins to allow general conclusions to be drawn.

Earlier studies have tended to see the British amphitheatres as a discrete group of small military and civilian amphitheatres of modest pretensions, but which could be compared as a whole. By considering the communities served by the amphitheatres, it has been possible to demonstrate that the structures fall into a number of sub-groups, and that different communities required different kinds of amphitheatre. This is most marked in the very clear contrast between the amphitheatres of the *civitas* capitals and the legionary fortresses, a major distinction first noted by Michael Fulford.[1]

Among the towns of Roman Britain, it is quite startling that as far as is known only London and the *civitas* capitals had amphitheatres. Two out of the earliest three *coloniae*, Gloucester and Lincoln, had no building for entertainment, while the third, Colchester, boasted a circus and a theatre but no amphitheatre. The partially excavated theatre is undated,[2] but Tacitus records such a building, which 'echoed with shrieks' during the Boudiccan revolt of AD 60.[3] It seems likely that the early theatre occupied the same site, adjacent to, and within the precinct of, the Temple of Claudius. Colchester may have been destined to be the centre for the organisation of the Imperial cult in the new province, like the cult complex at *Lugdunum*, though this is a modern assumption not backed by ancient sources.[4] This would mean that the theatre would be analogous to the *Lugdunum* amphitheatre, intended for cult gatherings, possibly provincial councils, and the festivals held in connection with the cult might have included *munera*. The Colchester theatre is not of the Gallic theatre-amphitheatre type, being closer to the standard classical form, however it would be unwise to dismiss the structure as possibly the earliest venue in Britain in which *munera* took place on this basis, as it is clear that theatres were used for such displays in Rome itself and in the east, particularly before the construction of the Colosseum.[5] If *munera* took place in the Colchester theatre, this would go a long way to explaining the wealth of gladiatorial imagery from the town, particularly the painted wall plaster (*colour plate 25*), and also the Hawkedon helmet (*96*), if it is to be interpreted as booty from the Boudiccan sack of Colchester.[6]

The other two urban theatres, at Verulamium and Canterbury (we know nothing of the theatre attested by the Brough-on-Humber inscription), are of the theatre-amphitheatre type in their first form, and the central post in the arena at Verulamium is suggestive of a tethering facility for arena spectacles, possibly for the execution of criminals or for animal baiting. The Verulamium theatre, like that at Colchester, is sited within the *temenos* of a religious sanctuary and is related closely to a temple, and there is no doubt in these instances that presentations in these buildings were of cultic importance. Both Canterbury and Verulamium were early *civitas* capitals, and Verulamium was swiftly promoted to the second rank of chartered towns as a *municipium*. Both settlements became Romanised towns in the first phase of the establishment of the British province in the pre-Flavian period, and it is possible that these facts contributed to the choice of building a theatre-amphitheatre rather than an amphitheatre in these places. The relative dates of the buildings, Verulamium *c.*AD 140 (though the site may have been reserved for the purpose since the foundation of the town) and Canterbury possibly in the Flavian period, make this unlikely and we should perhaps look tentatively to other explanations. The theatre-amphitheatre form is typical of the Gallic provinces, and found in very few places beyond. It may well have catered to a particularly Gaulish requirement, and its presence in these early south-eastern towns may perhaps reflect strong Gaulish influence, or even a large Gaulish population.

London was founded on neutral territory as a new town. Based upon a river crossing and as an ideal port site, and a potential centre for the road network of the new province, the creation of London must have involved official agency. London became a boom town for pioneers interested in exploiting this latest conquest. Incoming traders founded the town, which developed quickly, acquiring a rudimentary street grid even before the Boudiccan revolt. This new settlement had no past history in native settlement, and developed as a purely Roman place. Though the *Procurator* may have been based here before

AD 60, his office was certainly in London after the revolt, as was the rest of the provincial administration. London's suite of public buildings developed in a piecemeal way, probably as the result of a complex set of individual, corporate and personal benefactions. The amphitheatre was part of this phenomenon, which has aptly been described by John Creighton as the 'creation of the familiar'.[7] The construction of the amphitheatre shortly after AD 70, as attested by the dendrochronological dates, was part of the earliest group of monumental buildings, including the first *forum*, and may have been officially aided, as the stamped timbers used in the building suggest. The character of the building is wholly familiar from amphitheatres built elsewhere in the Roman Empire. It had a timber-framed structure, including an outer wall and probably a system of framed seating. It is different from the amphitheatres of the *civitas* capitals, and this difference is an aspect of that between a place where incomers were establishing patterns of behaviour and life with which they were familiar and comfortable[8] in a new setting, against places where an existing population were learning to adapt their social behaviour and environment to new forms.

The period during which Britain was gradually conquered and under which the south at least took on the trappings of a Roman province coincided with the golden age of amphitheatre building. The Flavian dynasty, from AD 69-96, under which so much of the conquest took place, was inextricably linked to the amphitheatre as a building form, not least because it was under Vespasian and Titus, the first two of the three Flavian emperors, that the Colosseum, properly the 'Flavian amphitheatre', was built. The best known of the governors of Britain in this period, Gn Julius Agricola (AD 78-84), carried Roman arms to the Moray Firth, but also encouraged Romanisation, as we are told by Tacitus. Perhaps amphitheatres were seen by the *civitates* at first as desirable aspects of the suite of Roman facilities which they were beginning to appreciate, their construction an expression of loyalty to the dynasty. However, the amphitheatres of the *civitas* capitals demonstrate what Alison Futrell[9] has termed an *interpretatio provincialis*, a provincial interpretation of the amphitheatre form. Futrell uses the term in the context of Gaul, where the spread of the amphitheatres in the province shows partially a strong identification with towns and urbanisation, but there is also a very large number of rural amphitheatres, usually at cult sites, and the larger amphitheatres are not necessarily in places of large population density. To this should be added the prevalence of a very Gaulish form, the theatre-amphitheatre or 'mixed edifice' type, whose few outliers include Verulamium. In Gaul Futrell concludes that the 'provincial amphitheatre was not merely superficial decoration for the new-fangled Roman town but rather served as an expression of local needs and enthusiasms'[10]. I believe that the amphitheatres of the *civitates* of Britain also demonstrate a clear *interpretatio provincialis* of the form and function of the amphitheatre. From the earliest example at Silchester, those for which we have evidence are very similar to each other. All were built on hollow or sloping ground in order to minimise the volume of spoil needed to raise the banks. The structure of the *cavea* in each case relies on the careful construction of earthworks and there are no outer walls. The one possible exception may have been the latest, Carmarthen, though this is far from certain, and even if there was a timber outer wall here, it would have been only on the low northern side. Silchester and Dorchester in their earliest forms showed a very simple shape, in the former circular, in the latter elongated within the limits of a pre-existing monument. In the past it has been suggested that military planning was required for public buildings in the early towns of Roman Britain. These amphitheatres would not have required such input and their difference to the legionary amphitheatres alone suggests that military help was not provided for their construction. As large earthwork structures they can be seen as direct descendants of an indigenous tradition of the construction of communal earthworks, stretching from the henge monuments of the Neolithic to the hill-forts of the Iron Age. Thus, though a desire to be seen as 'Romanising' the *civitas* by the construction of an amphitheatre might have been the motivation, no further help from the Roman authorities would be required in their construction. I have suggested (p. 52) that the construction of amphitheatres might have been through corporate civic effort by the *civitates*, encouraged and led by the tribal aristocratic oligarchy which formed the *ordo*, but this may effectively have been no departure from pre-Roman corporate or communal practice. Only the function and form of the earthwork has changed. Silchester is the clearest example of this. Centre of a *civitas* with a promiscuous attachment to Romanisation, Silchester rapidly acquired a suite of Roman-style buildings. The amphitheatre may have been the simplest to plan, because the mechanisms of construction fitted so easily into a well understood way of doing things, even if the form and function did not, resulting in the circular arena of the first phase. The remodelling of the Maumbury Rings henge to form the amphitheatre of Dorchester is particularly interesting if one sees the earthwork amphitheatres of the *civitas* capitals as part of an indigenous building tradition put to new uses. There is room to suspect that the henge might have been used for tribal meetings in the pre-Roman period and that the re-modelling was undertaken to convert an existing meeting place to fit into a new Roman milieu. This in turn may indicate that the other amphitheatres of the *civitas* capitals were also intended, at least in part, as meeting places for the *civitas*.

The form of *civitas* amphitheatres also suggests a provincial interpretation of the spectacles associated with the amphitheatre. Key to this, as Boon intimated[11] is the fact that the amphitheatres at Silchester, Cirencester and Carmarthen, and possibly that at Chichester, all have positive evidence for terraces, which can only have accommodated standing spectators. Boon's assertion that the Silchester stone phase amphitheatre was equipped with solid timber seating is not borne out by the evidence, and appears in the report as an admitted assumption.[12] This means that for all of the *civitas* amphitheatres for which there is evidence a standing audience must be envisaged, though probably with higher-ranking personages accommodated in tribunals near the ringside. This must mean that the full *munum legitimum*, an all-day affair featuring *venationes* in the morning, executions at midday and gladiatorial *munera* in the afternoon, is highly unlikely to have taken place, as this would require the audience to stand pretty much all day. This might also have to do with the prosaic factor of the British climate, which, as any cricket fan or Wimbledon-goer knows, is not universally favourable to all-day outdoor events.[13] This does not, of course mean that the three elements of the *munus legitimum* might not have occurred separately at different times, and we should consider the possibility that executions might have been the most frequent spectacle. At Silchester, the excavator makes much of the large quantity of horse bone among the faunal assemblage from the site, including a horse skull in the western recess opening from the arena.[14] This, it is suggested, might be evidence for various forms of equestrian spectacle.

The duration and character of events in these amphitheatres is one question, another relates to the frequency with which they might have been put on. At Silchester the arena deposits are characterised by episodes of silting interleaved by gravel lenses representing arena surfacing. This suggests long periods of disuse with very occasional episodes of usage. Similar evidence comes from the local pollen record, which shows the establishment of oak and ferns around the north entrance and the banks in the second century, declining during the replacement of the timber structure in stone, and then a further increase. This certainly indicates an informal and casual treatment of the building, which is inconsistent with frequent use.[15] This contrasts with London, where the arena was surfaced with alternate hard and soft surfaces, thought to have functioned together. These successive resurfacings do not appear to have included silts indicative of periodic disuse, the implication being that the London amphitheatre was used much more frequently than that of Silchester. In all of the urban amphitheatres the duration, frequency and character of spectacles would have been dependant on the enthusiasm on the inhabitants of the *civitas* to see such entertainments and the capacity of the purses of those willing to fund events. The humble scale of the urban structures has led to the conclusion that a full enthusiasm for amphitheatre spectacle never actually developed among the inhabitants of the British *civitates*, and that in Britain there was 'an underlying reluctance to assimilate the idea', which originated in cultural traditions in Roman Italy, and had become weaker as it crossed through Gaul and into Britain.[16] Whatever the provincial interpretation of spectacle might have been, a fundamental lack of interest in this aspect of Roman life in the *civitates* is probably the best explanation for the failure of the amphitheatres to develop beyond a very basic form.

The Gaulish type of the rural sanctuary accompanied by a theatre-amphitheatre does not really figure in Britain except at Gosbecks Farm near Colchester, where a temple complex includes a classical theatre, and possibly at Frilford. Whatever the fascinating structure at Frilford finally turns out to be, it is neither a Gaulish theatre-amphitheatre, nor an amphitheatre in the sense of others in Britain. Its excavators, however, see it as the expression of native religious practices couched within a new Roman structural repertoire. Drained and surfaced, and surrounded by a plastered and painted stone wall, the Frilford structure does appear like an arena, and it remains possible that ceremonies including *munera* took place here within a religious context.[17] The status of the banks around the arena and whether some form of terracing or seating was provided remains to be seen.

The two legionary amphitheatres at Caerleon and Chester are very different to those of the *civitates*. If, as is likely, there was an amphitheatre in York, it would more readily fit the legionary group, as York was always a legionary fortress with a civilian *canabae*, despite the fact that the *canabae* became a later *colonia* and briefly an Imperial capital under Septimius Severus. In York the presence of the legion would always have been a factor, as at Chester. We have also seen that the Richborough amphitheatre may just have been a late foundation, associated with the building of the fourth-century Saxon Shore fort and possibly even the functional replacement of the Caerleon amphitheatre when Legion II *Augusta* moved from Caerleon to Richborough. A major question concerning the Chester amphitheatre is why it achieved such a complex and ornate final form, and why Chester should boast the largest and most elaborate amphitheatre in Britain. This question links with that of the status of Chester by the early third century, a question that is still under debate. Certainly the amphitheatre was not the only exceptional structure in Roman Chester. The analysis of the recent excavations will ultimately address this question.[18] The Chester and Caerleon amphitheatres were stone built from the first, and through their architecture, particularly the style of entrances, demonstrate total familiarity with the form of the Roman amphitheatre. They were built by the legionaries, as attested by the centurial stones that record the centurions responsible for work gangs. As the legionaries were by definition Roman citizens, these structures were explicitly built by and for Roman citizens, and specifically by the army for the army. We have already touched on the idea of the Roman army as a community as well as an Imperial institution (p. 18) and mentioned the fact that the army was, when these amphitheatres were built, an almost entirely 'foreign' community in the new British province (p. 58). The legionary amphitheatres were built in the context of the military community, which was bound together by organisation, a system of ranking and also in a common experience of ritual. As Ian Haynes puts it:

> From the Euphrates to the Tyne, soldiers celebrated the same festivals and swore the same oaths. Through such rituals the entire army shared in the military ethos that originated in Rome herself.[19]

The catalogue of festivals celebrated by the *cohors XX Palmyrenorum* at Dura Europos is listed in the document known as the *Feriale Duranum* dated to the AD 220s. The list includes festivals of Roman deities, celebrations of the Imperial cult, involving deified emperors of the past as well as the reigning Severan dynasty, and also such military events as *honesta misso* (demobilisation) on 7 January and the *rosaliae signorum*, a festival of the standards, which took place in May. All of these festivals, many of which required animal sacrifice, may have been celebrated in the military amphitheatres and at least some of these festivals may have been accompanied by spectacles. As we have seen, *munera* may have performed a particularly important didactic role for the legions. Whatever the truth of this, we can be sure that *munera* were celebrated in the legionary amphitheatres, as these are the only two amphitheatre sites where sculpture and graffiti illustrating gladiatorial themes have been found (*94, 95*). The idea that the legions had their own 'stables' of gladiators is based on shaky ground – one classical reference and the Colchester vase (p. 170; *97*). However, the fact that a centurion of Legion I Minervia based in Bonn could boast of catching 50 bears for the arena in a six-month period[20] clearly shows that a concern for the arena and duties associated with it fell into the purview of the army. The amphitheatres of the auxiliaries were probably similar in function to those of the legionaries, although it is possible that they were built temporarily for specific and special events, an idea which has been advanced in connection with the examples in Germany.[21]

The military amphitheatres and the London amphitheatres are connected by the fact that they were built for communities most of whose members came from outside Britain. The London amphitheatre was part of the creation of a familiar ambience by those creating a new urban community of Roman type. The legionary amphitheatres were built by the legions to serve their established needs. The only real difference was that London was a new community, which had to establish itself and bind together pretty much from scratch, whereas the legions were existing communities, which came into the province as units, with established disciplines and ways of operating. The legions also possessed the

CONCLUSIONS: AMPHITHEATRES AND SPECTACLES IN BRITAIN

artisans and craftsmen needed to undertake major projects like amphitheatre building, and were the standard bearers of the Imperial mission, wedded to the Imperial ideal. Both in London and in the legions, the amphitheatre was probably experienced in the same way as among military and largely Roman communities elsewhere. It can be no coincidence that the deities associated with the amphitheatre elsewhere are seen in Britain exclusively at these three sites. In the *civitates*, the Romanised communities formed from the native British tribal structures and the amphitheatrical concept does not appear, from the nature of the buildings themselves, to have been widely accepted. This observation should, perhaps be moderated by the fact that objects portraying aspects of the arena were relatively common in Roman Britain, and clearly the arena had its enthusiasts in Britain as elsewhere. Many of the more expensive items, such as the mould-blown glass chariot and gladiator cups[22] were more than likely purchased as souvenir wares and the less expensive items such as decorated samian wares actually found at the Chester and London amphitheatres suggest the same thing.

The amphitheatres did not actively outlast the mid-fourth century, and they may well have succumbed to the change in attitudes which followed the widespread adoption of Christianity. Their later histories vary. In the west they may have been fortified settlements or refuges, as suggested for Chester, Caerleon and Cirencester. At Verulamium and London they became city dumps, and elsewhere there is no evidence. The use of Silchester and Dorchester as fortifications in the twelfth and seventeenth centuries respectively shows opportunistic reuse of features whose identity was long forgotten.

As a final note it is perhaps salutary that as recently as 1706, not 2000 years ago but only 300, 10,000 spectators resorted to Maumbury Rings to witness the burning of a 19-year-old woman, and that the last public execution in a Romano-British amphitheatre occurred only two and a half centuries ago.

APPENDIX: VISITING THE AMPHITHEATRES

The amphitheatre sites are generally located in historic towns or in attractive countryside areas. Though an itinerary solely for amphitheatre visiting is not really possible, the sites can certainly add interest to days out or holidays. The following directions are correct at the time of writing. The sites listed are those that are worth visiting, because there is something of the amphitheatre to be seen.

SOUTHERN ENGLAND

Charterhouse on Mendip (ST 506561)
From the west, and the A38 road between Bristol and Bridgewater, take the unclassified road eastwards signed to Shipham, then the road signed to Charterhouse. After some 5km a T-junction is reached, on which is the Charterhouse Centre for the Mendips Area of Outstanding Natural Beauty, where there is a car park. The other access is from Cheddar, via the B3135 Cheddar Gorge road, turning left on the B3371 and left on the unclassified road to Charterhouse, which also reaches the centre. From the centre, take the road northwards towards the B3134, taking the track called Rains Batch, which is first on the left. The site is in a field on the left towards the top of the hill before the twin radio masts are reached. It is possible to drive up to the masts, though the site is on the very pleasant, waymarked Charterhouse walking route. The earthwork is very clearly visible from the road, but is on private land and is not publicly accessible. Excellent information and walking guides to the AONB are available from the helpful staff at the Charterhouse Centre.

APPENDIX: VISITING THE AMPHITHEATRES

Cirencester (SU 016995)
From the main Swindon-Cirencester route, take the A419 Swindon Road, turning right onto the A419 Bristol road at a roundabout (signs to Stroud and Chippenham). Go straight on at a second roundabout, and climbing the hill, take the first left on Cotswold Avenue. The amphitheatre entrance is in a stone wall near an obelisk monument adjacent to a scout hut. Through the gap in the wall, the visitor enters a park area of undulating ground – the earthworks of Roman quarrying. Following the path leads to the entrance to the elliptical banked earthwork of the amphitheatre. There is limited parking on Cotswold Avenue, which is a quiet suburban street. Signposting to the site is currently particularly poor. The fine Corinium Museum in the town contains a very well-displayed collection of Roman material.

Chichester (SU 860050)
From the A27 coast road go into central Chichester on the A286. Parking is available in the Market Road car park. From the car park, pass through a gap in the wall on the east side, and cross the alley to the amphitheatre, in a field beyond. Coming from East Street, go through the city wall onto the road called The Hornet. An alley on the right leads to the end of Whyke Lane. The amphitheatre lies off the alley. All that can be seen of the amphitheatre is a bowl-like hollow in open space, though there is a good information board. Chichester is a beautiful small city, with a fine cathedral and a good District Museum.

Dorchester, Maumbury Rings (SY 694900)
From the southern bypass road, the A35, take the B3147 into the centre of Dorchester. The amphitheatre is on the right side of the road, at the junction of Maumbury Road and the B3147, Weymouth Avenue. Dorchester South railway station is on the town side of the amphitheatre. Opposite is a large car park, though this is the site of a market on Wednesdays and car-boot sales on Sundays. There are a number of alternative car parks. The amphitheatre survives extraordinarily well as a spectacular earthwork. It cannot have suffered a great deal since Stukeley's day, and one can still follow his description on site. It is situated in a public park and is fully accessible, free of charge. At the only surviving entrance, on the right side, there are timber-revetted cut steps allowing access to the crest of the banks (the park is a favourite dog-walking site and it is advisable to watch your footing!).

There are several other places of archaeological interest in the immediate vicinity, including Maiden Castle hillfort (English Heritage: admission charge), signposts to which are passed en route to the amphitheatre. The Dorset County Museum (admission charge) has extensive collections on Roman Dorset. It is within easy walking distance of the town centre, on High Street West, and has an excellent bookshop. The Colliton Park Roman townhouse is also worth a visit.

London (TQ 513281)

From Bank tube station go north along Princes Street, and at the top turn left onto Gresham Street. Guildhall Yard is third on the right. The outline of the amphitheatre is laid out in slabs on the pavement of Guildhall Yard. On the east side is the Guildhall art gallery, and the east entrance passage and part of the arena is impressively displayed in a well-lit and presented exhibition. Admission fee (adults £2.50, concessions £1, children under 16 free; all day on Fridays and from 3.30pm on other days: free) includes the Guildhall Art Gallery itself, which has some fine works, my own favourite being W.L. Wyllie's 'Opening of Tower Bridge in 1894'. The Museum of London, which displays all aspects of the city's history, is nearby on London Wall.

Richborough (TR 325602)

Richborough is on the edge of Sandwich, Kent. From the crossroads of the A256 and the A257 to the west of Sandwich, follow Ash Road towards the town centre. Across a level crossing take a left turn on Richborough Road, following a brown tourist sign to the Roman fort. Afer a couple of miles the Roman fort, with its car park and small visitor centre, with toilets, appears up the slope to the right. It is well signposted. The amphitheatre is on the left of Richborough Road and is accessible from the public footpath under the old railway bridge piers. The shape of the earthwork is clearly visible as a grass-covered oval bank. The site is in the guardianship of English Heritage, as is the fort site itself (admission charge to fort).

Silchester (SU 640625)

Take the A340 main road between Basingstoke and Reading, turn off at the brown tourist sign to Roman Silchester on Bramley Road. Take a left turn on Silchester Road, through Little London. Continue through Silchester village, past the Romans Hotel, turn right at a T-junction with a brown sign 'Roman Silchester'. Turn right at Wall Lane and the car park for Silchester Roman town is on the right. A small, chemical, portaloo-type toilet is available in the car park. A town trail leaflet showing routes and basic information is available free from a box on the fence. Walk through the centre of the town and go left to the amphitheatre. Alternatively reach the site via Wall Lane, past the car park, walking (or driving) round the impressive town defensive circuit. The *cavea* survives as tree-clad banks. The arena, now dry, thanks to drainage put in by English Heritage, is gravelled, and a few courses of the flint walling of the entrances and arena, as well as the niches in the walls to either side of the arena, are consolidated and displayed. Despite the recent work it remains easy to visualise the site as Stukeley saw it.

ENGLISH MIDLANDS

Chester (SJ 405663)
The Chester amphitheatre is situated on Little St John's Street, on the southern part of Chester's inner ring road. The street curves around the site on the east side of the 1950s Newgate Arch. There is a multi-storey car park close by at Pepper Street. From the city centre walk down St John's Street on the south side of East Gate, where the site is signposted. The site is on the far side of the road at the T-junction at the bottom of the street. The northern half of the site is open to visitors, and the principal east and north gate, the north-east quadrant of the *cavea* and the arena may be examined. The north-west quadrant has been the subject of the recent excavations, and at the time of writing is awaiting decisions on future display.

The Lunt, Baginton, Coventry (SP 345752)
Accessed from the A46 Coventry bypass, the location is indicated by brown tourist signs from the area of Coventry airport, along with the Midlands Air Museum. It is in the village of Baginton on Coventry Road. Visible are the reconstructed east gate, granaries and *gyrus* of the timber-built Roman fort. The *gyrus* gives an excellent impression of the arena of any timber-built amphitheatre, except, of course for the fact that there is no *cavea*. There is a car park and toilets at the site (adults £2, concessions £1, under 5s free).

WALES

Caerleon (ST 339906)
The site of Caerleon is well signposted from the M4 motorway with brown tourist signs. On entering Caerleon village, cross the River Usk. Cadw signs appear in the middle of the village. Pass the signs to the Roman fortress and

baths on the right, and continue to the next left-hand turn signposted to the amphitheatre. There is a large car and coach park, with public toilets. It is well worth visiting the museum at Caerleon, and also the other parts of the Roman fort which are displayed, but the amphitheatre is beyond doubt the jewel of this site. It is the most completely excavated and displayed of all of the British amphitheatres.

Carmarthen (SN 224120)

Follow the main A48 from Swansea, take the 'Town Centre' signs to the river bridge, cross the bridge and bear right around the base of the castle up Castle Hill. Turn right along Priory Street and straight on at the Old Oak roundabout. At the end of a terrace of houses on the left is a grass bank with a stone wall running up the side of it flanking a path. This brings the visitor to the east entrance of the arena. The arena walls and passage walls are reconstituted in modern drystone work. The north side is hollowed from a steep hillside, the south side is a low bank. The site is completely unsignposted but is publicly accessible and entry is free. Parking is on-street, just past the amphitheatre.

Tomen-y-Mur (SH 707387)

The site lies on fairly bleak open moorland some 3.5km north of the village of Trawsfynydd, on the A470 road between Ffestiniog and Dolgellau. Access is by way of an unclassified roadwhich turns eastward off the A470, just south of the junction with the A487 road to Porthmadog. The road has no signpost, and is easily missed, though there is an isolated cottage nearby. After some 3km there is a small car park with signage for the Snowdonia National Park and Tomen-y-Mur, just before a cattle grid. To reach the site, walk up the road, over the cattle grid, and the rather unprepossessing humps and bumps of the amphitheatre are on the right immediately after the cattle grid. The central arena is very boggy, and the site is overgrown, though standing in the arena (wear wellies!) the banks appear quite impressive.

NOTES

CHAPTER 1: INTRODUCTION

1. Stukeley, W., 1723 *Of the Roman amphitheatre at Dorchester*, in W. Stukleley, 1776, *Itinerarium Curiosum* (second ed. London), 163
2. Professor Mary Beard in her lecture 'Cutting Gladiators down to size' at the Chester conference *Roman amphitheatres and spectacula*, held in February 2007
3. Boon (1972), 99
4. Wheeler and Wheeler (1928)
5. Golvin (1988)
6. Bomgardner (1993), 379
7. Fulford (1989)
8. Bateman (1997)
9. Wilding (2005)

CHAPTER 2: ORIGINS AND DEVELOPMENT OF THE AMPHITHEATRE

1. Stukeley (1723), 163
2. Bomgardner (2000), 34-5
3. Livy, 39.22.2
4. Livy 44.18.8
5. Wiedemann (1992), 60. Classical references cited in notes 12-14
6. Valerius Maximus 2, 4.7
7. Wiedemann (1992), 6
8. Plutarch, *Caesar*, 5
9. Futtrell (1997), 4-6
10. Cassius Dio 43.22.3
11. Bomgardner (2000), 59
12. Pliny, *Historia Naturalis* 35.15; Stukeley (1723). Many have tried to explain how this might have worked. See Golvin (1988), pl 4: Bomgardner (2000), 36-7
13. Augustus, *Res Gestae*, 22.1
14. Wiedemann (1992), 9

15. Wiedemann (1992), 44: Dodge, H., forthcoming, 'Amphitheatres in the East' in Wilmott (forthcoming)
16. Wiedemann (1992), 42
17. Wiedemann (1992), 43
18. Futtrell (1997), 83
19. Wiedemann (1992), 43
20. For full text in translation see Futrell (2006), 177-8
21. Drinkwater (1983), 78-9
22. Futrell (1997), 89-91
23. Pliny, *Panegyric*, 33
24. For an excellent explanation of this complex concept see Wiedemann (1992), 35-7
25. Futtrell (1997), 75
26. Carroll (2001), 5
27. Drinkwater (1983), 151; Futrell (1997), 72
28. Wiedemann (1992), 47; Plass (1995), 25-8
29. Futrell (2006), 43
30. Cassius Dio 54.2.4

CHAPTER 3: DISCOVERY AND EXPLORATION

1. Stukeley (1723), 169
2. Giraldus Cambrensis, 1191 *The Itinerary of Archibishop Baldwin through Wales*, 5.3
3. Leland, John 15 7.138
4. Aubrey, J., 1668 *Monumenta Britannica* (ed J. Fowles, London 1980, 550-1)
5. Stukeley (1723), 163
6. Piggott, S., 1950 *William Stukeley, an eighteenth century antiquary* (Oxford), 73
7. Stukeley (1723), 163-75
8. Wiener, M.J., 2001 'Alice Arden to Bill Sikes: Changing Nightmares of Intimate Violence in England, 1558-1869', *Jour Brit Studies*, 40.2, 84-212
9. Stukeley (1723), 175
10. Stukeley (1723), 164
11. Gough, R., 1789 *Camden's Britannia* (London), 281
12. Anon 1821, *The History and Antiquities of Silchester in Hampshire* (Winchester) 9-11. The reference to seating terraces is one of a number. How it can be true that these were visible is something of a mystery. Perhaps they were simply cattle paths. See discussion by Boon (1990), 398
13. Grove-Lowe (1848)
14. Roach-Smith (1850), 161-8
15. Roach Smith (1850), 167
16. Stanley, W.O., 1874 'The Amphitheatre of Castell in Anglesey, *Archaeol Jour*, 31, 320-6
17. Royal Comission for Ancient and Historic Monuments (Wales), 1937, *An Inventory of the Ancient Monuments of Anglesey* (London), 105
18. Allen (1888), 267-8
19. Mitchell (1886), 9. Reference has been made to the alleged Bosham amphitheatre by Wilding (2005), 26
20. In his appendix to MacLauchlan, H., 1858 *Memoir written during a survey of the Roman Wall*, (Newcastle upon Tyne), 92-6
21. Bruce, J.C., 1867 *The Roman Wall* (third ed, London), 191
22. Archaeol Jour (1860) 'Proceedings', *Archaeol Jour*, 27, 345-6
23. Scarth (1858), 143-54
24. Rudder (1800)

25 Jour Brit Archaeol Assoc, 1869 'Proceedings of the Congress', *Jour Brit Archaeol Assoc*, 25, 106-8
26 Jour Brit Archaeol Assoc, 1870 'Proceedings of the Congress', *Jour Brit Archaeol Assoc*, 26, 184
27 Pennant, T., 1784 *Tour in Wales, vol ii*, (London), 112
28 Allen (1888), 267-8
29 Pitt Rivers (1887), 23-5, pl 3
30 Bosanquet, R.C., 1904 'Excavations on the line of the Roman Wall in Northumberland; The Roman Camp at Housesteads', *Archaeol Aeliana²*, 25, 192-300; Wilmott, T., forthcoming 'The Housesteads Amphitheatre', *Archaeol Aeliana*
31 Allcroft, A.H., 1908 *Earthwork of England* (London)
32 Allcroft (1908), 586
33 Allcroft (1908), 588
34 Allcroft (1908), 587
35 Allcroft (1908), 584-5
36 Allcroft (1908), 586
37 Allcroft (1908), 589-91
38 Allcroft (1908), 588, fn
39 Pope (1885), 66-9
40 Thompson, M.W., 1977 *General Pitt Rivers* (Bradford-on-Avon), 95
41 Bradley (1975), 1-97
42 Gray (1909), 118-37
43 Hawkes, J., 1982 *Mortimer Wheeler; adventurer in archaeology* (London), 96
44 Hawkes (1982), 100
45 Wheeler and Wheeler (1928), 111-218
46 Jackson, R., 1983 'The Chester gladiator rediscovered', *Britannia*, 14, 87-95
47 Williams (1929)
48 Wilmott, T., Garner, D. and Ainsworth, S. (2006)
49 Newstead, R. and Droop, J.P., 1932 'The Roman Amphitheatre at Chester', *Jour Chester Archaeol Soc*, new ser, 29, 5-40
50 Ashby, T., Hudd, A.E., and Martin, A.T., 1905, 'Excavations at Caerwent on the site of the Romano-British City Venta Silurum', *Archaeologia*, 59, 88-115
51 White, G.M., 1936 'The Chichester Amphitheatre: preliminary excavations', *Antiquaries J*, 16, 148-59
52 Kenyon, K.M., 1935, 'The Roman theatre at Verulamium, St Albans', *Archaeologia*, 84, 214-61
53 Lowther, A.W.G. 1935 *The Roman theatre at Verulamium* (London)
54 Ovens, G.L., 1951 'Carmarthen: ancient landmarks', *Carmarthen Antiquary*, 2, 67-9
55 Jones, G.B.D., 1969, 'Excavations at Carmarthen, 1968', *Carmarthen Antiquary*, 5, 2-5
56 Vatcher (1963)
57 Frere, S.S., 1970 'The Roman theatre at Canterbury', *Britannia*, 1, 83-113
58 Hobley, B., 1973 'Excavations at 'the Lunt' Roman military site, second interim report', *Birmingham and Warwicks Archaeol Soc Trans*, 85, 7-93
59 For full detail of the financial and political manoeuvring see Thompson (1975), 129-33
60 Thompson, F.H., 1975 'The excavation of the Roman amphitheatre at Chester', *Archaeologia*, 105, 127-239
61 Holbrook, N., 1998 'The Amphitheatre: Excavations directed by J.S. Wacher 1962-3 and A.D. McWhirr 1966', in N. Holbrook (ed), *Cirencester, the Roman town defences, public buildings and shops (Cirencester Excavations V)*, Cotswold Archaeological Trust (Cirencester), 145-75
62 Collingwood, R.G. and Richmond, I.A., 1969 *The Archaeology of Roman Britain*, (second, revised ed, London), 116-20, fig. 42
63 Hope, W.H. St J. and Stephenson, M., 1910 'Excavation about the site of the Roman town at Silchester, Hants in 1909', *Archaeologia*, 62, 322
64 Fulford (1989), 1, 6-7
65 Fulford, M., 1989 *The Silchester Amphitheatre; excavations of 1979-85*, Britannia Monograph Ser, 10 (London)

66 Bomgardner, D., 1991 'Amphitheatres on the fringe', *Jour Roman Archaeol*, 4, 282-94
67 Horne, E.A., 1977, 'Air Reconnaissance 1975-77', *Aerial Archaeology*, 1 16-20; Goodburn, R., 1979 'Roman Britain in 1978', *Britannia*, 10, 307
68 Hingley, R., 1985, 'Location, function and status: a Romano-British 'religious complex' at the Noah's Ark Inn, Frilford (Oxfordshire)', *Oxford Journal Archaeology*, 4, 201-214
69 Hingley (1985)
70 Bateman, N., 1997 'The London Amphitheatre: excavations 1987-1996', *Britannia*, 28, 50-85
71 Bateman (1989), 73-85, fig 6
72 Moloney, C., 1996 'Catterick Racecourse', *Current Archaeology*, 148, 128-32; Wilding, 2005, 50-1
73 By local archaeologist Dr W. Lonie: Keppie L.J.F., 1993, 'Scotland' in 'Roman Britain in 1992', *Britannia*, 24, 282
74 Keppie, L.J.F., 1994 'Scotland' in 'Roman Britain in 1993', *Britannia*, 25, 261; Clarke, S., Tebbs, A. and Wise, A., 1996 *Newstead 1996; the northern vicus and the amphitheatre, excavation and survey*, University of Bradford interim report (www.trimontium.freeserve.co.uk/bradford1.html)
75 Bishop, M.C. 1997, '"Gladiator's arena" found near Edinburgh', *British Archaeology*, June 1997, 5
76 Wilmott, Garner and Ainsworth (2006); Ainsworth, S. and Wilmott, T., 2005 *Chester Amphitheatre; from gladiators to gardens* (London)
77 Wilding, R., 2005 *Roman Amphitheatres in England and Wales* (Chester)
78 Wilmott, T. (ed), forthcoming, *Roman amphitheatres and spectacula; a 21st century perspective; papers from the Chester conference, 16th-18th February, 200*, BAR International Series (Oxford)

CHAPTER 4: DISTRIBUTION, TYPE AND FUNCTION

1 Stukeley (1723), 175
2 Sargent, A., 2002, 'The North-South Divide Revisited: Thoughts on the Character of Roman Britain', *Britannia*, 33, 220-6
3 Stukeley (1732), 125
4 As found for instance in Collingwood and Richmond (1969), 116-7; Johnson, A., 1983 *Roman Forts* (London), 219; Wilson, R., 1980 *Roman Forts* (London), 64
5 Thompson (1975), 128
6 Goldsworthy, A., 2003 *The complete Roman Army*, (London), 106; Le Bohec, Y., 1994 *The Roman Imperial Army* (London), 113, 235
7 Watson, G., 1969 *The Roman Soldier* (London), 147-8
8 Millett, M., 1990 *The Romanisation of Britain* (Cambridge), 87
9 Frere (1987), 65
10 Millet (1990), 87
11 Crummy, P., 2005, 'The Colchester Circus', *Current Archaeol*, 169
12 Millett (1990), 65-7
13 Wacher (1995), 255-7
14 Millett (1990), 69-71
15 Tacitus, *Annales*, 14:33
16 Millett (1990), 88-90; Wacher (1995), 88-90; Creighton (2006), 93-107
17 Marsden, P., 1987 *The Roman Forum Site in London* (London), 73
18 Bateman (1997), 67
19 Mattingly (2006), 19; Creighton (2006), 98-9
20 Several stamps reading ICLV, and MIBL: Bateman (1997), 54
21 Wacher (1995), 94
22 cf Millett, M., 1994, 'Evaluating Roman London', *Archaeol Jour*, 151, 427-35
23 Hopkins, K., 1980 'Taxes and trade in the Roman empire 200BC-400AD', *Jour Roman Studies*, 70, 101-25
24 RIB 1962; Frere, S.S., 1983, *Verulamium excavations, Vol II*, Soc Antiqs London Res Rep, 41 (London), 67-71

25 Frere, S.S., 1985 'Civic pride; a factor in Roman town planning', in F. Grew and B. Hobley, *Roman urban topography in Britain and the western empire*, CBA Res Rep, 59 (London), 34-6
26 Blagg, T.F.C., 1990 'Architectural munificence in Britain: the evidence of the inscriptions', *Britannia*, 21, 13-32
27 RIB 707
28 RIB 288
29 Bradley (1975), 38-9
30 Guzzo, P.G., 1998 *Pompeii* (Naples); Bomgardner (2000), 41-2; *CIL* 10.852
31 Bomgardner (2000), 241, fn 45
32 Mauri, A., 1955 *Studi e recherché sull'anfiteatro flavio Puteolano* (Naples), 85-9
33 *CIL* 13.1642. Quoted by Frere (1985), 35 (op cit, note 25)
34 Fulford (1989), 179
35 Millett (1990), 83
36 Wacher (1995), 524
37 It has been suggested that the Dorchester amphitheatre was a military structure which predated the foundation of the town, cf Bradley (1975), 76-7; Bateman (1997), 77
38 Fulford (1989), 192
39 Millett (1990), 83; RIB 92, 93
40 Wacher (1995), 259
41 White (1936), 158
42 Wacher (1995), 304
43 Holbrook (1998), 158
44 Wacher (1995), 391
45 Fulford (1989), 192
46 Bradley (1975), 79; Fulford (1989), 186
47 For this debate see Manley, J., 2002 *AD 43; the Roman invasion of Britain*; Grainge, G., 2005 *The Roman invasions of Britain*, (Tempus, Stroud)
48 Particularly in the Antonine itinerary which lists only a single Channel crossing – Boulogne to Richborough
49 Millett, M. and Wilmott, T., 2003 'Rethinking Richborough' in P. Wilson (ed) *The Archaeology of Roman Towns* (Oxford), 184-194
50 Roach-Smith, C., 1850 *The antiquities of Richborough, Reculver and Lympne* (London) 161-5
51 Martin, L., 2001, *Richborough amphitheatre, Kent: report on geophysical surveys, February 2001*, English Heritage centre for Archaeology Report, 30/2001
52 Fulford (1989), 193
53 Hingley (1985)
54 Futrell (1997), 70-73
55 Dunnett, R. (1971), 'The excavation of the Roman theatre at Gosbecks', *Britannia*, 2, 27-47
56 Kenyon (1935), 99; Grenier, A., 1958 *Manuel d'archaeologie Gallo Romaine III: L'architecture 2: Ludi et circenses, théâtres, amphithéâtres* (Paris), 880-85
57 Golvin (1988), 226. Futrell (1997) also uses the term 'mixed edifice' for this type
58 Golvin (1988), pl xlviii
59 Personal communication from Dr Zahrin Velickov
60 Carroll, M., 2001 *Romans, Celts and Germans; the German Provinces of Rome* (Tempus, Stroud), 52
61 Bomgardner (1993, 388) suggests this strongly for the British urban amphitheatres. Bateman (1997, 8) 1, does not think this likely, citing Millett (1990, 72) on the lack of evidence for the use of military staff on such projects
62 Golvin (1988), 156. Bomgardner (1993), 381, m.45, remains unsure of this conclusion
63 Le Roux, P., 1990 'L'amphithithéâtre et le soldat sous l'Empire Romaine' in C. Domergue, C. Landes and J-M Pallier, *Spectacula, I: gladiateurs et amphitheatres. Actes du colloque tenu a Toulouse et a Lattes le 26, 27 et 28 Mai 1987*, (Toulouse), 203-15: Bateman (1997), 81

THE ROMAN AMPHITHEATRE IN BRITAIN

64 Boon (1972), 99
65 Mattingley, D., 2006 *An Imperial possession: Britain in the Roman Empire* (London), 187
66 Le Bohec, Y., 1989 *The Roman Imperial Army* (London), 135
67 See the collected papers in Goldsworthy, A. and Haynes, I., 1999 *The Roman army as a community*, Jour Roman Archaeol Supplement Ser, 34 (Rhode Island)
68 Haynes (1999), 7
69 Goldsworthy, A., 2003 *The Complete Roman Army*, (London), 106: my italics in quote
70 Golvin (1988), 156
71 For a possible site indicated by the street plan, see Ottaway, P. (1993), *Roman York* (London), 33-4
72 RCHME, 1962 *Eburacvm, Rroman York* (London),135, 133
73 Collingwood and Richmond (1969), 116-7
74 Allen (1888)
75 Clarke, Tebbs and Wise (1996)
76 Fabricius, E., Winkelmann, F., Stade, K., various dates, *Der Obergermanisch-Rätische Limes des Römerreiches*. For Dambach, abt A, band vi, 42-3. For Zugmantel, abt A band ii, 73; abt B, band ii, taf 1
77 Schmotz, K., 2005 'Erste Arbeitsergebnisse zum Amphitheater von Künzing, Lkr. Degendorf', in K. Schmotz (ed), *Vorträge des 23. Niederbayerischen Archäologentages* (Deggendorf), 149-66; Schmotz, K., 2006, *Das hölzerne Amphitheater von Künzing, Lkr. Degendorf. Kenntnisstand und erste rekonstruktionnsätze nach abschliss de geländearbeiten im Jahr 2004*, in K Schmotz (ed), *Vorträge des 24. Niederbayerischen Archäologentages* (Deggendorf), 95-118
78 Crew, P., 1980 'Forden Gaer, Montomery', *Bull Board Celtic Studies*, 28 (1978-80), 730-41; Wilding (2005), 86
79 Bishop, M.C., 1997 '"Gladiator's arena" found near Edinburgh', *British Archaeology*, June 1997, 5
80 Hobley (1973), 32-4
81 Xenopon, *De re equestri*, iii, 5
82 Bomgardner (2000), 212; Jennison, G., 1937 *Animals for show and pleasure in Ancient Rome* (Manchester), 178
83 CIL 13.8174
84 CIL 13.12048
85 Fabricius, E., Winkelmann, F., Stade, K., *Der Obergermanisch-Rätische Limes des Römerreiches*. abt A band ii, 73
86 Jennison (1937), 148, 172
87 Bateman (1997), 80, n.154

CHAPTER 5: PLANNING, CONSTRUCTION AND ARCHITECTURE

1 Stukeley (1723), 166
2 Golvin, J.-C., 1988 *L'Amphithéâtre Romain* (Paris), pl 2
3 Golvin (1988); Hallier, G., 1990 'La géométrie des amphithéâtres militairs du Rhin et Danube', in *Akten des 14.Internationalen Limeskongresses in Carnuntum, Vienna*, 71-82; Wilson-Jones, M., 1993 'Designing amphitheatres', *Mitteilungen des Deutschen Archäologischen Instituts Römischen Abteilung*, 100, 394
4 Wilson-Jones (1993), 394
5 Ziebart *et al.* (2006)
6 Fulford (1989), 13
7 Bradley (1975), 54, fig. 16
8 Wilson-Jones (1993), 391
9 Wilson-Jones (1993), 394-5
10 Sunter in Fulford (1989), 170-1
11 Wilson-Jones (1993), 394-5

[12] Stukeley (1723), 166. He criticises interpretation of the Colosseum layout: 'I suspect Desgodetz, in laying down his plot of the *Collisaeum*, has without necessity employed no less than eight centres, which is a matter of great perplexity'
[13] Ziebart *et al.* (2006)
[14] Fulford (1989), 13
[15] Holbrook (1998)
[16] Thompson (1975)
[17] Wilmott, Garner and Ainsworth (2006)
[18] Bradley (1975), 43
[19] Sunter in Fulford (1989), 162; Bateman (1997), 54
[20] For this feature see many plans in Golvin (1988) and Bomgardner (2000), esp. 162-4; for Xanten-Birten see Lehner, H., 1910, 'Vetera; ausgrabungen in die Jahre 1908-1910', *Bonner Jahrbücher*, 119, 230-61
[21] Fulford (1989), 23, fig. 9
[22] Golvin (1988), 318-19; Jacobelli, L., 2003 *Gladiators at Pompeii* (Los Angeles), 58-61
[23] Boon, G.C., 1974 *Silchester: the roman town of Calleva* (Newton Abbott), 148
[24] Bradley (1975), 50
[25] Fulford (1989), 186
[26] Jennison (1937), 178
[27] Holbrook (1998)
[28] Fulford (1989), 179
[29] Bateman (1997), 54
[30] Bradley (1975), 58
[31] Sunter in Fulford (1989), 166-7, 170, 175
[32] Bradley (1975), 56
[33] Stukeley (1723), 174
[34] Gough, R., 1789 *Camden's Britannia* (London), 142
[35] Fulford (1989), 14, 17
[36] Little (1971)
[37] Boon (1990), 399
[38] Stukeley (1723), 178
[39] Golvin (1988), 381; Bomgardner (1993), 386
[40] Bateman (1997), 73
[41] Holbrook (1998), 173
[42] Sunter in Fulford (1989), 163
[43] Wright, J.A., 1929, 'Notes on the planning and setting out of the amphitheatre' in Wheeler and Wheeler (1928), 215-6
[44] Wilson-Jones (1993), 395
[45] Thompson (1975), fig. 52
[46] Hallier (1990)
[47] As at Avenches, see Bridel, P., 2004 *Aventicum XIII: L'Amphithéâtre d'Avenches*, I, *Cahiers d'Archéologie Romande*, 96, (Lausanne)
[48] Garner, D. and Wilmott, T., in prepration *The Roman Amphitheatre at Chester, excavations 2004-2006. Vol 1 the amphitheatre*, Grosvenor Museum Archaeological Report (Chester)

CHAPTER 6: THE SITES; THE SOUTH AND EAST

[1] Stukeley (1723), 175
[2] Wilding (2005)

3   Bateman (1997), (2000)
4   Ziebart *et al.* (2006)
5   Bateman (1997), 58
6   Bateman (1997), 67
7   Bateman (1997), 67
8   Bateman (2000), 28
9   Bateman (1997), 58
10 Esmonde-Cleary, A.S., 2000 'Greater London' in 'Roman Britain on 1999', *Britannia*, 31, 415
11 Stukeley (1776), 178
12 Fulford (1989)
13 Fulford (1989), 13-29, 161-7, 179-83
14 Sunter in Fulford (1989), 166-7
15 Sunter in Fulford (1989), 167
16 Fulford (1989), 47
17 Sunter in Fulford (1989), 175
18 Allcroft (1908), 584-5
19 Stukeley (1723)
20 Collingwood and Richmond (1969), 119
21 Bradley (1975), 2
22 Pope (1885)
23 Bradley (1975)
24 Bradley (1975), 7-38
24 Bradley (1975), 14
26 Bradley (1975), 45
27 Bradley (1975), 74
28 Bradley (1975), 79; Fulford (1989), 192
29 White (1936)
30 Wacher (1995), 265
31 Wheeler, L., 1988, 'Historical Background', in Holbrook (1998), 145-7
32 Rudder, S., 1779 *A new history of Gloucestershire*, Cirencester
33 Rudder, S., 1800, *History of the ancient town of Cirencester*, second edn, Cirencester
34 Skinner, J., 1824, Continuation of journal from Cheltenham to Birdlip and Cirencester, November 10th 1824, British Museum Add Ms 33679
35 JBAA (1869), 213
36 JBAA (1869), 106-8
37 Holbrook (1998), 145-75
38 Holbrook (1998), 173
39 Holbrook (1998), 153
40 Holbrook (1998), 161
41 Ovens (1951)
42 Jones (1969)
43 Jones (1969), 4
44 Little (1971)
45 Jones (1969), 4
46 Little (1971), 60
47 Wacher (1995), 391
48 James (2003), 18-20
49 Horne (1977); Goodburn, R., 1979 'Roman Britain in 1978', *Britannia*, 10, 307
50 Maxwell, G.S. and Wilson, D.R., 1987 'Air reconnaissance in Britain, 1977-84', *Britannia*, 18, 1-48
51 Wacher (1995), 249-50, followed by Bateman (1997), 76, fig. 6
52 Esmonde-Cleary, A.S., 1995 'East Anglia' in 'Roman Britain in 1999', *Britannia*, 31, 411

53 Cott (2002)
54 Ashby et al. (1905)
55 Wacher (1995), 398; Brewer, R.J., 1993 *Caerwent Roman Town*, Cadw guidebook (Cardiff), 53
56 Stukeley (1776), 125
57 Millett and Wilmott (2003)
58 Pearson, A., 2002, *The Roman Shore Forts* (Tempus, Stroud)
59 Martin, L., 2001 *Richborough amphitheatre, Kent; report on geophysical surveys, February 2001*, English Heritage Centre for Archaeology report 30/2001
60 Roach-Smith (1850)
61 Grove-Lowe (1848)
62 Kenyon (1935)
63 Lowther (1935)
64 Brannigan, K., 1987 *The Catuvellauni* (Stroud), 75
65 Wacher (1995), 228
66 Kenyon (1935), 218
67 Lowther (1935), 31-4
68 Brannigan, K., 1987 *The Catuvellauni* (Stroud), 77
69 Frere (1970)
70 Todd, M., 1994 'Charterhouse on Mendip: interim report on excavations 1994', *Somerset Archaeol and Nat Hist Proceedings*, 138, 75-9
71 Scarth (1858)
72 Allcroft (1908), 589-91
73 Gray (1909)
74 Gray (1909), 125
75 Gray (1909), pl. 3
76 Gray (1909), 127
77 Bradford and Goodchild 1939
78 Hingley (1985)
79 This account is compiled from the interim reports of the Marcham/Frilford project as follows: Gosden, C. and Lock, G., 2003 'Frilford: A Romano-British ritual pool in Oxfordshire?' *Current Archaeology*, 184, 156-9; Lock, G., Gosden, C., Griffiths, D., Daly, P., Trifkovic, V., and Marston, T., 2002 'Hillforts of the Ridgeway Project: excavations at Marcham/Frilford 2001' *South Midlands Archaeology*, 32, 69-83; Lock, G., Gosden, C., Griffiths, D., and Daly, P., 2003 'Hillforts of the Ridgeway Project: excavations at Marcham/Frilford 2002', *South Midlands Archaeology*, 33: 84-91; Lock, G. and Gosden, C., 2004 'The Ridgeway and Vale Project: Excavations at Marcham/Frilford 2003 – interim report', *South Midlands Archaeology* 34, 84-94; Gosden, C. and Lock, G., 2005 'The Vale and Ridgeway Project: excavations at Marcham/Frilford 2004', *South Midlands Archaeology*, 35, 94-105
80 Lock, G. and Gosden, C., 2006 *The Vale and Ridgeway Project: Excavations at Marcham/Frilford 2005: interim report*, www.arch.ox.ac.uk/research/research_projects/marcham
81 Vatcher (1963)
82 Pottery report by K. Annable in Vatcher (1963), 211-12
83 Vatcher (1963), 199
84 Pitt Rivers, Gen. A.L.F., 1887 *Excavations on Cranbourne Chase near Rushmore on the borders of Dorset and Wiltshire*, vol 1 (London), 23-5, pl. 3

CHAPTER 7: THE SITES: THE NORTH AND WEST

1 Stukeley (1723), 168
2 Jackson (1983)

3 Williams (1929)
4 Newstead and Droop (1932)
5 Thompson (1975)
6 Ainsworth and Wilmott (2005); Wilmott, Garner and Ainsworth (2006)
7 Personal communication from Dr Peter Hill
8 Boon (1987), 5
9 The other being Silchester
10 Weighall, A., 1926 *Wanderings in Roman Britain* (London), 279
11 Allcroft (1908), 587
12 Wheeler and Wheeler (1928), 111
13 Boon (1972), 80
14 Wheeler and Wheeler (1928), 113
15 Wheeler and Wheeler (1928), 115-8
16 Wheeler and Wheeler (1928), 115
17 Boon (1987), 63
18 Wheeler and Wheeler (1928), 135
19 Wheeler and Wheeler (1928), 123
20 As at Avenches, see Bridel, P., 2004 *Aventicum XIII: L'Amphithéâtre d'Avenches*, l, *Cahiers d'Archéologie Romande*, 96 (Lausanne)
21 As defined by Peter Hill, 2006 *The Construction of Hadrian's Wall*, (London), 41
22 The fire is mentioned by Boon (1987, 30); see Wheeler and Wheeler (1928), 116
23 Redating from Wheeler by Boon (1972, 45), who stresses that the contextual information of groupings of material needs to be treated with caution
24 Quote from Boon (1987, 64); see Wheeler and Wheeler (1928), 119
25 Wheeler and Wheeler (1928), 140
26 Miller, S.N., 1929, 'stamped tiles' in Wheeler and Wheeler (1928), 159-60
27 Richmond, I.A., 1950 'Excavations at the Roman Fort of Newstead', *Procs. Soc Antiqs Scotland*, 84, 1-38
28 By local archaeologist Dr W. Lonie; Keppie L.J.F., 1993, 'Scotland' in 'Roman Britain in 1992', *Britannia*, 24, 282
29 Keppie L.J.F., 1994, 'Scotland' in 'Roman Britain in 1993', *Britannia*, 25, 261; Clarke, S., Tebbs, A. and Wise, A., 1996 *Newstead 1996; the northern vicus and the amphitheatre, excavation and survey*, University of Bradford interim report (www.trimontium.freeserve.co.uk/bradford1.html)
30 Schmotz (2006); above
32 Jarrett (1968), 111-13
33 Guest, Lady Charlotte, 1877 *The Mabinogion* (Cardiff), 425
34 Jarrett, M.J., 1964 'Excavations at Tomen y Mur, 1962: interim report', *J Merioneth Historical and Record Soc*, 4, 171-5
35 Simpson, G., 1964 *Britons and the Roman Army*, (London)
36 Pennant, T., 1784 *Tour in Wales, vol ii*, (London), 112
37 Allen (1888)
38 Gresham (1938)
39 Wilding (2005), 110
40 Above
41 Hobley (1973)
42 Bishop (1997)
43 Neighbour (2002); (2007)
44 Jarrett, M.J., 1969 *The Roman Frontier in Wales* (Cardiff), 85-8
45 Crew (1980); Wilding (2005), 86
46 Breeze, D.J. 2006
47 Burnham, B.C., 'The Northern Counties' in 'Roman Britain in 2003', *Britannia*, 35, 273
48 Wilding (2005)
49 Bidwell, P., 1997 *Roman forts in Britain* (London), 105

50   Wacher (1995), 401-7
51   Dobinson, C., 1990-93, 'Field Survey at Aldborough', *Yorks Arch Soc Roman Antiquities Section Bulletin*, 7, 15; 8, 21; 9, 9; 10, 3
52   Collingwood, R.G., 1930 *The Archaeology of Roman Britain* (London), fig 42e
53   Smith (1984), 16; Wilding (2005), 22
54   Ecroyd-Smith, H. 1852 *Reliquae Isurianae* (London), 24
55   For example in Wacher 1995, 401-7; Charlesworth, D., 1970 *Aldborough Roman Town and Museum*, DoE official handbook (London)
56   Dobinson, C., 1995, *Aldborough Roman Town*, English Heritage guidebook (London), 5
57   '*Viator Militaris*', 1811 'A Roman Inscription from Aldborough in Yorkshire', *Gentleman's Magazine*, 1811, part 2, 312
58   Moloney, C., 1996 'Catterick Racecourse', *Current Archaeology*, 148, 128-32; Wilding, 2004, 50-1
59   Wilson, P.R., 2002 *Cataractonium, Roman Catterick and its hinterland: excavations and research, 1958-1997*, CBA Research Report 128, Part 1 (London), 30, 40-2
60   St Joseph, J.K., 1973, 'Air Reconnaissance in Britain', *J Roman Studies*, 43, 239-40
61   Davies, J.L. and Jones, R.H., 2002 'Recent research on Roman camps in Wales' in P. Freeman, J. Bennett, Z. Fiema and B. Hoffman (eds), *Limes XVIII; proceedings of the xviiith International Congress of Roman Frontier Studies held in Amman, Jordan (September 2000)* BAR Internat Ser 1084, (Oxford), 835-41
62   Gibson, A., 1999 *The Walton Basin Project; excavation and survey in a prehistoric landscape 1993-7*, CBA Research Report 118 (London), 7-8; Wilding (2004), 114
63   As suggested by Gibson (1999), 8

CHAPTER 8: THE ARENA SPECTACLE IN BRITAIN

1   Stukeley (1723), 174
2   Smith, C.R., 1854, *Collectanea Antiqua iii*, (London) 193-6; Haverfield, F., 1918 'Roman Leicester', *Archaeol Jour*, 75, 1-45
3   Weighall, A., 1926 *Wanderings in Roman Britain* (London)
4   Frere, S.S. and Tomlin, R.S.O., 1995 *The Roman Inscriptions of Britain, Vol 2, Fascicule 7 Graffiti on Samian Ware* (Oxford), RIB 2501.586
5   Todd, M., 1973 *The Coritani* (London), 66
6   Ibid; Frere, S.S., 1975, Review of B. Cunliffe, *The Regni* and M. Todd, *The Coritani*, *Antiquaries Jour*, 60, 145-6
7   Wacher (1995), 375
8   Frere, S.S., 1979 *Bignor Roman Villa: guidebook* (St Ives), 11; Wilding (2005), 18
9   Jennison (1937), 160
10 Pompeii: Jacobelli (2003), 49-51; Zliten: Ville (1965)
11 Bateman (1997), 58, fn 24
12 Smith, D.J., 1980, 'Mosaics' in I.M. Stead, *Rudston Roma Villa* (Leeds), 131-8; Smith, D.J., 1976 *The Roman mosaics from Rudston, Brantingham and Horkstow* (Kingston upon Hull)
13 Wilson, R.J.A., 2003 'The Rudston Venus mosaic revisited: a spear-bearing lion?', *Britannia*, 34, 288-91
14 Toynbee, J.M.C., 1948, 'Beasts and their names in the Roman Empire', *Papers of the British School at Rome,* ns 3, 24-36
15 Ward-Perkins, J.B. and Toynbee, J.M.C., 1949 'The Hunting Baths of Lepcis Magna', *Archaeologia*, 93, 165-95
16 Poinssot, L. and Quoniam, P., 1952 'Bêtes d'amphithéâtre sur trios mosaïques du Bardo, *Karthago*, 3, 129-65
17 Bomgardner 2000, 139; this mosaic also features the presiding deity Diana, who holds a millet stalk, and a number of leopards, all of whom have names
18 Rule, M. and Sturgess, K., 1974 *Brading Roman Villa* (Farnborough), 6

19 Price, J.E. and F.G.H., 1881 *A description of the remains of Roman buildings at Morton, near Brading, IW* (London)
20 Henig, M., 1984 *Art in Roman Britain* (Oxford), 220
21 Ling, R., 1991 'Brading, Brantingham and York; a new look at some fourth-century mosaics' *Britannia*, 22, 147-95; Witts, P., 1994 'Interpreting the Brading 'Abraxus' Mosaic', *Britannia*, 25, 111-17
22 For instance the Caesar Gallus (351-4) is recorded by Ammianus Marcellinus (xiv.7.2) as over fond of gladiatorial fights (Witts, op cit)
23 Pace, B., 1955 *I mosaici di Piazza Armerina* (Rome)
24 Toynbee, J.M.C., 1986 *The Roman art treasures from the temple of Mithras*, London Middlesex Archaeol Soc Special Paper, 7, 46
25 Puttnam, W.G. and Rainey, A., 1972 'Fourth interim report on excavations at Dewlish Roman vila, 1972 and on the mosaic in Room 11', *Proc dorset nature Hist Archaeol Soc*, 94, 81-6
26 Witts, op cit; Besaouch, A, 1985 'Nouvelles observations sur les sodalités Africaines', *CRAI* 453-75; Bomgardner, 2000, 139-41
27 Johnston, D.E., 1994 'North African influences in Romano-British mosaics' in P. Johnson, R. Ling and D.J. Smith (eds), *Fifth international colloquium on ancient mosaics*, Jour Roman Archaeol Supp Ser, 9 (Ann Arbor, Michigan), 295-306
28 RCHME, 1962 *Eburacvm, Rroman York* (London), 135, 133
29 RCHME, 1962 *Eburacvm, Rroman York* (London), 135, 133
30 Jackson, R, 1983 'The Chester gladiator rediscovered', *Britannia*, 14, 87-95
31 My italics. Juvenal, *Satires* viii, 203-5; Loeb Classical Library, 1918 *Juvenal and Persius* (London), 174-5. See also Junckelman, M., 2000 *'Familia Gladiatoria*, the heroes of the amphitheatre' in E. Köhne and C. Ewigleben, 2000 *Gladiators and Caesars; the power of spectacle in ancient Rome* (London), 31-74
32 Jackson, op cit, 92
33 Brewer, R.J. 1982 *Corpus Signorum Imperii Romani*, Vol 1, Britain, fasc 4, Wales, nos 37, 38
34 Painter, K.S., 1969, 'A Roman bronze helmet from Hawkedon, Suffolk', *Brit Mus Quarterly*, 33, 121-130
35 Robert, L., 1948 'Monuments de Gladiateurs dans l'Orient Grec', *Hellenica* 5, 77–99
36 Christou, D., 1996 *Kourion; its monuments and local museums* (Nicosia)
37 Junkelmann (2000)
38 Junkelmann (2000), 137
39 RIB 2503.119; Hull, M.R., 1963 *The Roman Potters' kilns of Colchester*, Soc Antiqs London Research Rep, 21 (London) 96
40 Jacobelli (2003), 49-51
41 Toynbee, J.M.C. (1964) *Art in Britain under the Romans* (Cambridge), 411-3
42 Ville, G., 1981, *La Gladiature en Occident des origins á la mort de Domitien* (Paris), 214
43 Suetonius, *Tiberius*, 72
44 Tacitus, *Annales*, 1.21
45 Ling, R., 1981 'The wall plaster from Balkerne Lane' in P. Crummy, *Colchester Archaeological Report 3: excavations at Lion Walk, Balkerne Lane an Middleborough, Colchester, Essex* (Colchester), 146-53
46 Junkelmann (2000), 76, 103
47 By D.S. Neal: cf Neal, D.S., 1965 'The *Figidarium* Mosaics' in A. Detsicas 1965, 'Excavations at Eccles 1964, third interim report' *Arch Cantiana*, 80, 69-91; Neal (1981), 76
48 Smith, D.J., 1975 'Roman mosaics in Britain before the fourth century', in *La Mosaïque Gréco-Romaine* (Centre de la Recherche Scientifique, Paris), 271
49 Frere, S.S., 1979 *Bignor Roman Villa: guidebook* (St Ives), 11
50 Foucher (1994)
51 Ville, G., 1965 'Essai de datation de la mosaïque des gladiateurs de Zliten', in *La mosaïque gréco-romaine, Editions du Centre National de la Recherche Scientifique, Paris*, 147–55
52 Junkelmann (2000) Madrid: 137, Verona: 107, Nennig: 88; Hope, C.A. and Whitehouse, H.V., 2003 'The Gladiator Jug from Ismant el-Kharab', in G.E. Brown and C.A. Hope (eds), *The Oasis Papers*, 3 (Oxford), 291-310

53 Hellmann, M-C, 1987 *Les représentations de gladiateurs sur les lampes romaines*, in C. Landes and D. Cazes (eds), *Les Gladiateurs*, (Lattes), 83–5
54 He has probably thrown his net, as in an image in a mosaic in the Archaeological Museum, Madrid; Junkelmann (2000), 137
55 Hull, M.R. (1963) *The Roman Potters' kilns of Colchester*, Soc Antiqs London Research Rep, 21 (London), 47-74
56 Ibid, 92-3, fig. 50
57 Hull, M.R., 1958 *Roman Colchester*, Soc Antiqs London Research Rep, 20 (London), 170, pl. xxxa
58 RIB 2419.18, 2419.19
59 Visy, Z., 1989 *A római limes Magyarorsázgon* (Budapest), 28
60 Köhne, E. and Ewigleben C., 2000 *Gladiators and Caesars; the power of spectacle in ancient Rome* (London), fig. 140
61 Bögli, H., 1989 *Aventicum; the Roman city and the museum*, (Avenches), 15
62 Friendship-Taylor, R. and Jackson, R. 2001 'A new gladiator find from Piddington, Northants', *Antiquity*, 75, 27-8
63 Allason-Jones, L. and Miket, R., 1984 *The Catalogue of small finds from South Shields Roman fort* (Newcastle-upon-Tyne)
64 Worrell, S., 2004 'Roman Britain in 2003; finds reported under the Portable Antiquities Scheme', *Britannia*, 35, 323-4
65 Boon, G.C., 1971, 'Some Roman objects from Carmarthen', *Carmarthen Antiquary*, 7, 136-9
66 Bird, J., 2004 'The decorated samian from the London amphitheatre', *Study Group for Roman Pottery, Newsletter 38*, December 2004
67 Wheeler and Wheeler (1928), 170, pl. xxxiv
68 For the best account of Nemesis see Hornum, M.B., 1993 *Nemesis, the Roman State and the Games* (Leiden)
69 Fear, A.T., 1991 'Religious graffiti in two Spanish amphitheatres', *Oxford Jour Archaeol*, 10, 123-5
70 Knight, J.K., 1998 *Caerleon Roman Fortress* (Cardiff), 36
71 Wheeler and Wheeler (1928), 113
72 Foucher (1994); Bomgardner (2000), 113
73 Foucher (1994)
74 Thompson (1975), 184
75 Boon (1972), 100
76 Tomlin, R.S.O. and Hassall, M.W.C. 'Inscriptions – Roman Britain in 2002', *Britannia*, 34, 362
77 Boon (1987), 41
78 Tertullian, *Apologia* 15.4; *Ad Nationes* 1.10.47; Kyle (1998), 155-8
79 Wheeler and Wheeler (1928), 161

CHAPTER 9: AFTER THE ROMANS

1 Bateman (2000), 40-1
2 Mattingly, D., 2006 *An imperial possession: Britain in the Roman Empire* (London), 376
3 White (1936), 156-7
4 Thompson (1975), 153-4
5 Cüppers, H., 1979 *Trier Amphitheatre* (Mainz), 26
6 Wilmott, Garner and Ainsworth (2006), 13
7 Matthews, K.J., 2003 'Chester's amphitheatre after Rome, a centre of Christian worship', *Cheshire History*, 43, 12-27
8 Wheeler and Wheeler (1928), 115
9 Wilmott, T., 1997 *Birdoswald; Excavtions on a Roman fort on Hadrian's Wall and its successor settlements, 1987-92*, English Heritage Archaeol Rep, 13 (London)

10. Barker P., 1999 *The Baths Basilica, Wroxeter Excavations 1966-90*, English Heritage Archaeol Rep, 8 (London)
11. Holbrook (1998), 174
12. Wacher (1995), 322
13. Wacher (1976), 16-17
14. Holbrook (1998) 175
15. Fulford (1989), 56
16. Fulford (1989), 57
17. Bateman (2000), 46-9
18. Ottaway, P., 1993 *Roman York* (London)
19. See the chapter on early Christian sources for the condemnation of the amphitheatre and the accounts of martyrdom in Futrell (2006), 160-88
20. Bateman (2000), 73
21. Thacker, A.P. and Lewis, C.P. (eds), 2003 *Victoria County History of Cheshire, Vol 5, Part 1, The City of Chester* (London), 88
22. Gray (1909), 227
23. Bradley (1975), 90
24. Roberts, I., 1990 *Pontefract Castle* (Wakefield)
25. Leland, John 15 7.138
26. Stukeley (1723), 175

CHAPTER 10: CONCLUSIONS: AMPHITHEATRES AND SPECTACLES IN BRITAIN

1. Fulford (1997), 187
2. Crummy, P., 1982 'The Roman theatre at Colchester', *Britannia*, 13, 299-302
3. Tacitus, *Annales*, xiv.32
4. Creighton (2006), 113
5. Bateman (1991), 76
6. Painter (1969)
7. Creighton (2006), 93-107
8. Creighton (2006), 107
9. Futrell (1997), 75
10. Futrell (1997), 76
11. Boon (1990), 399
12. Fulford (1989), 186
13. I would like to thank my wife for this observation!
14. Fulford (1989), 189
15. Fulford (1989), 191-3
16. Fulford (1989), 193
17. Gosden and Lock (2005)
18. Wilmott (forthcoming) 'New excavations at the Amphitheatre of the Legionary Fortress of Chester (Deva), Britain', in *Roman Frontier Studies XX* (Leon, Spain); Mason, D., 2000, *The Elliptical building; an image of the Roman world?*, Chester Archaeology Excavation Report, 12 (Chester); Mason, D.J.P., 'The status of Roman Chester; a reply' *J Chester Archaeol Soc*, new ser, 68, 53-9
19. Haynes (1999), 7
20. *CIL* 13.12048
21. Sommer, S. (forthcoming), 'The auxiliary amphitheatres of the Roman frontiers' in Wilmott, T. (ed) forthcoming
22. Mattingly (2006), 317

SELECT BIBLIOGRAPHY

Ainsworth, S. and Wilmott, T., 2005 *Chester Amphitheatre; from gladiators to gardens* (London)
Allcroft, A.H., 1908 *Earthwork of England* (London)
Allen, J.R., 1888 'Amphitheatre at Tomen y Mur, Merionethshire', *Arch Cambrensis*, 5, 267-8
Ashby, T., Hudd, A.E. and Martin, A.T., 1905 'Excavations at Caerwent on the site of the Romano-British City Venta Silurum', *Archaeologia*, 59, 88-115
Bateman, N., 1997 'The London Amphitheatre: excavations 1987-1996', *Britannia*, 28, 50-85
Bateman, N., 2000 *Gladiators at the Guildhall; the story of London's Roman amphitheatre*, (London)
Bishop, M.C. 1997, '"Gladiator's arena" found near Edinburgh', *British Archaeology*, June 1997, 5
Blagg, T.F.C., 1990 'Architectural munificence in Britain: the evidence of the inscriptions', *Britannia*, 21, 13-32
Bomgardner, D., 1991 'Amphitheatres on the fringe', *J Roman Archaeol*, 4, 282-94
Bomgardner, D., 1993 'A new era for amphitheatre studies', *J Roman Archaeol*, 6, 375-90
Bomgardner, D., 2000 *The story of the Roman amphitheatre* (London)
Boon, G.C., 1972 *Isca; the Roman legionary fortress at Caerleon, Monmouthshire* (Cardiff)
Boon, G.C., 1987 *The legionary fortress of Caerleon – Isca* (Cardiff)
Boon, G.C., 1990 'Silchester Amphitheatre (review)', *Britannia*, 21, 397-400
Bradley, R., 1975 'Maumbury Rings, Dorchester: the excavation of 1908-1913', *Archaeologia*, 105, 1-97
Carroll, M., 2001 *Romans, Celts and Germans; the German provinces of Rome* (Stroud)
Clarke, S., Tebbs, A. and Wise, A., 1996 *Newstead 1996; the northern vicus and the amphitheatre, excavation and survey*, University of Bradford interim report (www.trimontium.freeserve.co.uk/bradford1.html)
Collingwood, R.G., 1930 *The Archaeology of Roman Britain* (London)
Collingwood, R.G. and Richmond, I.A., 1969 *The Archaeology of Roman Britain*, (second, revised edn, London)
Cott, P.J., 2002 'Archaeological Geophysics in East Anglia', *Archaeological Prospection*, 9, 157-61
Creighton, J., 2006 *Britannia, the creation of a Roman province* (London)
Crew, P., 1980 'Forden Gaer, Montgomery', *Bull Board Celtic Studies*, 28 (1978-80), 730-41
Davies, J.L. and Jones, R.H., 2002 'Recent research on Roman camps in Wales' in P. Freeman, J. Bennett, Z. Fiema and B. Hoffman (eds), *Limes XVIII; proceedings of the xviiith International Congress of Roman Frontier Studies held in Amman, Jordan (September 2000)* BAR Internat Ser, 1084, (Oxford), 835-41
Dodge, H., forthcoming, 'The Amphitheatre in the East' in Wilmott
Drinkwater, J., 1983 *Roman Gaul* (London)
Foucher, L., 1994 'Diana-Nemesis, patronne del'amphithéâtre, in Romano-British mosaics' in P. Johnson, R. Ling and D.J. Smith (eds), *Fifth international colloquium on ancient mosaics*, J Roman Archaeol Supp Ser, 9 (Ann Arbor, Michigan), 229-37
Frere, S.S., 1970 'The Roman theatre at Canterbury', *Britannia*, 1, 83-113
Frere, S.S., 1985 'Civic pride; a factor in Roman town planning', in F. Grew and B. Hobley, *Roman urban topography in Britain and the western empire*, CBA Res Rep, 59 (London), 34-6

Fulford, M., 1989 *The Silchester Amphitheatre; excavations of 1979-85*, Britannia Monograph Ser, 10 (London)
Futrell, A., 1997 *Blood in the Arena* (Austin, Texas)
Futrell, A., 2006 *The Roman Games* (Oxford)
Garner, D. and Wilmott, T., in preparation *The Roman Amphitheatre at Chester, excavations 2004-2006. Vol 1 the amphitheatre*, Grosvenor Museum Archaeological Report (Chester)
Golvin, J.-C., 1988 *L'Amphithéâtre Romain* (Paris), pl. 2
Gosden, C. and Lock, G., 2005 'The Vale and Ridgeway Project: excavations at Marcham/Frilford 2004', *South Midlands Archaeology*, 35, 94-105
Gray, H. St G., 1909 'Excavations at the "amphitheatre", Charterhouse on Mendip, 1909', *Somerset Archaeol and Nat Hist Proceedings*, 55, 118-37
Grenier, A., 1958 *Manuel d'archaeologie Gallo Romaine III: L'architecture 2: Ludi et circenses, théâtres, amphithéâtres* (Paris), 880-5
Gresham, C.A., 1938 'The Roman fort of Tomen y Mur', *Arch Cambrensis*, 93, 192-211
Grove-Lowe, R., 1848 *A description of the Roman theatre at Verulamium* (St Albans)
Hallier, G., 1990 'La géométrie des amphithéâtresmilitairs du Rhin et Danube', in *Akten des 14.Internationalen Limeskongresses in Carnuntum, Vienna*, 71-82
Haynes, I., 1999, 'Introduction: the Roman army as a community', in A. Goldsworthy and I. Haynes, 1999 *The Roman army as a community*, J Roman Archaeol Supplement Ser, 34 (Rhode Island)
Hawkes, J., 1982 *Mortimer Wheeler; adventurer in archaeology* (London), 96
Hingley, R., 1985, 'Location, function and status: a Romano-British 'religious complex' at the Noah's Ark Inn, Frilford (Oxfordshire)', *Oxford Journal Archaeology*, 4, 201-14
Hobley, B., 1973 'Excavations at 'the Lunt' Roman military site, second interim report', *Birmingham and Warwicks Archaeol Soc Trans*, 85, 7-93
Holbrook, N., 1998 'The Amphitheatre: Excavations directed by J.S. Wacher 1962-3 and A.D. McWhirr 1966', in N. Holbrook (ed.), *Cirencester, the Roman town defences, public buildings and shops (Cirencester Excavations V)*, Cotswold Archaeological Trust (Cirencester), 145-75
Horne, E.A., 1977, 'Air Reconnaissance 1975-77 (Caistor St Edmund)', *Aerial Archaeology*, 1 16-20
Jackson, R, 1983 'The Chester gladiator rediscovered', *Britannia*, 14, 87-95
Jacobelli, L., 2003 *Gladiators at Pompeii* (Los Angeles), 58-61
James, H., 2003 *Roman Carmarthen: excavations 1978-1993*, Britannia Monogr Ser, 20, 18-20
Jarrett, M.G., 1968 *The Roman Frontier in Wales* (second edn, Cardiff)
Jennison, G, (1937) *Animals for show and pleasure in Ancient Rome* (Manchester), 178
Johnston, D.E., 1994 'North African influences in Romano-British mosaics' in P. Johnson, R. Ling and D.J. Smith (eds), *Fifth international colloquium on ancient mosaics*, J Roman Archaeol Supp Ser, 9 (Ann Arbor, Michigan), 295-306
Jones, G.B.D., 1969, 'Excavations at Carmarthen, 1968', *Carmarthen Antiquary*, 5, 2-5
Jour Brit Archaeol Assoc, 1869 'Proceedings of the Congress', *Jour Brit Archaeol Assoc*, 25, 106-8
Junkelmann, M., 2000 *Das Spiel mit dem Tod. So kämpften Roms Gladiatoren* (Mainz)
Kenyon, K.M., 1935, 'The Roman theatre at Verulamium, St Albans', *Archaeologia*, 84, 214-61
Kyle, D.G., 1998 *Spectacles of death in ancient Rome* (London)
Le Roux, P., 1990 'L'amphithithéâtre et le soldat sous l'Empire Romaine' in C. Domergue, C. Landes and J.-M. Pallier, *Spectacula, I: gladiateurs et amphitheatres. Actes du colloque tenu a Toulouse et a Lattes le 26, 27 et 28 Mai 1987*, (Toulouse), 203-15
Ling, R., 1981 'The wall plaster from Balkerne Lane' in P. Crummy, *Colchester Archaeological Report 3: excavations at Lion Walk, Balkerne Lane an Middleborough, Colchester, Essex* (Colchester), 146-53
Little, J.H., 1971, 'The Carmarthen Amphitheatre', *Carmarthen Antiquary*, 7, 58-63
Lock, G. and Gosden, C., 2006 *The Vale and Ridgeway Project: Excavations at Marcham/Frilford 2005: interim report*, www.arch.ox.ac.uk/research/research_projects/marcham
Lowther, A., 1935, *The Roman theatre at Verulamium; reconstruction* (London)
Martin, L., 2001, *Richborough amphitheatre, Kent: report on geophysical surveys, February 2001*, English Heritage centre for Archaeology Report, 30/2001

Mattingley, D., 2006 *An Imperial possession: Britain in the Roman Empire* (London), 187
Maxwell, G.S. and Wilson, D.R., 1987 'Air Reconnaissance in Britain 1977-84', *Britannia*, 18, 43-4
Millett, M., 1990 *The Romanisation of Britain* (Cambridge)
Millett, M. and Wilmott, T., 2003 'Rethinking Richborough' in P. Wilson (ed.) *The Archaeology of Roman Towns* (Oxford), 184-94
Moloney, C., 1996 'Catterick Racecourse', *Current Archaeology*, 148, 128-32
Neal, D.S., 1981 *Roman Mosaics in Britain*, Britannia Monograph 1 (London), 76
Neighbour, T., 2002 'Excavations on the "amphitheatre" and other areas east of Inveresk fort', in M.C. Bishop (ed.), *Roman Inveresk; past, present and future*, (Duns), 41-51
Neighbour, T., 2007, 'A semi-elliptical timber-framed structure at Inveresk (the most northerly amphitheatre in the Empire?)', *Britannia*, 37, 125-40
Newstead, R. and Droop, J.P., 1932 'The Roman Amphitheatre at Chester', *Jour Chester Archaeol Soc*, new ser, 29, 5-40
Painter, K.S., 1969, 'A Roman bronze helmet from Hawkedon, Suffolk', *Brit Mus Quarterly*, 33, 121-130
Pitt Rivers, Gen. A.L.F., 1887 *Excavations on Cranbourne Chase near Rushmore on the borders of Dorset and Wiltshire*, vol 1 (London), 23-5, pl. 3
Plass, P., 1995 *The Game of Death in Ancient Rome* (London)
Pope, A., 1885 'The amphitheatre at Dorchester', *Proc Dorset Natur Hist Archaeol Fld Club*, 8, 66-9
Roach-Smith, C., 1850 *The antiquities of Richborough, Reculver and Lympne* (London) 161-5
Rudder, S., 1800, *History of the ancient town of Cirencester*, second edn, Cirencester
Scarth, Rev. H.M., 1858 'Some account of the investigation of barrows on the line of the Roman road between Old Sarum and the port at the mouth of the River Axe, supposed to be the *Ad Axum* of Ravennas', *Archaeol Jour*, 16, 143-54
Schmotz, K., 2006, *Das hölzerne Amphitheater von Künzing, Lkr. Degendorf. Kenntnisstand und erste rekonstruktionnsätze nach abschliss de gelädearbeiten im Jahr 2004*, in K. Schmotz (ed), *Vorträge des 24. Niederbayerischen Archäologentages* (Deggendorf), 95-118
Stukeley, W., 1723 *Of the Roman amphitheatre at Dorchester* (London)
Stukeley, W., 1776 *Itinerarium Curiosum* (second edn London), 163
Thompson, F.H., 1975 'The excavation of the Roman amphitheatre at Chester', *Archaeologia*, 105, 127-239
Vatcher, F. de M., 1963 'The excavation of the Roman earthwork at Winterslow, Wilts', *Antiqs J*, 43, 198-217
Ville, G., 1965 'Essai de datation de la mosaïque des gladiateurs de Zliten', in *La mosaïque gréco-romaine*, Editions du Centre National de la Recherche Scientifique, Paris, 147–55
Wacher, J., 1995 *The Towns of Roman Britain* (second edn, London)
Wheeler, R.E.M. and Wheeler, T.V., 1928 'The Roman Amphitheatre at Caerleon, Monmouthshire', *Archaeologia*, 78, 111-218
White, G.M., 1936 'The Chichester Amphitheatre: preliminary excavations', *Antiquaries J*, 16, 148-59
Wiedemann, T., 1992 *Emperors and Gladiators* (London)
Wilding, R., 2005 *Roman Amphitheatres in England and Wales* (Chester)
Williams, W.J., 1929 'Roman Amphitheatre in the Ursuline Convent School Grounds', *Jour Chester Archaeol Soc*, new ser, 28, 218-9
Wilmott, T. (ed), forthcoming, *Roman amphitheatres and spectacula; a 21st century perspective; papers from the Chester conference, 16th-18th February, 200*, BAR International Series (Oxford)
Wilmott, T., Garner, D. and Ainsworth, S., 2006 'The Roman Amphitheatre at Chester; an interim account', *English Heritage Hist Rev*, 1, 7-23
Wilson, P.R., 2002 *Cataractonium, Roman Catterick and its hinterland: excavations and research, 1958-1997*, CBA Research Report 128, Part 1 (London), 30, 40-2
Wilson-Jones, M., 1993 'Designing amphitheatres', *Mitteilungen des Deutschen Archäologischen Instituts Römischen Abteilung*, 100, 391-42
Ziebart, M., Arthur, J., Bateman, N., Rauxloh, P., Lees, D. and Brown, J., 2006 'Determination of the parameters of the Guildhall amphitheatre ellipse in London', *J Archaeol Sci*, 2006, 1-10

INDEX

Illustrations are on page numbers highlighted in **bold**. The main sections on each site are highlighted in ***bold italic***.

Aldborough, Yorkshire, supposed amphitheatre at ***158***
Allcroft, A. Hadrian 31-3
amphitheatres
 urban 47, 62
 rural 56
 legionary 57
 auxiliary 59
Arles, France, amphitheatre at **17**
armour, Hawkedon helmet 168, **169**
Army, Roman 18-19, 58, 81
Aquincum, Hungary, two amphitheatres at 59
Aubrey, John 22
Augst, Switzerland, amphitheatre/theatre 19, 57
Augustus, Emperor 12

Baginton, Warwickshire, The Lunt fort, *gyrus* at 37, 61, 67, ***155-6***
Bateman, Nick 9, 41, 61
Bignor villa, Sussex, gladiator mosaic 163, 172-3
Bomgdaner, David 9, 40, 80
Bonn, Germany, inscription from 61
Boon, G.C. 8, 58, 79
Bosanquet, R.C. 31
Bosham, Sussex, supposed amphitheatre at 27
Brading villa, Isle of Wight, hunting mosaic at 164
Bradley, Richard 33, 64
Brough-on-Humber, theatre inscription at **51**
Bruce, J. Collingwood 28

Caerleon, Gwent, amphitheatre at 21, 35, 57, 81, 85-6, ***143-50***
 graffiti from 168
Caerwent, amphitheatre at 36, 55, ***118***
Caesar, C Julius, spectacles 12, 13
Caister St Edmund, Norfolk, amphitheatre at 40, ***117-8***
Canterbury, theatre at 37, 57, **127**
Capua, Italy, amphitheatre at 13, **89**
Carceres 71-2, 162
Carnuntum, Austria, the two amphitheatres at 59
Carmarthen, amphitheatre at 37, 45, 54, 74, **76**, ***115-17***
 knife handle from 178
Catterick, North Yorkshire, supposed amphitheatre at 42, 159-60
cavea 74, 87
Channing, Mary, execution of 22, 197
Charterhouse-on-Mendip, Somerset, amphitheatre at 28, 32, 34, 38, 56, 89, ***127-30***
Chester, Cheshire, amphitheatre at 35, 37, **38**, 42-3, 57, 66, 81, **89**, ***135-43***
 around amphitheatre 178-9
 latrines 178
 shrine 178
 post Roman 184, 186-8
Chesters, Hadrian's Wall, possible *gyrus* at 61, ***158***

220

Chichester, Sussex, amphitheatre at 36, 44, 54, **108-10**
Christian martyrdom, in Gaul 17
  of Aaron and Julius 185
Cicero, M Tullius, law on *munera* 13
Cirencester, Gloucestershire, amphitheatre at 24, 29, 38, 54, 72, **73**, 77, **78**, **110-15**
  post-Roman 185-6
civitas capitals 49
churches, near amphitheatre sites 186-8
clasp knives 176-8
clibani 178
Collingwood, R.C. 38, 58
Colchester
  foundation 48
  theatre at 48, 179
  vase from 169-70
  gladiator wall-painting from 171
coloniae 48
Colosseum 12, 15, **16**
Condate, Lugdunum, Imperial cult and amphitheatre 17, 48
Corbridge, Northumberland, clasp knife from 178
Curio, M Scribonius, double theatre of 14
curse tablets 181

Dambach, Germany, auxiliary amphitheatre at 60
dating 55
decoration, architectural 87
Diana, cult of 180
Dorchester, amphitheatre at **23**, **25**, 33, 52, 63, 67, 70, **103-8**
  post Roman 189
  gallows at 23, 188

Eccles villa, Kent, gladiatorial mosaic from 172
entrances 70, 72, 78, 85-6

Frilford, Oxfordshire, ?amphitheatre at 40, 56, **130-2**
Forden Gaer, Montgomerys, possible *gyrus* at 61, **157**
Fulford, Prof. Michael 9, 40

Garner, Dan 42
Giraldus Cambrensis 21
Gladiator, Lucius, at Leicester 161
  retiarius, relief from Chester 166-7
  wall-painting at Colchester 171
  depicted on mosaics 171-3
  depicted on clasp knives 176-7
  depicted on pottery 169
Gloucester, foundation 48
Golvin, J-Cl. 9, 61, 80
Gosbecks Farm, Colchester, theatre and sanctuary at 56
graffiti, gladiatorial from Caerleon **168**
  on pot sherd from Leicester 161
Grey, H. St George 33
gyrus 61

Hawkedon, gladiator's helmet from 168, **169**
Housesteads, Hadrian's Wall, supposed amphitheatre at 28, 31, 32

Imperial cult 17, 48, 179
Inscriptions, dedicatory 52
  religious 180
  curse tablets 181
Inveresk, Midlothian, possible amphitheatre/ *gyrus* at 42, 44, 61, **156**

Jackson, Ralph 166

Kenyon, Kathleen 36, 57
Künzing, Bavaria, auxiliary amphitheatre at **60**, 89, **90**

Leicester, inscription from 161
Leland, John 22
Limes 18
Lincoln, foundation 48
Llanidan, Anglesey, supposed amphitheatre at 27
London, amphitheatre at **41**, 42, 54, 64, **67**, **69**, 71, 72, **75**, **92-97**
  post-Roman 183, 186
  foundation and origins 49
  Cripplegate fort 50
Lowe, R. Grove 26, 30
Lowther, Anthony 36
Ludi 38, 45
Lugdunum see *Condate*
Lunt fort see Baginton

McWhirr, Alan 38
Matthews, Keith 42
Mercury, cult of 181
mosaics 162-6, 171-3
  north African influence on 165

Mambury Rings see Dorchester
munera, history of 12
   in Gaul 17
   in Britain **166-73**
   ?at Colchester 48
   depicted on pottery 173-5
   depicted on glass 175
   depicted in mosaic 171-3
munus legitimum 15

Nemesis, cult of 179
Nero, Emperor 15
Newstead, amphitheatre at 42, 60, 89, **151-2**

Ovens, G.L. 37

Paestum, Italy, amphitheatre at 13, 67, **68**, 84
Pera, D Brutus, *munus* in memory of 12
Piddington, Northamptonshire, clasp knife from 176
Pitt Rivers, General 30
planning 63, 83
Pompeii, Italy, amphitheatre at **13**, 52, 163
Pozzuoli, Italy, amphitheatre at 13, **14**, 52, **53**

religion 179
Richborough, Kent, amphitheatre at 22, 24, **26**, **27**, 45, 55, **119-21**
Richmond, I.A. 38, 58
Rudder, Samuel 29
Rudston villa, North Yorkshire, Venus mosaic 164

Scaurus, M Aemilius, *venation* 12
Scarth, Rev. H.M. 28, 29
sculpture 166-7
seating 75, 87
estimates of numbers 80
shrine 178
Silchester, Hampshire, amphitheatre at 24, **25**, **40**, 52, 63, 67, **68**, 70, **71**, **72-3**, 74, **75**, 77, **97-103**
   post-Roman 186, 188
Smith, C. Roach 26
snack food 178
Sofia, Bulgaria, theatre and amphitheatre at 57
South Shields, Tyne and Wear, clasp knife from 177
souvenirs 179
Stanley, W. Owen 27
stairs 77, 84

structures
   timber 66, 91
   masonry 70, 84
Stukeley, William 22, 45, 64, 80

Taurus, C Statilius, amphitheatre built by 14
Telegenii, symbols of 165
terraces 78-9
tethering block 162
theatre-amphitheatres
   in Gaul **19**, 20, 57
   at Verulamium 36, 56
Thompson, F. Hugh 37, 42
Tomen-y-Mur, amphitheatre at 27, 30, 38, 60, 89, **153-5**
Trajan's Column 18, **87**
tribunals 80

venations
   history of 11
   in Britain **162-6**
   depicted on pottery 171
   depicted on mosaic 163
Verulamium
   theatre at 26, 36, 57, **122-7**
   supposed amphitheatre at 30
   foundation of *municipium* 49
   forum and basilica at 50
Vespasian, Emperor 15
Vindolanda, Northumberland, painted glass vessel 173
vivaria 61

Wacher, John 38
Walton, Radnors, supposed amphitheatre at **160**
Wheeler, Sir Mortimer and Mrs T.V. 35
Wilding, Roy 43
Williams, W.J. 35
Wilmott, Tony 42
Winterslow, Wiltshire, supposed amphitheatre at 40, 56, **132-3**
Woodcutts, Dorset, supposed amphitheatre at 30, 56, **133**
Wren, Sir Christopher 22

York, possible amphitheatre at 59
   bone slip from 166

Zugmantel, Germany, auxiliary amphitheatre at 60

Also available from Tempus Publishing

**Chester AD 400-1066
From Roman Fortress to English Town**

David Mason

978 0 7524 4100 9   £17.99

This is the most up-to-date general account of Chester from the late Roman period to the Norman Conquest. Its author tells the story of Chester; its disappearance into obscurity during the 'Dark Ages', its emergence as an important religious, commercial and military settlement in the Kingdom of Mercia and the everyday life of its people leading up to the advent of Norman rule.

Roman Dorset

Bill Putnam

978 0 7524 4104 7   £17.99

At the time of the Roman invasion present-day Dorset was part of the territory of the Durotriges. The Second Legion Augusta was responsible for the conquest of this area and Bill Putnam charts the remarkable extent to which Roman ideas, life and language were adopted in the years following this conquest. This book is the result of 40 years of fieldwork and research by the author.

**Defying Rome
The Rebels of Roman Britain**

Guy de la Bédoyère

978 0 7524 4440 6   £17.99

Rome's power was under constant challenge and nowhere moreso than in Britain. From the beginning to the end of Roman rule in Britain a succession of idealists and chancers, most famously Boudica, tried to expel Rome and recover their lost power. This book covers 14 rebellions and explains why Britain was such a hot-bed of dissent.

A Roman Frontier Fort in Scotland
Elginhaugh

William S. Hanson

978 0 7524 4113 9 £17.99

Elginhaugh is the only completely excavated timber-built auxiliary fort in the Roman Empire. Here the excavator, Prof. W.S. Hanson tells the story of its discovery and excavation, interprets the evidence and discusses the nature of military life on the furthest northern frontier of the Empire in the first century AD and its impact on the local area.

Britannia Prima
Britain's Last Roman Province

Roger White

978 0 7524 1967 1 £19.99

This important work counters the widely held view that when the legions left Britain the Roman way of life disappeared with them. In fact Britannia Prima – broadly the west of Britain – had from the fourth to the sixth centuries a distinctive Romano-British character and successfully resisted significant Anglo-Saxon invasion longer than any other area of Britain.

The End of Antiquity
Archaeology, Society and Religion
AD 235-700

Jeremy K. Knight

978 0 7524 4082 8 £17.99

This is a masterful study of the transition from the Classical world to Medieval Europe and has won widespread critical acclaim.

'For this well written, well illsutrated and scholarly book, he has placed all students of Late Antiquity in his debt' – *Antiquaries Journal*

www.thehistorypress.co.uk